"This excellent collection of essays on diverse social issues pertaining to planned events is both timely and distinctive. The binding themes of events as transformative phenomena, within the frame of UN Sustainability Goals, shed light on critical topics including health, safety, equality, human rights and cultural identity. Students and practitioners will find the contributors' arguments to be thought-provoking and the practical implications highly relevant, while the quizzes are a valuable resource for teachers."

Donald Getz, *Professor Emeritus, The University of Calgary, Alberta, Canada*

"This timely collection offers a thought-provoking and insightful look at those wider societal issues that impact the design, delivery, and legacy of staging events. International, interdisciplinary, and underpinned by theory, individual chapters provide rigorous scrutiny of the staging of events and their intentional, and unexpected, outcomes. Readers will be energized and challenged by the material which will serve as a catalyst for the continued growth of the study of events."

Alan Fyall, *PhD, Visit Orlando Endowed Chair of Tourism Marketing, University of Central Florida, USA*

"The book titled *Events and Society* is presenting a holistic approach to understanding the world of all types of events focusing primarily on sport events such as the Olympic Games but also cultural events. The book's four sections focusing on how events transform people, places, experiences, identities and the environment offer intriguing insights from experts in the field. A must-read for academics and professionals working in the event space!"

Kyriaki (Kiki) Kaplanidou, *PhD, Professor and Director of Graduate Sport Event Management Certificate, Graduate Coordinator, College of Health and Human Performance, University of Florida, USA*

"This extensive book provides rich insights into the transformational role of events in society. It analyses important but often undiscussed topics affecting events from a community, grassroots level to mega events. Original and thought-provoking areas such as loneliness; diversity; displacement; identity and belonging are part of the narrative and supported with engaging case studies. A compelling read for anyone interested in the sociological impacts of festivals and events!"

Dr Jane Ali-Knight, *Professor in Festival and Event Management, The Business School, Edinburgh Napier University, Scotland*

EVENTS AND SOCIETY

Events of all shapes and sizes play an important part in all of our lives. They are fun, frivolous, and often allow us to escape from our everyday lives – and they are also fascinating to study and examine in a more serious way, to understand what they mean and what they do for us – individually and collectively. *Events in Society*, therefore, explores the social impact and sociological implications of designing, planning, and delivering events – cultural events like the Edinburgh Fringe Festival; sporting events like the Olympic and Paralympic Games and FIFA World Cup; to music festivals like Glastonbury.

Thirty carefully selected contributions feature, written by global experts in a short and succinct way that are easy to digest, covering a variety of disciplines, fields, contexts, and cases. Every chapter explores a critical issue or debate based on real-life events, and contextualises this within the key theoretical debates, managerial, and policy implications. Throughout, there are linkages to the UN Sustainable Development Goals, as well as interactive features to aid understanding and spur critical thinking, including learning objectives, quiz questions, and debate questions per chapter.

Some of the topics covered include:

- Uniting nations and people
- Personal experiences and transformations
- Social critique and explorations
- Activism
- Programming and representation
- Health, safety, and security
- Identity and gender
- LGBTQ+
- Environmentalism
- Displacement and exclusion
- Education and participation
- Community development
- Disability and accessibility

This innovative, topical, engaging, and comprehensive book is an essential reading and teaching resource for all students and lecturers in events that are easy to integrate into educational programmes.

Mike Duignan is a Professor at the Sorbonne, University of Paris 1, France, and the Director of Research, Intelligence, and Education at Trivandi, UK. Since 2021, Mike has been the Editor-in-Chief of the leading peer-reviewed journal for the study and analysis of events, *Event Management Journal*. Formerly, he was a tenured Associate Professor at the University of Central Florida, USA; the Director of the UK Olympic Studies Centre; and a Reader and Head of Department at the University of Surrey, UK.

Routledge "How Events Transform Society" Series

Events of all shapes and sizes are witnessing significant growth – locally, regionally, nationally, internationally – shaping our lives, economies, and society-at-large in profound and complex ways.

Books in this series are cutting edge and intellectually stimulating, with a balance between theory and application. Titles are accessible and content easily digestible for students, academics, and practitioners. Taking a flip classroom approach, these can easily be integrated as a week of teaching, with interactive activities such as classroom quizzes, debate questions, and further reading to situate theory in real-life practices.

Each book in the series includes approximately 30 carefully crafted case studies written by leading academics and practitioners globally, that present complex scholarly arguments as concise and accessible chapter-based articles. Each short topical chapter explores a critical issue or debate based on real-life events related to the overarching theme, and contextualises this within the key theoretical debates, managerial and policy implications and links to SDGs.

Events and Society
Bridging Theory and Practice
Edited by Mike Duignan

For more information about this series, please visit: www.routledge.com/tourism/series/RPISEF

EVENTS AND SOCIETY

Bridging Theory and Practice

Edited by Mike Duignan

LONDON AND NEW YORK

Designed cover image: Getty Images

First published 2025
by Routledge
4 Park Square, Milton Park, Abingdon, Oxon OX14 4RN

and by Routledge
605 Third Avenue, New York, NY 10158

Routledge is an imprint of the Taylor & Francis Group, an informa business

British Library Cataloguing-in-Publication Data
A catalogue record for this book is available from the British Library

ISBN: 978-1-032-78621-6 (hbk)
ISBN: 978-1-032-78620-9 (pbk)
ISBN: 978-1-003-48872-9 (ebk)

DOI: 10.4324/9781003488729

Typeset in Berthold Akzidenz Grotesk
by codeMantra

This book is dedicated to my beautiful mother, Carol Ann Duignan, who passed away on the 14th November, 2023.

CONTENTS

FIGURES

CONTRIBUTORS

Beck Banks, Warren Wilson College, USA. Assistant Professor of Communications, specializing in transgender media and representation studies, often focusing on rural areas and activism efforts.

Richard Betts, Professor, University of Exeter, UK. Richard is Chair in Climate Impacts at the University of Exeter, and Head of Climate Impacts in the Met Office Hadley Centre.

Trudy Barber, University of Portsmouth, UK. Dr Barber is a pioneering academic in digital culture, known for her research on virtual reality, cybersexuality and immersive technologies, influencing the intersection of technology and human experience.

Ian Brittain, Associate Professor, Coventry University, UK. Ian is an internationally recognized expert in the study of disability and Paralympic sport, and has attended five summer Paralympic Games, from Sydney to Rio.

Chris Brown, University of Hertfordshire, UK. An expert in disability sport and founder of the Disability Sport Info podcast, Chris lectures in sport development. His PhD investigated the sport participation legacies of the London 2012 Paralympics.

John Bustard, Ulster University, UK, is a senior lecturer in digital transformation.

Robin Canniford, University of Galway, Ireland, is Professor in Marketing.

Piyusha Chatterjee, University of Glasgow, UK. Research Associate on the Deindustrialization and Politics of Our Time (DePOT) project, School of Modern Languages and Cultures. Piyusha Chatterjee is an oral historian working on gender and labour in the context of deindustrialization and global economic restructuring since the 1960s. In 2024, she received the Leverhulme Early Career Fellowship at the University of Glasgow.

Karen Davies, Cardiff Metropolitan University (Welsh Centre for Tourism Research), UK. Dr Davies is a senior lecturer in events management, with a keen interest in research surrounding festivals and cultural events and inclusivity, particularly in relation to those living in poverty.

Michele K. Donnelly, Associate Professor, Department of Sport Management, Brock University, Canada. Donnelly's sociological research agenda addresses social inequalities, particularly gender, primarily using qualitative empirical studies of major multi-sport events (e.g., the Olympic Games), as well as alternative and understudied social practices (e.g., roller derby, skateboarding). Donnelly is the author of *Gender Equality and the Olympic Programme* (Routledge, 2022).

Mathew Dowling, School of Sport, Exercise and Health Sciences, Loughborough University, UK. Dr Dowling is a senior lecturer in sport management. His research interests focus on sport policy and governance, organizational theory, professionalization, comparative methodology and government involvement in sport.

Mike Duignan, Trivandi, UK and University of Paris 1 (Pantheon-Sorbonne), France. Mike is the Director of Research, Intelligence and Education at Trivandi and Professeur at the University of Paris 1 (Pantheon-Sorbonne), focusing on managing major events and their economic and social impacts on the people and places that host them.

Giana Eckhardt, King's College London, UK. Giana is Professor of Marketing, and Vice Dean of Executive Education and External Engagement.

Nicole Ferdinand, Senior Lecturer, Oxford Brookes University, UK.

Lina Fadel, Heriot-Watt University, UK. Assistant Professor in Social Research Methods. Her interests include (auto)ethnographies of migration, anticolonial and creative methods, and the complexities of othering in migration contexts.

Coen Heijes, University of Groningen, the Netherlands. Coen Heijes specializes in presentist, interdisciplinary approaches to leadership, ethics, diversity studies and 21st-century challenges and how these interact with Shakespeare studies.

Tim Hill, University of Bath, UK. Tim is a senior lecturer in marketing.

Michael Hughes, School of Environmental and Conservation Sciences, Murdoch University, Australia. Michael has over 25 years' experience teaching and researching in the field of environmental management, with a particular focus on nature-based recreation and protected area management.

Alison Hutton, Western Sydney University, Australia. Ally's work primarily focuses on emergency health care in high-visibility events, both planned (mass gatherings) and unplanned (disasters). Her work into the psychosocial nature of mass gatherings is used globally at large events.

Keith Johnston, Orgues Létourneau, Canada. Keith's research on 17th- and 18th-century Italian theatre has appeared in *Eighteenth-Century Life*, *Music & Letters* and *Intersections*.

Cheryl Jones, School of Education, Murdoch University, Australia. Cheryl has a background in sociology, culture studies and educational psychology. Her research interests include the social nature of emotions and their function in collaborative contexts, including global environmental matters.

Amelie Katczynski, Deakin University, Alfred Deakin Institute for Citizenship and Globalisation, Australia. Amelie's research background is in geographies of human wellbeing and the anthropology of reproduction. She has worked in Germany and Australia, and now conducts ethnographic fieldwork at a public health school in Lao PDR.

Niki Koutrou, University of Sunderland in London, UK. Dr Koutrou is a principal lecturer whose research interrogates sustainable community sport programmes, civil society sustainability and volunteering, and Olympic/sport event legacies.

Judith Mair, Associate Professor, University of Queensland, Australia. Judith's work aims to understand and enhance the positive impacts of tourism and events on the communities and societies that host them.

Kevin Markwell, Faculty of Business, Law and Arts, Southern Cross University, Australia. Kevin is a cultural geographer with an interest in the intersections of leisure, tourism and LGBT identities. He has focused particularly on events as sites for individual and collective identity formation.

Pauline Marsh, Wicking Dementia Research and Education Centre, University of Tasmania, Australia. Pauline's research centres on solving seemingly intractable social problems by working closely with communities on Lutruwita/Tasmania, where she leads the Nature Connection Storytelling Project and the Venture Out Research Group.

Jim Macbeth, Sociology and Tourism, Murdoch University, Australia. Jim was a foundation staff member of Murdoch in 1975, specializing in social inquiry and sociology. He established tourism there, and is Head of the School of Social Sciences and Humanities.

Brian McCullough, University of Michigan, USA. He is an Associate Professor and Program Chair of Sport Management in the School of.

Nduka Mntambo, Netherlands Film Academy, Amsterdam University of the Arts. Nduka Mntambo is an artist and academic whose work spans spatial practices, experimental filmmaking, and artistic research. He is currently Head of the Masters in Film at the Academy.

David Murphy, University of Strathclyde, UK. David has published widely on modern and contemporary Francophone West African culture, including *The First World Festival of Negro Arts, Dakar 1966: Contexts and Legacies* (2016).

Stephen Murphy, Trinity College, Dublin, Ireland. Stephen is Assistant Professor in Marketing at Trinity Business School.

David Newsome, School of Environmental and Conservation Sciences, Murdoch University, Australia. David's interests focus on nature-based tourism, with a particular emphasis on the environmental impacts of recreation and tourism and the sustainability of tourism in national parks and nature reserves.

Verity Postlethwaite, Loughborough University, UK. Dr Postlethwaite is a Vice-Chancellor Independent Research Fellow. Her fellowship uses an interdisciplinary approach and focuses on the use of events as catalysts for social and community change in the UK, Japan, and Australia.

David Roberts, Innis College, University of Toronto, Canada. David is Director and Associate Professor, teaching stream, in the Urban Studies Program.

Sean Spence, Royal Military College of Canada. Sean is a pracademic within the hospitality and live events space. He does security risk management consulting, teaching and researching within the events industry. He is currently working on a security risk management textbook for live events.

Elaine Stratford, Geography, Planning, and Spatial Sciences, University of Tasmania, Australia. Elaine's research, higher degree supervision, and learning and teaching activities are motivated by trying to understand the conditions in which people flourish in place, in their movements, in daily life, and over their life-course.

Pauline Marsh, Professor, School of Geography, Planning, and Spatial Sciences, University of Tasmania, Australia.

Adam Talbot, University of the West of Scotland, UK. Adam is a lecturer in event management. His research covers protest and human rights in the context of sport mega-events.

Eleni Theodoraki, University College Dublin, Ireland. Dr Theodoraki is a Professor of Sport Management. Her research draws on organization and social theory, and explores issues of governance, policy, strategy development, effectiveness, and sustainability. Eleni has worked for organizing committees for the Olympic Games, and was commissioner for sustainability for London 2012.

Ayanna Thompson, Arizona State University, USA. Professor Thompson is a scholar of Shakespeare, race, and performance. Her research employs historicist, theoretical, pedagogical, and practical lenses to ask how race operates in performance and as a performance.

Christine Van Winkle, Professor of Recreation Management, University of Manitoba, Canada. Dr Van Winkle cares deeply about the role of festivals, parks, museums, and interpretative centres in our community; and, as such, has dedicated her career as a researcher to exploring visitors' experiences in these tourism and leisure settings.

Nigel L. Williams, PMP, University of Portsmouth, UK. Nigel is a Professor in Responsible Project and Systems Management, and Associate Dean for Research and Innovation at the Faculty of Business and Law.

FOREWORD

At its least this book is a collection of evidence-based essays, providing an objective lens on the nature, credibility and legacy of the global events industry. At its best it can be viewed as a demand for scrutiny, a call for action on how we assess, where we place value, what is important and how and where our money is being spent.

It is not true when politicians say there is no money. What is true is that choices are made about how to spend public money, our money. A politician once said to me, "Shona, on the doorsteps, no one ever asks me about the arts." It is time to talk openly about how much is spent on major events, which events and why. Why is it that major sporting events – peripatetic one-offs with heavy carbon bootprints and that single broadcast moment – are coveted and attract investment of tens of millions? In the case of the Olympics, billions are spent. In comparison annual, home-grown arts festivals and cultural events with sustained social, cultural and economic impact have to jump through bureaucratic hoops and promise to solve all the ills of world to secure tens of thousands or a few hundred thousand at best. Isn't there a better legacy than new buildings, a one-off media moment? Isn't real legacy a change in and for the people, a sustained benefit that aims for minimal damage to climate and place and maximum economic and social benefit for local and global participants?

The excellent series of chapters in this book illustrate that large parts of the global events industry are driven by big scale, big money and big extraction, with dubious legacy or social capital left in their wake.

I have spent 35 years working on arts events, and I share here a couple of illustrations from my own experience.

Belfast – Imagine!

In 1999 I headed up Belfast's bid to be European Capital of Culture – Imagine Belfast. Even the bidding process needed to be a citywide re-imagining of what was uniquely Belfast and what more the city could be. It was one year after the signing of the Good Friday Agreement. There was no money, no administrative structure and no real belief from the city leadership. Belfast wasn't ready and didn't win (Liverpool did), and there was a bomb-scare in front of the bus the day the jury came to visit. But … the authenticity of the process did create a number of firsts, and a cultural strategy for Belfast that was at least partially delivered. It was the first time that artists and creatives had been given paid roles in shaping a major civic initiative. It was the first time the citizens had been widely consulted on a cultural vision for a re-imagined Belfast. It was the first time a serious proposition had been put forward to mark that Belfast had built the *Titanic*, and the only time the iconic Harland & Wolff shipyard cranes were allowed to be repurposed as an art installation. Crucially, it was the first time that the "peace walls", some 20 miles of them separating the city's communities, were mentioned with a positive aspiration to one day bring them down. (The Northern Ireland peace walls were built throughout the conflict knows as the Troubles as a means of separating two warring communities.)

In spite of not winning, there is a legacy, the Titanic Exhibition Centre was built and opened in 2012, celebrating some 7.5 million visits by 2023. The Lyric Theatre was rebuilt, the Opera House extended and the Ulster Hall refurbished. Belfast is comfortable with building projects; and these at least were locally rooted, creating employment and a platform for local creative talent. The harder work of taking down the psychological barriers that divide people and in turn the physical walls that are such a scar and manifestation of old divisions – that would have required creative thinking, imagination and sustained investment.

As one chapter in this book recommends – policy makers should pay more attention to the positive effects of shared civic experiences and community connection and interaction, rather than narrowly targeted events or built-environment legacy projects.

So hope for a great sea-change
On the far side of revenge.
Believe that a further shore
Is reachable from here.
Believe in miracles
And cures and healing wells.

Seamus Heaney's powerful words from *The Cure at Troy* became the narrative for Derry-Londonderry's year as UK City of Culture. The poem perfectly encapsulated the aspiration of the twin themes of the year, joyous celebration and purposeful enquiry. The first, a desire to re-present a city that had only been pictured as a city of conflict with a dark past as a place of joy and humanity; and the second to not forget or hide from that past, but to look at it through a different lens. Heaney, himself a Nobel Prize winner, was schooled in Derry, and was an authentic choice for a spirit guide.

The City of Culture bid was won in the same year that former UK Prime Minister David Cameron made a public apology for the atrocity of Bloody Sunday. The scale of the challenge of creating a new story was highlighted in 2011 when Derry's new Peace Bridge was opened. It was a vital and beautiful piece of new infrastructure, loaded with symbolism and creating the first pedestrian walkway between two sides of the city that had previously been bridged only for cars, not people. The main national broadcast that night introduced this uplifting moment as "a new sectarian interface for Derry", and intercut the news piece with scenes of rioting – that had happened in Belfast a year earlier. Such was the determination to trap Derry in an old narrative.

In my first media interview as Chief Executive of the Culture Company (the organisation established to deliver Derry's UK City of Culture year), it was put to me: "Well you failed in Belfast, what makes you think you can make a success in Derry?"

It should be noted that no money comes with winning a City of Culture bid, just the leverage of the title. On my first day in the job in April 2011, I was given a Blackberry a second-hand laptop and a fundraising challenge of £20 million. There was no office, no team and very little financial commitment. And the designated year was 2013. We raised the money, but we had to plead, beg, cajole and account for every penny through layers of bureaucratic oversight in triplicate.

And yet what happened was authentic and in its own way transformational.

Our first objective was to create a programme that would be ambitious and brave and outward-reaching, but also would be bespoke to Derry-Londonderry and say something of the cultural fabric of the place and its past, present and future. The programme was a balance of large-scale public events, with long-term educational and community-based initiatives. The education and communities element of the programme was a process of development, not an event. The whole programme focused on quality artistic, sporting and discursive experiences that were not designed along sectarian lines or on outdated high art/low art dividing lines.

We took risks in structuring the team, and our approach was new: the emphasis was on programming and content, and that is where we placed the most significant resource. There was no single curator, but a team with different backgrounds, interests and experiences. And it worked – it brought different voices and curatorial approaches.

We gave out money. We got others to give out money. Democratised the curation of the year with cultural partners, visual artists, community workers. But kept a clear narrative.

To deliver on the potential it was crucial that the Culture Company was not the sole agent, but a central hub for partnership working, generating ideas and enabling support. The programme was inclusive and respectful of cultural diversity. There was so much to celebrate joyously.

The very first event of the year, built on a Derry tradition of the monthly mayor's tea dance, brought together 1000 of the city's senior citizens in style to dance to big band music on a rainy Saturday afternoon in January – and dance they did.

The show by choreographer and dancer Hofesh Shecter was loud and visceral and moving and energizing, with the sound of metal guitars and drums. The fusion of local musicians with world-class dancers performing Shecter's *Political Mother* at Ebrington was a real "wow" moment.

The 21st of June – Music City Day. From the dawn chorus – with choirs from Donegal and Derry singing to accompany the dawn at An Grianán, its ancient stones turning gold as the sun came up – this was special. The city woke to a sky orchestra – on a most serene morning, ten hot air balloons silently took to the skies and then floated over the city playing orchestral music to rouse the people below. All day long music came from everywhere, poured on to the streets and seemed to seep through the pores of the buildings and the people. The city celebrated the 100th anniversary of "Danny Boy", singing it together on Guildhall Square. Derry-Londonderry is the most musical of cities.

Thousands of people came from near and far, 179,000 of them to witness as Artichoke – producers of bespoke public arts events – brought their genius to the city and transformed buildings, streetscapes and parks through light and fire. The Fire Garden in St Columb's Park had a spiritual beauty about it that took me back there four nights in a row, and was profound and moving to experience.

Lenanshee was a beautiful musical production that put young people with special needs at the heart of the programme in a poignant and brilliantly worked out tale of fairy folk and legend. A child-like wonder descended over even the most determined of adults as the fire-breathing menace of the Loch Ness monster made its eerie way up the River Foyle to do battle with its old foe Columba, in the *Return of Colmcille*. A fantastic spectacle that saw Walk The Plank, the brilliant outdoor arts company, recruit and rehearse with local artists and residents for over a year.

Old places and ideas were transformed psychologically and physically through art. The Turner Prize did not take place in a gallery, but in a disused former military barracks. The police – who only a year earlier would have had to wear flak jackets and drive Saracen armoured carriers – were on bicycles, and their band headed the parade of the All-Ireland Fleadh (Ireland's biggest annual celebration of traditional music, which came north to Derry for the first time in 2013). Over 1000 local women aged from 18 to 80 put on their wedding dresses and attempted a Guinness World Record for the largest number of brides on a bridge, raising a huge amount of money for breast cancer research in the process.

The hallmarks of the year were participation, inclusion, quality and equity.

A peaceful future with culture as the driver

In Derry-Londonderry, the city celebrated a year of unprecedented cultural participation, positive media coverage, new visitors and peaceful public gatherings. The year 2013 opened the door, gave a glimpse of the galvanising role that culture can play in regeneration, in vibrancy, in the creative economy and, crucially, in peace-building and the possibility of a shared future.

We need a way to measure differently. If we invest £10 million in culture, how much do we save in policing and security, or on mental health and well-being?

Broadcaster and author Melvyn Bragg was in Derry, saying:

> It feels great, it feels a sort of triumph of the human spirit, it's wonderful and it shows the democratic power of culture that it can bring everybody together and because it doesn't matter who you are if you like this sort of music or that sort of music you don't ask what religion people are, or what gender they are or what colour they are – you like the music. And it's wonderful imaginative democracy, and it's terrific that Derry has seized that crown, it's just great.

And, as one local man put it:

> On a daily basis I can see the real legacy it has left behind. City of Culture afforded many the platform to challenge old prejudices and extend boundaries. As a result it has achieved more for good relations in this city than perhaps we have managed in the previous 15 since the Good Friday Agreement. Any early cynics were blown away by the sheer magnitude, variety and scale of the programme of events. The city is simply much more integrated as a result.

Edinburgh: The Holy Grail – even when you have it, you can't see that you have it

I have been privileged to head up the Edinburgh Festival Fringe Society since 2016, supporting the Edinburgh Fringe – an event which, if assessed objectively, would probably meet every target that is identified in the chapters of this book as desirable from a major event. The mantra of the Edinburgh Festival Fringe is "to give anyone a stage and everyone a seat", which is fundamentally about inclusion. It has been running since 1947 and is a creative global phenomenon, unique in the world. It is an annual festival and performing arts marketplace that attracts some 3700 shows from over 60 countries, across 260 venues, for 50,000 performances throughout the month of August. It covers all genres of the performing arts – from theatre to comedy, contemporary dance, music, cabaret, circus, street performance and more – and involves those at the start of their creative journey as well as household names. It is by far the biggest of a rich tapestry of six festivals that all take place at the same time – the Edinburgh Military Tattoo and the Edinburgh International, Book, Art and Film Festivals. Collectively we make a local and global melting pot of creativity on the scale of a FIFA World Cup, and second only to the Olympics in terms of ticketed events. And we bring a return to the city of around £500 million, every year.

The chapter on the Fringe in this book speaks to the importance of sense of place, connection and identity. It is doubtful that the Fringe would have lasted over 75 years and evolved as it has without the particularity of Edinburgh. With its fabric and landscape – castle, cobbles, closes, wynds – it is a city of discovery hosting a festival that aims for the same. Fringe just wouldn't be the same in any other city. It is the way the festival inhabits, seeps in, becomes part of it all that make the event and the city somehow synonymous. The Edinburgh Fringe Festival was the catalyst for what has become a global movement, with some 400 Fringe festivals across the world and immeasurable mentions on media and broadcast outlets from Fringe alumni.

> It begins and ends with Edinburgh:
> its closes and taverns, venues in caverns
> and waiting in line for a show.
> That feeling of belonging
> in a crowd of perfect strangers.
> The Fringe that calls Edinburgh home.
>
> (extract from Fringe Blueprint 2017 – 70th anniversary)

Whether it's the democratic process and collective decision-making that sets the guidelines for street performers at the Edinburgh Fringe or the prop swap shops, local sourcing and commitment to print reduction, or the social interaction and shared interest, standing in line talking about shows – the Fringe speaks to Scottish values of inclusion, freedom of expression, cultural democracy and welcome.

However, it is not perfect; it is constantly evolving, has challenges of over-commercialism and needs to stay true to its roots of open access. But it is a values-led event, holding its participants to core principles of putting artists first, being open to all and looking out for each other and the planet.

Imagine if there was actual investment; how we could massively engage every community: enhance students' experience; encourage visitors to traverse Scotland; support volunteers; work with schools, care homes and hospitals. At a fraction of the cost of a cycling or FIFA or Olympic event, we could have sustained, positive and transformative change for local people and visitors alike.

Success needs supportive local government policy-making that provides balance between the needs of local residents and the benefits that an annual event of scale brings. As another contributor in this book contends, legacy doesn't happen on its own – it needs commitment, education, training, infrastructure sustained knowledge, expertise, strategies and initiatives.

I have worked in the arts, and specifically events, for 35 years, from film festivals and community Halloween celebrations to Cities of Culture and the Edinburgh Fringe. I have seen the Hindu Puja season in Bengal, where large-scale installations transform places and the life-size clay sculptures that are paraded through the streets are made year-round by local artisans. Whether it's the Kite Festival in Jogjakarta, the Bridgewater Carnival or the festivals in my local villages, the Lammas Fair in Ballycastle or the Portaferry Gala week, I believe in the transformational power of events, but some events more than others.

There is a direct correlation between cultural participation and health, life expectancy and quality of life. In turn, the healthiest economies in Europe are in those countries with the greatest cultural participation and creativity. Cultural participation provides the context for innovation and experimentation. Innovation and experimentation equals a wealthy economy. And therein lies the direct link between culture and economic benefit. But it requires long-term investment, trust and belief in people, and creative thinking at the heart of learning and training and skills.

It seems we look to the arts, and will create culturally driven regenerative programmes, in times of greatest need. Edinburgh's festivals were created as a means of healing and reconnection after the horrors of the Second World War. Derry, Glasgow and Liverpool won City of Culture titles in response to the need for social and economic reinvention. When COVID struck we turned to movies and TV box sets, and moments of joy were brought by musicians on the balconies of Italy or the synchronised playing of "Sunshine on Leith" from the tower blocks at Edinburgh's docks. What if this kind of healing and joy could be achieved in a sustained way and not only as a response to tragedy?

There are measures of success that are harder to evaluate but that bring real meaning and impact.

A sports journalist wrote in the *Derry Journal* in June 2013: "there is a success story happening in Derry that no spreadsheet, graph or accountant will ever be able to measure".

There was so much more to 2013 than buildings or economic return; after all, we took our guiding narrative from a poet rather than an economist. As Seamus Heaney reminded us in a speech just before his death that year:

> We are not simply a credit rating or an economy, but a history and a culture, a human population, rather than a statistical phenomenon.

Shona McCarthy
Chief Executive, Edinburgh Festival Fringe Society

PREFACE

In an era of rapid transformation, the education of the next generation of effective and socially conscious leaders is evolving at an unprecedented pace. The challenge lies in conveying complex ideas in a simplified manner, particularly within the intricate context of events, especially major and mega events. It is imperative to strike a balance between academic rigour and practical application, a balance that is essential for both educators and practitioners in the field. This book, *Events and Society*, is crafted with this goal in mind – making complex ideas accessible for busy students and even busier professionals who are deeply involved in managing the events they deliver.

The aim of this book is to create an accessible and intellectually stimulating resource focused on the crucial societal issues surrounding the planning, delivery, and legacy of hosting events. It is designed for students, academics, and practitioners alike. By bridging the gap between theoretical understanding and practical application, this book aspires to facilitate a deeper comprehension of the multifaceted nature of events and their impact on society.

Over the past decade there has been a proliferation of open-access and highly accessible short pieces related to event studies, authored by scholars worldwide. These pieces, characterized by their clear articulation of complex ideas, serve as ideal teaching material. The accessibility of these writings, crafted to be easily understood and integrated into learning and teaching, forms the unique selling point of this book. In the post-COVID era, educators are seeking high-quality content that can capture the attention and imagination of students. The short chapters in this book can be seamlessly integrated into weekly teaching modules, complete with activities that bring cases and examples to life.

The interdisciplinary nature of this book series honours diverse theoretical ideas and concepts drawn from a wide range of disciplines. Each chapter presents guiding theoretical ideas at the outset, and the volume maintains a balance between theory and practice throughout all chapters. By adopting a rigorous and disciplined approach to the study of leisure-related topics, we can make more general claims about how leisure serves as a unique incubator and social microcosm, contributing to disciplinary ideas and concepts. This approach will improve leisure-related research and attract attention from well-established authors in other fields, encouraging them to take the study and analysis of leisure seriously. This discipline-led approach is vital for the intellectual contribution of this book, addressing a wide array of critical and contemporary issues pertinent to learning, teaching, and research units in universities worldwide. These include field-level programmes in leisure (e.g., tourism, events, sports, hospitality) and broader school-level programs (e.g., business schools, built environment) that substantively engage with leisure-related research, contexts, and cases.

A significant development in event studies is the recognition that thousands, if not tens of thousands, of scholars globally write about events without primarily identifying as "event scholars". To advance our understanding of the power and potential of events on society, we must incorporate this intellectual analysis into the orbit of event studies. This integration is crucial for developing a more plural conception of events. Event studies encompass a diverse range of fields and disciplines, examining various types of events (e.g., sports, cultural, business, tribal, ritualistic, pilgrimages) and utilizing disciplinary perspectives such as history, anthropology, sociology, and economics.

ACKNOWLEDGEMENTS

I want to thank all the authors for submitting their interesting work on events, their contribution to the production of this book, for being open to feedback, and for being part of a diverse set of chapters that honour the power and potential of events for transforming places, people, experiences, identity and perspectives, and our environment.

INTRODUCTION

Mike Duignan

We know, intuitively, that events are powerful drivers of social change. We invest time, energy, and sometimes billions of dollars in the hope that they will transform the fortunes, lives, and livelihoods of the people and places that host them. Whether it's a local village fete or the grandest mega-event, we understand their impact. We feel it and we see it. Grassroots events excel at bringing people together and building social cohesion, while mega-events bring significant social and economic transformation to neighborhoods, business districts, and the nation at large over extended periods.

It is self-evident that not all transformation is beneficial. Each event is unique, with its own set of stakeholders, challenges, histories, and objectives. There is no universal "one-size-fits-all" event that achieves universally positive outcomes. Some benefits come at the expense of others. This is sometimes justified, sometimes less so. While most would argue that outcomes need not be a zero-sum game, in some contexts they are, especially where opportunity and resources are scarce. Events and their complex stakeholder networks must reflect on how to optimize benefits for those intended to benefit and mitigate harm to others.

As my friend Danny O'Brien says, events are "seed capital" – what owners and organizers do with them is what truly matters. Yet, it still surprises me how ignorant some are to this plain fact, often expecting positive social outcomes to occur with little or no attention, especially in the case of major and mega-events. This book honors a wide range of events, big and small, cultural, business, and sporting, across various cultural settings. They all share one common focus: being transformational – whether for the people affected, the places impacted, the experiences had, individual or group identity and representation, and, ultimately, for our environment.

Events serve as transformational "rites of passage" and tools for reconfiguring organizational fields. They impact industrial fields (e.g., tourism,

DOI: 10.4324/9781003488729-1

hospitality, and leisure industries), geographical fields (e.g., event-led urban and rural development and regeneration), and social fields (e.g., advancing social movements such as #MeToo and #BlackLivesMatter). Scholars across all fields and disciplines contribute to contemporary conversations and, in doing so, enrich event studies. This book aims to harness this wealth of knowledge, illustrating the significant impact of events-related research and fostering a more comprehensive understanding of their role in society.

The key social themes that are addressed across the book include:

- **Social Connection and Loneliness**: The role of festivals and events in fostering community solidarity and combating social isolation.
- **Cultural Identity and Belonging**: How events can transform individuals' sense of place, self, and community, and promote cultural expression and inclusivity.
- **Health and Well-being**: The impact of sports and physical activity promoted through events, and the challenges in translating elite sports success into grassroots participation.
- **Disability and Inclusion**: The effects of events like the Paralympics on societal perceptions of disability and the lived experiences of people with disabilities.
- **Volunteering and Community Engagement**: The long-term impacts of event volunteering programs and the importance of integrating these initiatives into broader community engagement strategies.
- **Economic Inequality and Displacement**: The uneven distribution of benefits from hosting mega-events, often leading to the displacement and marginalization of vulnerable communities.
- **Sustainability and Environmental Impact**: The environmental challenges and sustainable practices associated with hosting large-scale events.
- **Digital and Technological Innovation**: The influence of digital technologies, such as virtual reality and smartphones, on the event experience and audience engagement.
- **Safety and Security**: The importance of robust security measures and risk management practices in ensuring the safety of event attendees.
- **LGBTQ+ Visibility and Rights**: The significance of Pride events in promoting visibility and acceptance of LGBTQ+ individuals, particularly in non-urban areas.
- **Historical and Cultural Preservation**: Using historical events and cultural traditions to inform contemporary event planning and foster a sense of continuity and respect for heritage.

This book comprises 30 chapters, each addressing diverse and interconnected topics related to the societal implications of hosting events. Each chapter follows a consistent structure, beginning with the aim and learning objective(s), followed by theoretical focuses and the significance of these perspectives. Similarly, practical focuses and their significance are also outlined. The main body of each chapter consists of an 800- to 2000-word argument. Following the argument, chapters include managerial, policy, and/or research implications, explicitly mapping how they relate to the UN Sustainable Development Goals. Each chapter concludes with a series of quizzes to test knowledge and debate questions to engage learners in discussing and interrogating the argument.

I outline the focus and key argument(s) of each chapter in turn below.

Chapter 1 How festival encounters transform lives and landscapes – and why we should care

This chapter explores the transformative power of festivals on individuals and landscapes. It introduces the concept of "festival landscapes," where the physical and emotional interactions between people and their surroundings foster deep connections and care. The authors illustrate these transformations using the example of Lutruwita/Tasmania, showing how festivals can alter participants' sense of place, self, and others. The chapter emphasizes the importance of understanding these dynamics for festival organizers, policymakers, and researchers to enhance the positive impacts of festivals.

Chapter 2 City festivals and social connection: post-plague lessons from 17th-century Naples

This chapter examines how civic festivals in 17th-century Naples helped combat loneliness and foster social connections during the post-plague period. It suggests that similar approaches could be beneficial in modern post-pandemic contexts. By using historical sources, the chapter demonstrates how these festivals promoted community solidarity and well-being across different socio-economic classes. It argues that incorporating historical insights into contemporary event planning can address issues of loneliness and social isolation effectively.

Chapter 3 London 2012: did it inspire a generation?

This chapter critically assesses the claim that the London 2012 Olympics would "inspire a generation." It reviews the legacy of the event, particularly focusing on national sports participation trends before and after the Games. The chapter finds mixed evidence regarding the "demonstration effect," where elite sports are supposed to inspire grassroots participation. It concludes that, while the Games were a catalyst for enhancing the UK's elite sport infrastructure, the broader claim of inspiring widespread participation among the general population remains unproven.

Chapter 4 What did London 2012 mean for the Paralympics and the lives of people with disabilities?

This chapter evaluates the impact of the London 2012 Paralympic Games on perceptions of disability and the lives of disabled people. It highlights both positive and negative outcomes, noting significant advancements in elite parasports and disability awareness. However, it also points out that many disabled people continue to face significant societal barriers. The chapter emphasizes the need for ongoing efforts beyond the Games to achieve meaningful social change for people with disabilities.

Chapter 5 Has the London 2012 volunteering programme engendered a sustainable and wider volunteering legacy in the UK?

This chapter investigates the long-term impact of the London 2012 Games on volunteering in the UK. It discusses how the "Games Makers" program aimed to create a lasting volunteer culture. The chapter finds that, while there were immediate increases in volunteer participation, sustaining this momentum has been challenging. It highlights the importance of integrating volunteering initiatives into broader community engagement strategies to ensure a lasting legacy.

Chapter 6 A critical review of the Paralympic Games' potential to increase disabled people's sport participation

This chapter critically examines the potential of the Paralympic Games to boost sports participation among disabled people. It finds limited evidence supporting the idea that the Games significantly increase grassroots participation. The chapter suggests that, while the Paralympics can raise awareness and inspire some individuals, broader and more inclusive initiatives are necessary to achieve substantial and lasting increases in participation levels among disabled people.

Chapter 7 How does hosting the Olympics benefit local communities? An examination of Tokyo 2020

This chapter explores the social impacts of hosting the Tokyo 2020 Olympics on local communities. It discusses the concept of "mega-event legacy," focusing on both short-term and long-term social effects. The chapter critiques the negative impacts, such as displacement and rising living costs, while also considering potential benefits like improved infrastructure and increased international visibility. It calls for more strategic planning to maximize positive legacies and mitigate adverse effects on local residents.

Chapter 8 Does Carnival still come first in Rio even when the Olympics come to town?

This chapter compares the impacts of the Rio Carnival, a hallmark cultural event, with the 2016 Rio Olympics, a mega-sporting event. It discusses the social, cultural, and economic influences of these events on Rio de Janeiro and its residents. The chapter highlights that, while the Olympics provided infrastructure improvements and economic boosts, the Carnival, deeply rooted in Brazilian culture, plays a more significant role in promoting social cohesion, cultural expression, and economic survival for local communities. The Carnival's annual recurrence contrasts with the transient nature of the Olympics, emphasizing the need for ethical and sustainable event management that respects local traditions and benefits all stakeholders.

Chapter 9 Creating queer spaces: small-town Prides grow in numbers and popularity

This chapter explores the emergence and impact of Pride celebrations in small towns and rural areas, challenging the notion that LGBTQ+ culture is predominantly urban. It uses queer rurality theory to highlight the significance of these regional Prides, which provide essential support and visibility to queer individuals outside metropolitan areas. These events foster a sense of belonging and community, countering the isolation often experienced in rural settings. The chapter also addresses the challenges faced by organizers, such as resistance from local communities, but ultimately celebrates the resilience and positive impact of small-town Prides on their participants and broader society.

Chapter 10 Olympics for whom? Winners and losers of mega-events

This chapter critically examines the uneven distribution of benefits and harms resulting from hosting the Olympic Games. Using the framework of the right to the city, it argues that, while these events can bring infrastructural and economic benefits, they often exacerbate inequalities by favoring affluent areas and displacing marginalized communities. Case studies from various Olympic Games illustrate how the rhetoric of positive legacies often masks the adverse impacts on local residents. The chapter calls for more inclusive and equitable approaches to planning and hosting mega-events to ensure they truly benefit all urban inhabitants.

Chapter 11 Who benefits when a city hosts the World Cup?

This chapter delves into the consequences of hosting the FIFA World Cup, questioning who truly benefits from such a mega-event. It argues that, while the World Cup can enhance a city's global profile and infrastructure, it often leads to financial strain, displacement, and increased inequality. The chapter discusses the motivations behind cities' bids to host the World Cup, the common economic and social impacts, and proposes alternative planning strategies that prioritize equitable development and long-term benefits for all residents, rather than just the elites.

Chapter 12 How hosting the Olympics can lead to displacement

This chapter explores the phenomenon of displacement caused by the Olympics. It uses the concept of "accumulation by dispossession" to describe how hosting the Games often results in the eviction of low-income residents to make way for event infrastructure. Historical examples from Seoul, Atlanta, and Rio de Janeiro highlight the scale of forced evictions and the socio-economic consequences for affected communities. The chapter stresses the need for policies that protect residents' rights and ensure that the benefits of hosting mega-events are equitably distributed, avoiding further marginalization of vulnerable populations

Chapter 13 Marginalization, displacement, and exclusion in Montreal's cultural economy

Focusing on Montreal, this chapter investigates how the city's cultural economy, particularly outdoor festivals and busking, can marginalize and displace vulnerable groups. Through oral history interviews with long-time buskers, it reveals the challenges they face due to regulatory practices and urban transformation. The chapter argues that, while cultural events contribute to the city's vibrancy and economy, they often exclude those who are socially and economically marginalized. It calls for a more inclusive approach to urban planning and event management that considers the needs of all residents, ensuring equitable access to economic opportunities and public spaces.

Chapter 14 The roar of the crowd: how fans create electric atmospheres

The vibrant energy of mega-events lies in the electric atmosphere created by fans. This chapter delves into the social interactions that fuel these dynamic environments. It explores how organizers and fans co-create atmosphere before, during, and after events, emphasizing the importance of these collaborative efforts. As economies recover from the COVID-19 pandemic, understanding and enhancing the ambiance of mega-events is crucial for their success and lasting impact.

Chapter 15 Could virtual reality change gigs forever?

This chapter discusses the transformative potential of virtual reality (VR) and artificial intelligence (AI) in the context of live music events. It explores how these technologies can create immersive experiences that challenge traditional notions of live performances. The chapter introduces the concept of avatar performance and the uncanny valley, where digital representations may evoke feelings of unease. Through examples such as ABBA's virtual concerts, the chapter examines the future of audience engagement and the implications of these technologies on the music industry. It raises questions about the balance between technological innovation and the preservation of the live music experience.

Chapter 16 Looking beyond the screen: smartphone effects on festival engagement

This chapter investigates the impact of mobile devices on festival experiences. It applies the Unified Theory of Acceptance and Use of Technology 2 (UTAUT2) to understand how and why people use their phones during festivals. The chapter highlights the dual role of smartphones, which can both enhance and detract from festival engagement. It offers practical strategies for managing phone usage to foster communal interaction and improve attendee satisfaction. The discussion prompts readers to reflect on their digital habits, and encourages mindful use of technology to enrich social experiences at festivals.

Chapter 17 The need for live event security risk management practices in a post-COVID-19 world

This chapter emphasizes the importance of robust security risk management in the live events industry, particularly in the post-pandemic context. It outlines the lack of professionalism and adequate government regulation as significant security risks. The chapter argues for stronger public–private intelligence partnerships to protect attendees from threats such as terrorism, crowd surges, and other safety hazards. By examining incidents like the Fyre Festival and the Manchester Arena bombing, the chapter illustrates the dire consequences of inadequate security measures, and underscores the need for comprehensive risk management policies.

Chapter 18 Strategies for event managers to safeguard against deadly crowds

This chapter explores methods for event managers to foster cooperative crowding and enhance crowd safety. It emphasizes the importance of trust and collaboration among key stakeholders, including event managers, security personnel, and public officials. The chapter discusses the concept of cooperative crowding, where positive crowd behavior is encouraged through shared understanding and strategic planning. By analyzing incidents like the Astroworld tragedy, the chapter highlights the need for proactive crowd management strategies to prevent deadly surges and ensure the safety of attendees.

Chapter 19 Black Pete: an annual tradition or a national embarrassment?

This chapter examines the contentious Dutch tradition of Black Pete and its implications for systemic racism. It analyzes evolving Dutch attitudes towards Black Pete and the broader debate on blackface traditions worldwide. The chapter highlights the damaging effects of such traditions, and calls for a global reckoning to address racial stereotypes and promote equality. Through the lens of the Black Lives Matter movement, it discusses the ongoing efforts to challenge and change these cultural practices in the Netherlands and beyond.

Chapter 20 Contradictions and complexities: the Sydney Gay and Lesbian Mardi Gras, LGBT tourism events and social reform

This chapter critically examines the Sydney Gay and Lesbian Mardi Gras (SGLMG) and its dual role as a community-based celebration and a commercialized tourism event. It explores the historical significance of the parade for LGBTQ+ communities and the complexities arising from its integration into the tourism economy. The chapter discusses the tensions between maintaining the event's original political and social reform goals and the pressures of commercial interests. It highlights the challenges of ensuring that the Mardi Gras remains a platform for advocacy while also contributing to economic growth.

Chapter 21 Events and social media: the #Euro2020 online firestorm

This chapter investigates the powerful influence of social media on events, focusing on the #Euro2020 online firestorm following England's loss in the Euro 2020 final. It examines how social media platforms can amplify both positive and negative aspects of events. The chapter discusses the phenomenon of online firestorms, characterized by a surge of negative word-of-mouth and harassment. It highlights the role of social media in spreading racist abuse towards players and the broader societal implications. The chapter calls for proactive measures to manage online behavior and protect individuals from harassment during major events.

Chapter 22 #genderequalOlympics? Critical analysis of gender equality and the Olympic Games as a major multi-sport event

Chapter 22 critically examines the International Olympic Committee's (IOC) claims of achieving gender equality at the Olympic Games. This chapter scrutinizes the assertion that the Paris 2024 Summer Olympics would be the first "gender equal" Games due to equal athlete quotas for men and women. By exploring concepts such as gender parity and balance, this chapter aims to reveal the complexities and shortcomings of the IOC's approach to fostering gender equality in sports.

Chapter 23 Staging the African renaissance at Africa's first Black cultural festival

This chapter explores the First World Festival of Negro Arts, held in Dakar, Senegal, in 1966, highlighting its role in fostering a shared Pan-African culture and identity. It examines the festival's significance in the political context of African decolonization and the Cold War. The chapter argues that such events are not merely cultural gatherings but platforms that perform and produce Pan-African ideals, thereby promoting cultural and political unity. It calls for a revival of these festivals to enhance cultural, economic, and political collaboration across the African continent and diaspora.

Chapter 24 Transformative events: a migrant narrative of identity and belonging at the Edinburgh Festival Fringe

This chapter presents a personal case study of a Syrian scholar performing research on stage at the Edinburgh Festival Fringe. It explores how narrative performances can challenge stereotypes and singular narratives about migration, fostering a sense of belonging and identity among migrants. The chapter emphasizes the transformative power of storytelling events in creating inclusive spaces and promoting social change. It highlights the importance of narrative performance as a method of engaging public audiences and addressing issues of migration and displacement.

Chapter 25 Chale let's go: the case of the Chale Wote Street Art Festival

Focusing on the Chale Wote Street Art Festival in Accra, Ghana, this chapter examines how public art festivals can transform marginalized urban spaces and challenge conventional narratives. It discusses the festival as a catalyst for social change, using artistic projects and participatory engagements to reimagine public spaces. The chapter emphasizes the festival's role in producing knowledge and fostering cultural and social reimagining, particularly within the context of the Global South.

Chapter 26 Glastonbury and climate change: how the world's most iconic music festival puts the spotlight on climate challenges and solutions

This chapter discusses the environmental initiatives of the UK's Glastonbury Festival, highlighting its role in raising awareness about climate change. It explores how the festival integrates sustainability into its operations and promotes environmental consciousness among attendees. The chapter argues that festivals like Glastonbury can serve as powerful platforms for advocating climate action and demonstrating practical solutions to environmental challenges. It emphasizes the need for event organizers to adopt sustainable practices to minimize their ecological footprint.

Chapter 27 Concerns about the social implications of sporting events in natural areas

This chapter examines the social impacts of hosting sporting events in natural areas, focusing on the potential conflicts between environmental conservation and recreational use. It discusses the challenges of balancing the economic benefits of such events with the need to protect natural landscapes and biodiversity. The chapter calls for more comprehensive planning and management strategies to ensure that sporting events do not compromise the ecological integrity of natural areas. It highlights the importance of stakeholder engagement and sustainable tourism practices to address these issues.

Chapter 28 The good, the bad, and the noisy: the paradox(s) created by motorized events in green spaces

This chapter explores the complexities of hosting motorized events in green spaces, highlighting the conflicting values involved. It uses social capital theory and environmental science to examine the social, political, and ecological impacts of these events. The chapter emphasizes the need for a nuanced understanding of value conflicts and the importance of adopting sustainable event planning practices. It calls for a more critical approach to evaluating the benefits and drawbacks of motorized events in protected areas, considering issues of diversity, equity, and environmental sustainability.

Chapter 29 London 2012: what the Olympic Games' legacy of sustainability means for events today

This chapter assesses the sustainability legacy of the London 2012 Olympic Games, focusing on its impact on contemporary event management practices. It discusses the initiatives implemented to promote environmental sustainability during the Games and their long-term effects on the events industry. The chapter highlights the importance of integrating sustainability into all aspects of event planning and operations. It argues that the lessons learned from London 2012 can guide future events in achieving more sustainable outcomes and contribute to broader environmental goals.

Chapter 30 March Madness and the environmental impacts of sport events

This chapter investigates the environmental impacts of the US National Collegiate Athletic Association (NCAA) March Madness tournament, focusing on the carbon footprint and resource consumption associated with large-scale sporting events. It examines the challenges of balancing the economic and social benefits of such events with their environmental costs. The chapter calls for the adoption of green event management practices, including carbon offsetting, waste reduction, and sustainable transportation options. It emphasizes the role of stakeholders, including organizers, sponsors, and attendees, in minimizing the ecological footprint of sports events.

SECTION

1 TRANSFORMING PEOPLE

1 HOW FESTIVAL ENCOUNTERS TRANSFORM LIVES AND LANDSCAPES – AND WHY WE SHOULD CARE

Amelie Katczynski, Elaine Stratford and Pauline Marsh

AIM

To explore how encounters between people and landscapes at festivals are transformative, and to examine how they can engender relations of care.

DOI: 10.4324/9781003488729-3

LEARNING OBJECTIVES

LEARNING OBJECTIVES

1. Introduce the 'festival landscape' concept;
2. Illustrate how transformations of landscapes and people occur in practice, drawing on the example of Lutruwita/Tasmania; and
3. Show how the transformative dynamics of festival landscapes can mobilize relations of care.

Theoretical focus and significance

Theoretically, this chapter examines how festival landscapes transform individuals' sense of place, self, and other through embodied encounters. It also explores how individuals, in turn, transform festival landscapes. Additionally, the chapter considers the implications of these transformations for the relationships of care between people and landscapes.

Practical focus and significance

Practically, this chapter focuses on examining interactions between people and festival landscapes in Lutruwita/Tasmania that showcase relations of care. The significance of this examination lies in highlighting readily applicable ideas and insights for festival organizers, policy makers, and researchers who aim to foster relations of care in festival landscapes.

TOPIC – HOW FESTIVAL ENCOUNTERS TRANSFORM LIVES AND LANDSCAPES – AND WHY WE SHOULD CARE

Have you ever felt transformed at a festival? Perhaps you pitched your tent in a vast open paddock, or slept nestled among the trees in a forest? Maybe you felt sand run through your toes as you danced on golden beaches, or heard music rhythms bounce off the walls in a buzzing city? More than just party backdrops, festival landscapes are places that can transform our sense of place, self, and other. And, as we work and play in and with festival landscapes, inhabit their ecosystems, and journey on their paths, we also leave traces of ourselves (Ingold 1993). In this chapter, we focus on these potential transformations and questions about care that they evoke. We ask: how might encounters between people and landscapes at festivals transform both, and how can both engender relations of care?

Lutruwita/Tasmania is an Australian island-state well known internationally for its picturesque landscapes and ecological diversity.[1] A rich festival calendar mobilizes these attributes and the hundreds of thousands of people who travel to and through the state for festivals (Godde 2023). We completed in-depth interviews with seven festival organizers, performers, and attendees (Katczynski et al. 2022a). Here, we outline key findings from that study about how participants' interactions with festival landscapes of Lutruwita transform their sense of place, self, and other in ways that engender relations of care. We link our findings to broader theoretical contexts and point towards how our study's insights may help inform the work by festival producers and staff, policy makers, and attendees.

Festival landscapes

Our conception of 'festival landscape' is based in theoretical discussions by human geographers and social science festival research that employs the term. Wylie (2007, 1) distinguishes between studying landscapes as a 'scene we are looking at from afar' and as 'a world we are living in.' The second approach stresses experiences of closeness and entwinement (Ryan & Wollan 2013) and, we suggest, can further insights into how people–landscape interactions can engender relations of care. It links with studies on relationships between people and the more-than-human world as embodied encounters (Simonsen et al. 2017) that are created by multi-sensory, experiential, cognitive, and emotional engagements (see Simonsen 2007; Merleau-Ponty 2002 [1962]). We argue that this people/landscape interconnectedness brings opportunities and motivations to care.

Embodied work: transforming landscapes

Experiences of care were evident in our participants' descriptions of hands-on work to shape and transform festival landscapes. Crafting his disc jockey (DJ) stage at a bush doof (Figure 1.1),[2] one participant used existing features so as to not impose: 'If you use what's already there, then [the stage] blends in with that whole environment and ties in to … how people feel in it.' People also cared for installations to become 'naturally reabsorbed' in their environs. Sometimes, this re-absorption started unexpectedly: after its installation (Figure 1.2), one artist found her rock labyrinth scattered by sheep trotting on their usual route. Such experiences illuminate the animated, uncontrollable elements of festival landscapes, and may prompt festival producers and staff to accommodate other species.

Figure 1.1 Stage at a bush doof, Lutruwita/Tasmania. Author own image.

Figure 1.2 Rock labyrinth at the Fractangular Festival, Katree Designs. Author own image.

Although festival experiences can connect people to place (Duffy et al. 2011), all festival landscapes are ephemeral – they continually change (Atha 2018). People's repeated festival attendance can yield awareness of and concerns about change. One festival organizer told us: 'Since 2013 ... every summer [the site] just got drier and drier and drier ... 2020 was the driest year of all. There was no creek. There was just a stagnant puddle.' In this vein, studies suggest that people more likely show environmentally caring behaviours when they feel attached to a festival landscape (Alonso-Vazquez et al. 2019). In a time of 'deep uncertainty' (Whiting & Green 2024) characterized by extreme weather events, health crises such as COVID-19, and increasing costs of living and public liability insurance, many renowned festivals are not surviving. Festival producers and organizers may work together with policy makers to explore how to nonetheless invite recurring embodied interactions between people and landscapes that promote caring attachments.

People's encounters transformed

The idea that festival landscapes can strengthen inter-human relationships is not new, and can be linked to Durkheim's (1976 [1912]) early work on how rituals revive collective consciousness. For our participants, a sense of community was intertwined with bodily experiences: 'When you go and you camp, you get burnt together, you get wet together, you dance together ... it creates ... an embrace for me.' Moreover, when participants camped and partied out in the open, exposure to the elements, or what Ingold (2007, p. 19) calls 'the weather world,' enhanced a sense of interconnectedness, even between strangers. This outcome is what Simonsen (2007, p. 176) calls the 'affective space' of festivals: spaces when and where we feel more 'open to the world and aware of its "affect" on us.'

Among our participants, physical features of festival landscapes supported spontaneous encounters: large green spaces, secluded tents filled with costumes, comfortable lounges. 'Bumping into' others evoked a feeling of social openness and fluidity – of 'throwntogetherness,' to use a term from Massey (2005). Meeting basic needs also brought people together: 'You had to climb down to the river over these rocks and then fill your water bottle from the river. And there was a little queue, everybody waiting and having a little chat,' one attendee recalled. Spontaneous encounters can magnify 'creative social powers' (Leal 2016, p. 596): festivals provide opportunities to extend bonds or simply to practise getting on together – important alternatives in times when widespread antagonistic politics create hostile environments (Gawlewicz & Yiftachel 2022). Regional festivals can offer particular possibilities for 'infrastructures of care' to emerge (Duffy & Stratford, in press), and festival organizers may consider how to work with landscapes to mobilize care instead of hostility.

Changing sense of self

How our participants encountered others and developed care-full considerations for landscapes was also linked to shifts in their own sense of self. These shifts often stemmed from a sense of departure from everyday lives (Fjær & Tutenges 2017). As people leave home, travel to a festival, and cross the gate, they step into a space bounded by fences, gates, and fixed dates that (somewhat ironically) prompt many to feel free.

Our participants emphasized two major shifts from the everyday. The first was a sense of changing sociality, which one festival-goer called a removal of 'social expectations that come with adulthood' and finding 'a more authentic version of yourself - or at least a freer one.' People felt free to dress more 'out there' or do 'silly things' that are usually 'socially taboo.' Carnival-like landscapes signal a temporary lift of social order (see Bakhtin 1984 [1965]). Sometimes, they blur gender norms: one participant who takes big eyeshadow palettes to festivals gets asked by heterosexual men, 'Oh, could you do my make-up for me?' Transgression or experimentation is mostly bounded to a festival's time and place (Ravenscroft & Gilchrist 2009). But, sometimes, effects linger: 'I started to wear clothes for joy a lot more ... to be a little bit more original,' one avid festival-goer said.

The second shift was a sense of being 'close to nature' - a changing spatiality. Remote or rural festival settings prompted people to feel 'connected to the landscape' or 'surrounded ... in a beautiful way.' One performer felt his 'circadian rhythms tapped in' when watching the sun rise or set.

These findings are consistent with research showing that embodied experiences of engagement in non-human surrounds are a pathway to a stronger sense of connection with nature (Richardson 2023). Strong nature connections are associated with an increased likelihood to take steps to care for the environment. Festival organizers and policy makers may consider how to facilitate access to remote and rural environments in ways that mobilize care instead of harm.

Concluding remarks

This chapter focused on embodied relationships of closeness between people and festival landscapes, and how they might engender care. However, we acknowledge that distance and disconnection make us care too: when we are not there yet, no more, or never will be (again) (Katczynski et al. 2022b; see Milligan & Wiles, 2010). Of course, landscapes and humans are not always transformed in positive ways by festivals. Environmental degradation, sexual violence, drug abuse, and discrimination associated with festivals demonstrate a distinct lack of care. These 'transformations' call for society-wide changes that no event can fix. Nevertheless, our work suggests that place-based, in-depth studies are valuable to help festival producers, organizers, performers, and attendees mobilize the transformative powers of festival landscapes as care-full places that can help reshape our world.[3]

Managerial implications

The fact that it is possible to foster and steer care-full interactions between people and festival landscapes by caring for existing features of landscapes and their more-than-human inhabitants, and to promote respectful human and inter-species and ecosystemic interactions.

Policy implications

Festival event policies should be mindful that, while protecting environments from degradation, locking people out of landscapes can exclude them from potentially meaningful relationships with that landscape. Policies might focus on what frameworks are needed to more effectively influence the quality of recurring events, and on what is needed to manage one-off or less regular events.

Research implications

The research implications of this chapter recognise that place-based studies are needed to help people understand the absence or presence of specific practices of care in encounters between people and landscapes in order to provide festival producers and staff with relevant knowledge about how such care manifests.

QUIZ QUESTIONS

1. What are two different conceptual views about what (festival) landscapes are?
2. What is a common approach in the social sciences to study encounters between people and festival landscapes?
3. In this study, when people created festival stages or art, how did they show care for place?
4. What kinds of experiences with a festival landscape made people care about others?
5. What was it about a festival landscape that made people feel free, and how did they express this freedom?

Table 1.1 Alignment to United Nations Sustainable Development Goals

Goal	How
Good health and well-being	A positive sense of self and connections people build with landscapes and others at festivals can promote well-being. Spending time in the green and blue spaces of festival landscapes that have clean water and air can affect people's health positively.
Decent work and economic growth	Working and recreating in and with festival landscapes in creative and care-full ways can be a satisfying and healthy activity. If people attend festivals because they feel connected to landscapes, their (recurring) attendance can support event economies.
Reduced inequality	Encounters between strangers at festivals open opportunities to engage with diverse others, and may lead to relationships of practical support to counter inequalities.
Responsible consumption and production	People's engagement with landscapes as they create and attend festivals can build a sense of interconnectedness and desire to care for environments. This may lead to responsible patterns of consumption and production around festival events.
Climate action	As people observe changes in a festival landscape, or experience severe weather events, their climate awareness can grow and may inspire them to act to mitigate climate change.

DEBATE QUESTIONS

1. If bodily interactions at festivals are so transformative, is it possible for online events to also affect people's relationships to place and others?
2. The authors described the boundedness of festivals as ironically also evoking a sense of freedom. Can you think of examples where events' fences and gates have opposite effects?
3. Festivals and events in general create a lot of pollution. What do you think needs to happen to reduce care-less behaviours towards environmental landscapes?
4. In your mind, is it tokenistic or disrespectful to experiment with different social roles at festivals – for example, dressing up like someone with a different sexuality or ethnicity?
5. Can care-full interactions between humans and ecosystems or humans and other species be 'managed' at a festival? If yes, how?

NOTES

1 Lutruwita is the *palawa kani* Indigenous term for the area European colonizers named Tasmania.
2 Bush doofs are electronic music events associated with Australian youth culture (Canosa & Bennet 2021).
3 Our findings were particular to the setting of Lutruwita/Tasmania and the time of interviews (during the COVID-19 pandemic) that shaped people's recollections (see Katczynski et al. 2022a).

REFERENCES

Alonso-Vazquez, M., Packer, J., Fairley, F., & Hughes, K. (2019). The Role of Place Attachment and Festival Attachment in Influencing Attendees' Environmentally Responsible Behaviours at Music Festivals. *Tourism Recreation Research 44*(1), 91–102.

Atha, M. (2018). Ephemeral Landscapes. In Howard, P., Thompson, I., Waterton, E., Atha, M. (Eds.), *The Routledge Companion to Landscape Studies* (pp. 113–126). Routledge.

Bakhtin, M., (1984; 1965). *Rabelais and His World.* Indiana University Press.

Canosa, A. & Bennett, A. (2021). Urban Vibes in a Rural Setting: A Study of the Bush Doof Scene in Byron Shire. *Journal of Youth Studies 24*(3), 388–403. https://doi.org/10.1080/13676261.2020.1730772.

Duffy, M., Waitt, G., Gorman-Murray, A., & Gibson, C. (2011). Bodily Rhythms: Corporeal Capacities to Engage with Festival Spaces. *Emotion, Space and Society 4*, 17–24. https://doi.org/10.1016/j.emospa.2010.03.004.

Duffy, M., Stratford, E. (in press). Regional Arts Festivals as Infrastructures of Care. In C.P. Boyd, L.E. Boyle, S.L. Bell, E. Högström, J. Evans, A. Paul, & R. Foley (Eds.), *Routledge Handbook on Spaces of Mental Health and Wellbeing* (Chapter 29). Routledge.

Durkheim, E. (1912; 1976). *The Elementary Forms of Religious Life* (transl. by Joseph Ward Swain, second edition). Allen & Unwin.

Fjær, E.G., & Tutenges, S. (2017). Departies: Conceptualizing Extended Youth Parties. *Journal of Youth Studies 20*(2), 200–215.

Gawlewicz, A., & Yiftachel, O. (2022). 'Throwntogetherness' in Hostile Environments: Migration and the Remaking of Urban Citizenship. *City 26*(2–3), 346–358. https://doi.org/10.1080/13604813.2022.2056350.

Godde, C. (2023, June 26). Midwinter Festival Dark Mofo Posts Attendance Record. *Daily Adviser.* https://www.dailyadvertiser.com.au/story/8247121/midwinter-festival-dark-mofo-posts-attendance-record/.

Ingold, T. (1993). The Temporality of the Landscape. *World Archaeology 25*(2), 152–174.

Ingold, T. (2007). Earth, Sky, Wind, and Weather. *Journal of the Royal Anthropological Institute 13,* 19–38.

Katczynski, A., Stratford, E., & Marsh, P. (2022a). Tracing Memories and Meanings of Festival Landscapes during the COVID-19 Pandemic. *Emotion Space and Society 44*, 100903. https://doi.org/10.1016/j.emospa.2022.100903.

Katczynski, A., Stratford, E., & Marsh, P. (2022b). Absence and Distance: Reflections on Festival Landscapes in a Pandemic. *Social and Cultural Geography 24*(10, 1808–1826. https://doi.org/10.1080/14649365.2022.2107230.

Leal, J. (2016). Festivals, Group Making, Remaking and Unmaking. *Ethnos: Journal of Anthropology 81*, 584–599. https://doi.org/10.1080/00141844.2014.989870.

Massey, D. (2005). *For Space.* SAGE Publications.

Merleau-Ponty, M. (2002; 1962). *Phenomenology of Perception* (transl. by Colin Smith). Routledge.

Milligan, C., & Wiles, J. (2010). Landscapes of care. *Progress in Human Geography 34*, 736–754. https://doi.org/10.1177/0309132510364556.

Ravenscroft, N., & Gilchrist, P. (2009). Spaces of Transgression: Governance, Discipline and Reworking the Carnivalesque. *Leisure Studies 28*(1), 35–49. https://doi.org/10.1080/02614360802127243.

Richardson, M. (2023). *Reconnection: Fixing our Broken Relationship with Nature.* Pelagic Publishing.

Ryan, A. W., & Wollan, G. (2013). Festivals, Landscapes, and Aesthetic Engagement: A Phenomenological Approach to Four Norwegian Festivals. *Norsk Geografisk Tidsskrift Norwegian Journal of Geography* 67, 99–112. https://doi.org/10.1080/00291951.2013.784352.

Simonsen, K. 2007. Practice, Spatiality and Embodied Emotions: An Outline of a Geography of Practice. *Human Affairs 17,* 168–181. https://doi.org/10.2478/v10023-007-0015-8.

Simonsen, K., Koefoed, L., & de Neergaard, M. (2017). Festival as Embodied Encounters: On 'Kulturhavn' in Copenhagen. *Journal of Intercultural Studies 38*(6), 637–650. https://doi.org/10.1080/07256868.2017.1386633.

Whiting, S., & Green, B. (2024, February 15). Why are so many Australian music festivals being cancelled? *The Conversation.* https://theconve.rsation.com/why-are-so-many-australian-music-festivals-being-cancelled-223559

Wylie, J. (2007). *Landscape: Key Ideas in Geography*. Routledge.

2 CITY FESTIVALS AND SOCIAL CONNECTION

Post-plague lessons from 17th-century Naples

Keith Johnston

AIM

The aim of this chapter is to promote civic festivals, such as those celebrated in Naples in the 17th century, as an effective means of combating loneliness and isolation in modern, post-pandemic life.

DOI: 10.4324/9781003488729-4

LEARNING OBJECTIVES

LEARNING OBJECTIVES

1. Explain how civic festivals fostered social connection in early modern Naples.
2. Demonstrate how historical practices might inspire solutions to the current crisis of loneliness.
3. Show how critical historical approaches can inform planning and policy decisions.

Theoretical focus and significance

The theoretical focus of this chapter is on the use of historical sources and critical historiography to understand patterns of human behavior, especially in the wake of social disturbances like the epidemic spread of disease. This theoretical focus opens up new avenues to creatively explore the past for practices that ameliorate human suffering.

Practical focus and significance

The practical focus of this chapter is on demonstrating the ways that civic festivals fostered social connection in early modern Naples. The practical significance of this chapter is its suggestion that community events that embrace the solemn and celebratory and involve all socio-economic classes may have positive effects on a community's health and well-being.

TOPIC – CITY FESTIVALS AND SOCIAL CONNECTION: POST-PLAGUE LESSONS FROM 17TH-CENTURY NAPLES

The plague has passed, but an epidemic rages on. The World Health Organization officially ended the Covid-19 public health emergency of international concern (PHEIC) on May 5, 2023. However, what could have been a cause for celebration was anything but. "[T]he ending of the PHEIC is a bit of a collective shrug," Victoria Fan, a Fellow at the Center for Global Development, told *Vox* on the day of the announcement. "Many countries have already moved on, and have other political and policy priorities, with rising debt and inflation and all sorts of other types of crises that have floated to the top" (Landman, 2023). In fact, just two days earlier the Office of the US Surgeon General released a report with a title that says it all: "Our Epidemic of Loneliness and Isolation" (2023).

This epidemic began long before Covid-19 familiarized the world with "social distancing." The Prime Minister of the UK famously appointed a so-called "Minister of Loneliness" in 2018 in the wake of a report from Member of Parliament (MP) Rachel Reeves, who had come to some grim conclusions about the state of modern life. "In the last few decades," she said at the time, "loneliness has escalated from personal misfortune into a social epidemic" (Policy Exchange, 2017).

It doesn't have to be this way. History furnishes us with many examples of how other societies have combated the atomism and anomie that can follow on the heels of devastating epidemics, threatening to tear apart communities already rife with trouble. One of the most instructive examples might be that of the hurly-burly Italian port city of Naples, which drew on a thriving tradition of festivals to help put itself back together following a calamitous epidemic of bubonic plague that began in the spring of 1656. That December, as the disease retreated, the city celebrated a ten-day festival of mourning, thanksgiving, and great celebration. "After such calamity," says a contemporary Jesuit account, the city celebrated a festival that was "if not the greatest, as is often said, then at least, no one can deny, one not unequal to those seen in Naples in the midst of its greatest happiness" (Anon., 1660, p. 168). Should a future plague ever ravage the globe, sending us back into our homes for goodness knows how long, perhaps a festival might offer some of the communal comfort we crave.

City festivals were anything but new to Naples in 1656. The December event was, in fact, already on the calendar to celebrate the conception of the Virgin Mary on December 8. A year of outrageous suffering simply changed its focus. Like the many festivals before it, this one recruited nearly every order of society to participate in processions, devotions, performances, speeches, and celebrations that filled each day with the buzz of activity. Artisans built spectacularly ornate altars, neighborhood politicians organized local festivities, the military let loose the thunderous roar of artillery, composers wrote new musical works. It was "as much a spectacle of beauty as of piety," our Jesuit author writes: "Not a simple tribute, but a full triumph" (Anon., 1660, p. 167).

The December festival began appropriately with a solemn service at the cathedral to venerate a new saint, Francis Xavier, who was named protector of the city. The previous June the city officials tasked with combating the epidemic had prayed to the saint in desperation as the plague spread recklessly through the city. Sitting before a new statue of Xavier encrusted with jewels, the deputies of health acknowledged their debt to him for interceding as the sound of four choirs resonated throughout the cathedral in a work of great thanksgiving, the *Te Deum*. "In the number and quality of singers, it was the best of the whole festival," writes our Jesuit source (Anon., 1660, p. 159).

The thoroughly religious nature of 17th-century art and life can be striking to modern sensibilities. In addition to setting policy regarding quarantine and the *seicento* equivalent of social distancing, the deputies of health had recommended that city rulers commission artist Mattia Preti to paint frescoes of saints that would be mounted above each of the city gates to guard against the disease (Clifton, 1994). (They weren't completed in time, but wood-cut prints of Preti's proposed designs circulated in Neapolitan households for private protection.)

The visibility of religious practice has receded from the civic sphere in our more secular, pluralistic age. But the problems wrought by contagion in Naples are distressingly familiar. Conspiracy theories circulated that the virus was "artificially spread to kill the people" in response to an uprising nine years earlier, officials dithered for months about quarantine policies, allowing the disease to spread unchecked (Pasquale, 1668, p. 27). When they did clamp down, the eerie silence of empty streets and shuttered businesses set in. As one observer recalled, "the whole city had become a tomb" (Pasquale, 1668, p. 40).

After Saturday's cathedral service and a Sunday of solemn religious processions, the sober character of the festival surrendered to "the great rejoicing of fireworks and lights" (Anon., 1660, p. 165). The rest of the week similarly featured occasions for music, fireworks, fellowship, and civic connection. Each neighborhood (or rather, each administrative district) crafted banners of blue taffeta featuring scenes embroidered in gold thread. They were carried at the head of processions of torch-bearing politicians, nobles, and citizens—spectacles of civic pride our Jesuit source implies softened hearts made hard after a year of suffering. ("The city was a scene of great tenderness," he writes [Anon., 1660, p., 166].)

The festival was most likely an occasion to let loose and indulge in some less-than-pious behavior as well. Accounts of other festivals detail the drinking, fighting, and criminality that can happen when humans gather in the streets (Guarini, 2017). The earlier uprising in 1647 had in fact begun amidst preparations for a festival. The viceroyalty nevertheless understood the importance of these events to Neapolitan life. As a city with significant economic, political and religious divisions, festivals could help knit together a social fabric frayed by inequality, incivility, and disease.

Festivals also admittedly served to glorify and strengthen a repressive autocratic foreign regime. (Naples was then under Spanish control.) Let's not shy away from the indignities suffered by the vast majority of the population—the poor, the enslaved, the persecuted—at the hands of the ruling elite and their opportunistic collaborators. Historians continue to debate whether such state-sanctioned festivals were, in the end, part of a cynical "bread and circuses" approach to social control or part of a more humane concession to Neapolitan community and tradition. John Marino (2011) favors the former interpretation; Gabriel Guarino (2013) the latter.

Such debates should remind us to be thoughtful about how we use state funds to remember the dead and look to the future. But they shouldn't deter us from acknowledging what large civic celebrations can provide. What was true in Naples four centuries ago remains true today: at their best, festivals brought people together in common purpose; helped foster social bonds between communities and classes; and tied the present to a civic history that had endured for centuries.

As the US Surgeon General, Vivek H. Murthy, reminds us, finding new ways to create fellow feeling in our communities is an urgent task. "If we fail to do so, we will pay an ever-increasing price in the form of our individual and collective health and well-being," he warns. "Instead of coming together to take on the great challenges before us, we will further retreat to our corners–angry, sick, and alone" (Office of the Surgeon General, 2023, p. 4). No one should want to return to life as it was in 17th-century Naples, either before or after the plague. But, for an eight-day festival, it's worth an imaginative visit: they just might have been on to something.

Policy implications

This chapter suggests that policy makers should pay more attention to the positive effects of shared civic experiences rather than narrowly targeted events or built-environment legacy projects.

Research implications

This chapter suggests researchers should continue to develop quantitative research into the effects and possible benefits of large, intercultural civic celebrations on health, well-being and political civility.

QUIZ QUESTIONS

1. Why did cities erect plague columns in the 17th century?
2. Though the Covid-19 pandemic has ended, what "epidemic" is our modern society still battling?
3. What were three activities or events of the Neapolitan festival of December 1656?
4. What positive effects do contemporary accounts suggest resulted from the celebration of this festival?
5. What effects have modern scholars suggested resulted from the celebration of similar festivals?

DEBATE QUESTIONS

1. Is modern society suffering from an "epidemic of loneliness and isolation"?
2. Can modern pluralistic societies mourn loss in the same way as religiously uniform polities did in the past?
3. Do we have modern forms of civic gathering that are superior to festivals of the early modern period?

Table 2.1 Alignment to United Nations Sustainable Development Goals

Goal	How
Good Health and Well-Being	Festivals foster social connection and combat modern drivers of despair, especially loneliness and isolation.
Decent Work and Economic Growth	Festivals provide jobs and material support to several sectors of the economy, especially tourism, trade, and the visual and performing arts.
Peace, Justice and, Strong Institutions	Festivals develop fellow feeling and civic-minded approaches to cultural spending that provide the foundation for a less polarized political environment.

REFERENCES

Anon. (1660). *Scelta d'alcuni miracoli operati da S. Francesco Saverio apostolo del Giapone della Compagnia di Giesù in Napoli e suo regno*. Gratz: Widmanstetter.

Clifton, J. (1994). Mattia Preti's frescoes for the city gates of Naples. *The Art Bulletin*, *76*(3), 479–501.

Guarino, G. (2013). Public rituals and festivals in Naples, 1503–1799. In T. Astarita (Ed.), *A companion to early modern Naples* (pp. 257–280). Boston, MA: Brill.

Landman, Keren. (May 5, 2023). What the ending of the WHO's Covid emergency does (and doesn't) change. *Vox*. Retrieved April 17, 2024, from https://www.vox.com/science/2023/5/5/23712380/covid-emergency-ends-world-health-organization.

Marino, J.A. (2011). *Becoming Neapolitan: Citizen culture in baroque Naples*. Baltimore, MD: Johns Hopkins University Press.

Office of the Surgeon General. (2023). *Our epidemic of loneliness and isolation: The U.S. Surgeon General's advisory on the healing effects of social connection and community*. Washington, DC: US Department of Health and Human Services.

Pasquale, N. (1668). *À posteri della peste di Napoli e suo regno nell'anno 1656*. Naples: Luc'Antonio di Fusco.

Policy Exchange. (2017, December 11). *Transcript: Rachel Reeves MP – throwing a new light on loneliness*. Retrieved April 17, 2024, from https://policyexchange.org.uk/events/rachel-reeves-mp-throwing-a-new-light-on-loneliness/.

3 LONDON 2012: Did it inspire a generation?

Mathew Dowling

AIM

The aim of this chapter is to interrogate the central claim that hosting the London 2012 Summer Olympic Games would 'inspire a generation'.

DOI: 10.4324/9781003488729-5

LEARNING OBJECTIVES

LEARNING OBJECTIVES

1. To explore the 'inspire a generation' motto used as a central justification for hosting the London 2012 Olympic Games.
2. To analyse the legacy claims surrounding the hosting of the London 2012 Olympic Games.
3. To review the national participation trends pre- and post-hosting of the London 2012 Olympic Games.

Theoretical focus and significance

The chapter draws upon the sport policy and management literature in general, with a particular focus on studies that have examined the impact of mega-events on host nations and the concept of the demonstration or trickle-down effect. The chapter itself is largely atheoretical, but it is important to discuss the concept of legacy as a recently emergent phenomenon often utilized to justify mega-event expenditure.

Practical focus and significance

The chapter predominantly focuses on and integrates the claimed versus realized legacies of hosting mega-sporting events. The chapter assesses the often taken-for-granted assumptions surrounding the demonstration effect – i.e. the process whereby people are inspired by elite sport, sports people and events to actively participate themselves. Many assume this to be the case for hosting or spectating mega-sporting events, but there is a growing body of evidence to suggest otherwise.

TOPIC – LONDON 2012: DID IT INSPIRE A GENERATION?

The purpose of this chapter is to interrogate the central claim that hosting the London 2012 Summer Olympic Games would 'inspire a generation'. This now infamous tagline not only spoke directly to political ambitions to solve the UK's growing obesity epidemic, but was also reflective of the country's desire to rejuvenate its own image on the international stage. In unveiling the London 2012 Olympic motto, Lord Sebastian (Seb) Coe, chair of the London Organizing Committee of the Olympic and Paralympic Games (LOGOC), insisted that "every one of those individual performances will create a symphony of inspiration that will create lasting change" (Gibson, 2012). In similar fashion, the former Minister for Sport and then chair of the

British Olympic Association, Colin Moynihan, claimed that "London 2012 will motivate a whole generation of young people as they seek to emulate their Team GB heroes both on and off the sporting field" (LOCOG, 2007, para 15). The tagline was also a shrewd move on the part of Seb Coe and LOGOC in that it directly appealed to the original values of Olympism and the International Olympic Committee's (IOC) charter to 'encourage effort', 'preserve human dignity' and 'develop harmony'.

What exactly did Seb Coe and others mean by saying hosting the Games would 'inspire a generation? If by this he meant increasing participation among children and young people as a direct result of bidding for and hosting the Games, otherwise known as the 'trickle-down' or 'demonstration effect' (De Bosscher et al., 2013; Weed et al., 2015) – a process whereby, in this case, people are inspired by elite sport, sports people and events to actively participate themselves – then evidence for this, at best, is inconclusive or, at worst, appears to have failed spectacularly.

A closer inspection of the available national participation data at the time supports this viewpoint. The most comprehensive data comes from the *Taking Part Survey*, an annual face-to-face household assessment of adults aged 16 and over and children aged 5–15 in England (since discontinued and replaced by the *Active Lives Children and Young People Survey*). The Taking Part Survey demonstrates a decline in children's participation between 2008/9 and 2017/18 (as shown in Figure 3.1 and 3.2).

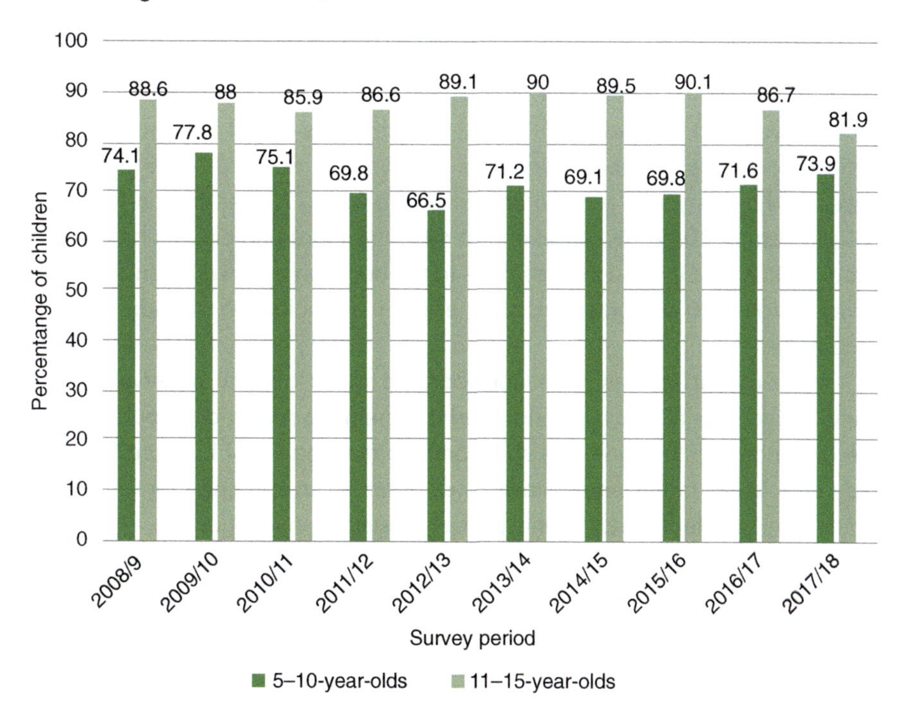

Figure 3.1 Percentage of children participating in sport in the previous week, 2008/9 to 2017/18. Author own figure (based on DCMS, n.d.).

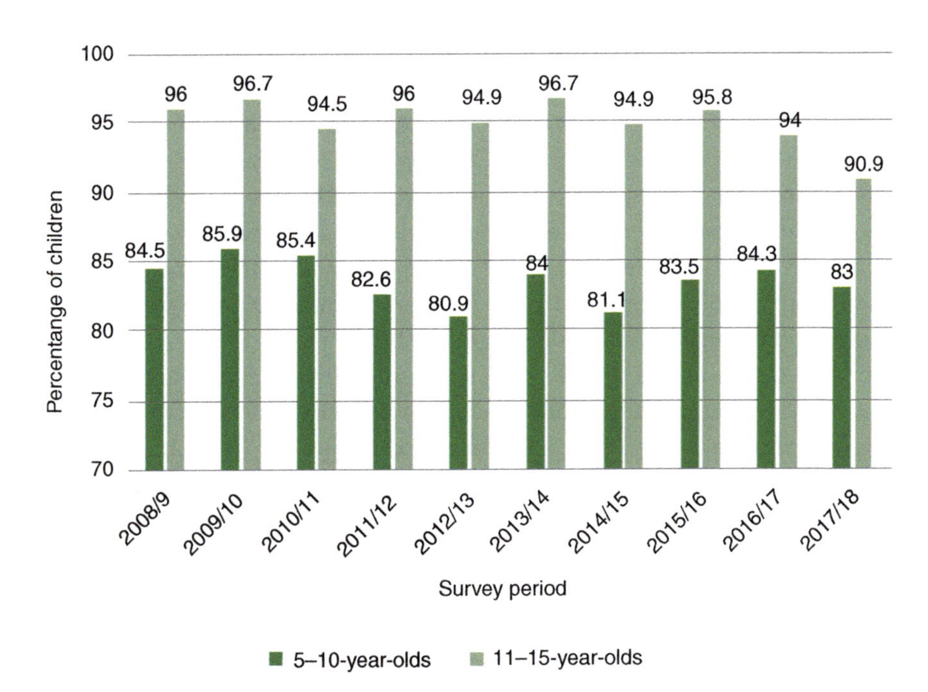

Figure 3.2 Percentage of children participating in sport in the previous four weeks, 2008/9 to 2017/18 (based on DCMS, n.d.).

During the period 2008–2010, the Labour government set a national participation target of 2 million more people active by 2012 (DCMS, 2008). Data from Sport England's *Active People Survey*, an annual telephone-based assessment of over 160,000 adults (+16), reveal that this target was not achieved. Participation rates of those considered active (i.e. doing 3 × 30 minutes of moderate–high physical activity) only changed from 17.1 per cent in 2008/9 to 17.9 per cent in 2012/13, representing 440,000 more participants before compared to after the Olympic Games. Due to the decision by government to change surveys from 2018 onwards, longer-term participation trends are not discernible.

More recent studies have corroborated these general observations. For example, Weed et al. (2015) conducted a systematic review of all publicly available evidence to interrogate the sport participation legacy of London 2012. The study concluded rather emphatically that "there is no evidence for an inherent demonstration effect" and "if the primary justification for hosting an Olympic Games is the potential impact on sport participation, the Games are a bad investment" (p. 195). This finding is also consistent with other host cities. A recent comparative study of mass participation legacies of hosting the Summer Olympic Games from Atlanta 1996 to Tokyo 2020(+1) demonstrated that there was no evidence that hosting the Olympic and Paralympic Summer Games had increased participation in the long term (Harris & Dowling, 2021). The study also revealed the inherent complexities of attempting to identify and meaningfully compare participation data: host cities/countries either completely lack robust and reliable measures or change the way they measure participation, making it difficult to compare changes in participation over time (particularly pre- and post-Games) – with this lack of standardized measures making it impossible to compare one edition of the Games to another.

Alternatively, by 'inspire a generation' did Seb Coe mean the next generation of elite athletes to continue the legacy of Team GB at future Olympics? If so, undoubtedly the Games were a catalyst for further developing the UK's elite sport system into a world-class medal-producing factory. The specific policy claims of the Conservative government at the time were contained within, but not explicitly articulated as, legacy plans, seeking to "create a world-leading sporting nation" (DCMS, 2008, p. 8), with the hosting of the Olympic Games acting as a catalyst. This intended policy outcome was also reinforced by the then Minister for Sport and the Olympics, Hugh Robertson, in the lead to host the Games, who claimed that "hosting the London 2012 Olympic and Paralympic Games will be the catalyst for a revolution in British sport at all levels over the next decade" (DCMS, 2012). Regarding elite sport success, Team GB delivered – at least in medal count. In Atlanta 1996, it finished in 36th place, just behind Ethiopia and ahead of Belarus, with 1 gold, 8 silver and 6 bronze medals. In London 2012, Team GB finished 3rd, with 29 gold, 18 silver and 18 bronze. Even more impressively, Great Britain and Northern Ireland has managed to surpass these figures in subsequent editions of the Games. In terms of elite sport, London 2012 was therefore an important milestone in the nation's development of its elite sport infrastructure.

Perhaps then the ingenuity in the tagline 'inspire a generation' is its deliberate ambiguity and malleability. We should therefore accept that this was (and over a decade later still remains) a rhetorical device used by politicians and leaders to rationalize and justify the astronomical costs of hosting the world's largest multi-sport, mega-event. The London 2012 Olympic Games cost US$15 billion according to one estimate, representing a 75 per cent overrun and making it the most expensive Summer Olympics at the time (Flyvberg et al., 2016).

Rather than a tangible and realizable legacy outcome, the tagline was a rhetorical device employed to convince the British people, the taxpayer, that there would at least be some return on investment or longer-term benefit for hosting the largest sport development project ever conceived. During the closing ceremony, Lord Coe rather modestly claimed, "when our time came we did it right ... today sees the closing of a wonderful Games in a wonderful city, we lit the flame and lit up the world" (IOC, 2012). If by "did it right" he meant hosting the games at enormous taxpayer expense, then yes. If by "did it right" he meant delivering on the original legacy plans to inspire a generation to take up sport and physical activity, then the evidence emerging over a decade later suggests otherwise.

Managerial implications

It is important to be cautious about legacy claims surrounding hosting mega-sporting events, and have a good grasp of available participation data when attempting to evaluate the long-term impact of mega-sporting events on participation in sport and physical activity. Standardized and longitudinal data is needed to make meaningful comparisons of the impact of mega-sporting events on participation; and, even then, causality claims are problematic.

Policy implications

Policy makers should be more transparent and realistic about the potential legacy outcomes surrounding the hosting of mega-sporting events. It is also important to ensure that effective systems of evaluation are put in place to assess policy outcomes.

Research implications

More empirical research is needed to better understand the relationship between mega-events and sport and physical activity participation. A body of evidence is also needed to independently assess the claimed legacies of these types of events.

QUIZ QUESTIONS

1. What was the motto for the London 2012 Olympic Games?
2. What is the best available data to assess sport participation trends before and after hosting a mega-event?
3. According to national participation surveys, did participation increase or decrease after hosting the London 2012 Olympic Games?
4. What have recent studies suggested about the relationship between hosting mega-events and sport participation?

DEBATE QUESTIONS

1. Did London 2012 'inspire a generation'?
2. Does hosting mega-events lead to an increase in sport participation?
3. What types of legacies are claimed by host cities/nations when hosting mega-events?

Table 3.1 Alignment to United Nations Sustainable Development Goals

Goal	How
Good Health and Well-Being	The chapter examines the relationship between sport and physical activity participation and the hosting of mega-events as potential vehicles for promoting health and wellbeing.

REFERENCES

DCMS. (2008). *Playing to win: A new era for sport.* London: UK Department for Culture, Media and Sport.

DCMS. (2012, May 12). *London 2012 the spark for transformation of British sport – from elite to grassroots* [press release]. UK Department for Culture, Media and Sport. https://www.gov.uk/government/news/london-2012-the-spark-for-transformation-of-british-sport-from-elite-to-grassroots.

DCMS. (n.d.). *Taking part: statistical releases.* UK Department for Culture, Media and Sport. https://www.gov.uk/government/collections/sat--2.

De Bosscher, V., Sotiriadou, P., & Van Bottenburg, M. (2013). Scrutinizing the sport pyramid metaphor: An examination of the relationship between elite success and mass participation in Flanders. *International Journal of Sport Policy and Politics*, *5*(3), 319–339.

Flyvberg, B., Budzier, A., & Stewart, A. (2016, July). The Oxford Olympics Study 2016: Cost and cost overrun at the games. *Said Business School Research Papers.* https://dx.doi.org/10.2139/ssrn.2804554.

Gibson, O. (2012, April 18). Lord Coe unveils London Olympics motto: 'Inspire a generation'. *TheGuardian*.https://www.theguardian.com/sport/2012/apr/18/lord-coe-london-olympics-motto.

Harris, S., & Dowling, M. (2021) (Eds.). *Sport participation and Olympic legacies.* Routledge.

IOC. (2012, August 13). London 2012 opening and closing ceremony. https://www.olympic.org/news/london-2012-opening-and-closing-ceremony.

LOCOG. (2007). *Press release: Five years to go to the start of the London 2012 Games.* http://www.london2012.com/news/media-releases/2007/2007-07/five-yearsto-go-to-the-start-of-the-london-2012-games.php.

Weed, M., Coren, E., Fiore, J., Wellard, I., Chatziefstathiou, D., Mansfield, L., & Dowse, S. (2015). The Olympic Games and raising sport participation: A systematic review of evidence and an interrogation of policy for a demonstration effect. *European Sport Management Quarterly*, *15*(2), 195–226.

4 WHAT DID LONDON 2012 MEAN FOR THE PARALYMPICS AND THE LIVES OF PEOPLE WITH DISABILITIES?

Verity Postlethwaite, Ian Brittain and Mike Duignan

AIM

The aim of the chapter is to offer positive and negative implications of the London 2012 Paralympic Games on sporting and societal contexts in the United Kingdom.

DOI: 10.4324/9781003488729-6

LEARNING OBJECTIVES

LEARNING OBJECTIVES

1. Discuss the major achievements of the London 2012 Paralympic Games in relation to changing the perception of people with disabilities.
2. Identify positive and negative implications of the London 2012 Paralympic Games.
3. Differentiate between impacts and changes on sporting and societal contexts in relation to disability.

Theoretical focus and significance

This chapter's theoretical focus is on the evolving concept of disability, presenting a pluralistic understanding of shifts in perceptions surrounding disability. Examining multiple perspectives on these changes is essential for adding depth and diversity to our understanding of how events impact communities. Additionally, it is crucial to determine whether an event's impact on a community pertains to the sporting context or to broader societal contexts.

Practical focus and significance

This chapter's practical focus is on various programmes and examples illustrating whether people with disabilities benefited from the actions and aims of the London 2012 Paralympic Games. It is crucial to critically reflect on the positive and negative impacts of the Games to better understand how to leverage events to influence broader societal issues, such as the perception and lived experiences of disabled people.

TOPIC – LONDON 2012'S LEGACY BOOSTED PARALYMPIC SPORT, BUT DISABLED PEOPLE'S LIVES HAVE WORSENED

For the planners of the London 2012 Olympic and Paralympic Games, a central aim was to transform how non-disabled people—and society at large—perceive disabled individuals in the long term. Key political figures, including then Prime Minister Tony Blair, London mayor Ken Livingstone, and Sebastian Coe, chairman of the London Organizing Committee, emphasized diversity and inclusion in the London legacy plans (DCMS, 2011). They believed that hosting such events had the potential to address pervasive social issues (Duignan, 2021).

The extent to which London 2012 fulfilled its promises for disabled people is a matter of perspective. The UK government and many involved in organizing the London 2012 Paralympic Games proclaimed the event a great success (DCMS, 2015). However, experts and organizations representing disabled people offer a contrasting view. As medical historian Anne Borsay (2004) highlighted in her book *Disability and Social Policy in Britain Since 1750: A History of Exclusion*, disabled individuals in Britain–and globally–were often regarded as second-class citizens before 2012, and largely remain so. Likewise, research by Brittain et al. (2019) shows that people with disabilities continue to face marginalization due to physical barriers, negative attitudes, and lack of access to essential resources such as education, employment, and housing. This issue was similarly identified in the lead-up to the Tokyo 2020 Olympics and Paralympics in Japan (Ha and Sieg, 2016).

The London 2012 legacy plans for disabled people, outlined by the government (DCMS, 2011), were grounded in the "social model" of disability (Scope, n.d.). Unlike the medical model, which attributes disability to an individual's impairments, the social model argues that societal barriers disable individuals. The goal was to shift societal attitudes to enable disabled people to lead fulfilling lives. These legacy plans had three primary aims: (1) to improve access to goods, services, and employment for disabled people; (2) to work with the media to positively highlight the contributions and talents of disabled individuals; and (3) to support their participation in sport and community activities.

Limited successes can be attributed to the London Games, particularly in elite parasports and education. High-level advocates in sport and politics used the London 2012 Paralympics to influence infrastructure and education around disability (Postlethwaite, 2020). Ex-Paralympians Tanni Grey-Thompson and Chris Holmes, now members of the House of Lords, continue to push for change (Pring, 2013). During London 2012, the "Get Set" education programme (IPC, 2011) was the first to incorporate Paralympic values in the national school curriculum, setting a precedent for the globally successful "I'm Possible" Paralympic educational resource. Research indicates that Olympic host cities and national Paralympic committees have utilized lessons from London 2012 to enhance the visibility of the Paralympic movement and its role in sport and society (Pourkiani et al., 2022). Domestically, UK Sport and Sport England have prioritized and funded both elite and grassroots sport for disabled people. The Great Britain and Northern Ireland Paralympic team has benefited from increased funding and continued success in subsequent Games.

However, transforming societal attitudes toward disabled people and increasing their community participation remains unmet goals. Research shows that the London 2012 Paralympics had a minimal impact on the number of disabled individuals participating in sport (Brown, 2019). In 2018, the Activity

Alliance reported that nearly 50 per cent of disabled people feared losing their welfare benefits if they were seen to be physically active. Moreover, the lives of disabled people have worsened since 2012 (Brittain et al., 2019). The aftermath of the 2008 global economic crash exacerbated poverty, exclusion, and the risk of abuse for disabled individuals worldwide.

The COVID-19 pandemic has further aggravated these challenges, and disabled people have been disproportionately affected (Kubenz and Kiwan, 2021). The UK Office of National Statistics (2021) reported that disabled individuals accounted for 6 in every 10 COVID-related deaths in the UK in 2021. Consequently, journalist and disability activist Frances Ryan (2020, p. 3) stated that disabled people in the UK now endure "nine times the burden of cuts compared to the average citizen, with those with severe disabilities being hit ... nineteen times harder."

The International Paralympic Committee (IPC) campaigns, "WeThe15" (www.wethe15.org/) and "The Valuable 500" (www.thevaluable500.com), acknowledge the broader societal context in which mega-events occur (Brittain and Beacom, 2016). These campaigns recognize that events alone cannot achieve the transformational social change often claimed for them. While the Paralympic Games can initiate discussions about disability issues due to their extensive media coverage, one major sporting event every four years is insufficient for driving substantial change.

Managerial implications

The managerial implications of this chapter emphasize the need to separately consider both sport/event-related and societal-related outputs and outcomes for events that aim to influence and improve community conditions. These aspects are not mutually exclusive but require distinct consideration. The London 2012 Paralympics, for example, successfully enhanced sporting outcomes for disabled individuals but did not significantly mitigate broader societal challenges faced by disabled people.

Policy implications

Policy makers should take into account the broader policy frameworks within which an event operates. In the case of the London 2012 Paralympic Games, austerity measures and other negative policy changes affecting disabled communities hindered the event's potential to act as a catalyst for societal change.

Research implications

Further research is needed to explore how the Paralympics and other parasport events can influence both sporting and societal outcomes for disabled individuals. Key questions remain regarding how to effectively track and demonstrate changes in perceptions.

QUIZ QUESTIONS

1. What was the key aim of the London 2012 Paralympic Games beyond the sporting event?
2. What were major outcomes from the London 2012 Paralympic Games?
3. What negative impacts and implications from the London 2012 Paralympic Games have been identified for disabled people?
4. Who are some of the major voices in the debate around the Paralympic Games?

DEBATE QUESTIONS

1. How can we measure perception change from an event?
2. Do the Paralympics (and other parasport events) have the ability to influence broader societal perceptions of disabled people?
3. What can events in the future learn from the London 2012 Paralympic Games?

Table 4.1 Alignment to United Nations Sustainable Development Goals

Objective	How
No Poverty	Disabled people not mentioned specifically here and, yes, one of the groups most likely to suffer poverty. Those in poverty unlikely to prioritize sport or even physical activity.
Zero Hunger	Hunger is both a cause of (e.g. malnutrition) and a result of disability (via poverty). Hungry people are unlikely to play sport.
Good Health and Well-being	Sport is potentially a route to good health and well-being (both physical and mental), but lack of knowledge regarding how to include various impairments hinders this route for many disabled people.

(*Continued*)

Table 4.1 (Continued)

Objective	How
Quality Education	Education is key – both generally (allowing access to jobs etc.) and specifically for non-disabled people regarding, e.g., the rights of disabled people or how attitudes impact the lives of disabled people (positively and negatively)s.
Gender Equality	Disabled females often face double discrimination that can severely impact their access to all areas of life, including sport.
Clean Water and Sanitation	Closely linked to poverty and hunger, and potentially a cause of some disabilities, this can be a barrier to sport, especially in hot climates where hydration is paramount.
Affordable and Clean Energy	Again, potentially a cause (ill health from lack of warmth) and a result of disability (poverty, lack of access to economic capital). This will also affect running costs for sports facilities that may put access charges beyond the reach of disabled people.
Decent Work and Economic Growth	Disabled people are often denied access to work of any kind due to fear or discrimination. Without the economic capital to support themselves provided by employment, access to sport becomes increasingly hard, if not impossible.
Industry, Innovation and Infrastructure	Disabled people are often also denied access to credit, increasing the likelihood of poverty and hunger and reducing the likelihood of sports participation.
Reduced Inequality	One of the few goals to specifically mention disability. However, in most countries inequality is actually increasing, with disabled people often one of the groups hardest hit. This then negatively impacts possible sports participation.
Sustainable Cities and Communities	Unclear in places whether "access to" includes accessibility in physical terms, although goal 11.2 does mention accessible transport—a key requisite of disabled people being able to participate in sport.
Responsible Consumption and Production	Disabled people are also citizens and have a role to play in responsible consumption and production, including organizations such as the IPC, to ensure food waste is minimized at Paralympic Games and regional and world championships.
Climate Action	Climate disasters can be major causes of disability, and disabled people and disability sport organizations have a role to play in fighting climate change.
Life Below Water	Disabled people can also play a role in conserving the marine environment, particularly those involved in marine-based sports such as sailing or adapted surfing.
Life on Land	Organizers of disability sport and disability sporting bodies and their members have a responsibility to ensure sustainable use of the environment in which they operate.

(*Continued*)

Table 4.1 (Continued)

Objective	How
Peace and Justice Strong Institutions	Perhaps one of the most important goals for disabled people (from which others may improve), but also perhaps the weakest/most overlooked. Organizations such as the IPC need to use their media reach to promote human rights and social justice for all disabled people as well as collaborate with bodies such as the IOC to do the same.
Partnerships to Achieve the Goal	The IPC, through collaborations such as WeThe15, entities such as the Sport and Rights Alliance (SRA), coalitions like the Centre for Sport and Human Rights (CSHR), and through its own development arm, the Agitos Foundation, can play a role in helping countries meet their development commitments, particularly in regard to disabled people.

REFERENCES

Activity Alliance. (2018). *The activity trap: Benefits or being fit?* https://www.activityalliance.org.uk/news/4430-the-activity-trap-benefits-or-being-fit.

Borsay, A. (2004). *Disability and social policy in Britain since 1750: A history of exclusion.* Palgrave Macmillan.

Brittain, I., & Beacom, A. (2016). Leveraging the London 2012 Paralympic Games: What legacy for disabled people? *Journal of Sport and Social Issues*, *40*(6), 499–521. https://doi.org/10.1177/0193723516655580.

Brittain, I., Biscaia, R., & Gérard, S. (2019). Ableism as a regulator of social practice and disabled peoples' self-determination to participate in sport and physical activity. *Leisure Studies*, *39*(2), 209–224. https://doi.org/10.1080/02614367.2019.1694569.

Brown, C. (2019). "I still think we've got mountains to climb": Evaluating the grassroots sport participation legacy of the London 2012 Paralympic Games for disabled people in England. (Doctoral dissertation, University of Kent).

DCMS. (2011). *London 2012: A legacy for disabled people – April 2011*. UK Department for Culture, Media and Sport. https://www.gov.uk/government/publications/london-2012-a-legacy-for-disabled-people-april-2011.

DCMS. (2015). *A new strategy for sport: Consultation paper.* UK Department for Culture, Media and Sport. https://assets.publishing.service.gov.uk/government/uploads/system/uploads/attachment_data/file/450712/1619-F_Sports_Strategy_ACCESSIBLE.pdf.

Duignan, M. B. (2021). Utilizing field theory to examine mega-event-led development. *Event Management*, *25*(6), 705–720. https://doi.org/10.3727/152599520X15894679115583.

Ha, K. & Sieg, L. (2016). Japan confronts disability stigma after silence over murder victims' names. *Reuters.* https://www.reuters.com/article/us-japan-disabled-idUSKCN11M0AM.

IPC. (2011). *Schools get set for London 2012 with grants to plan their games.* International Paralympic Committee. https://www.paralympic.org/news/schools-get-set-london-2012-grants-plan-their-games.

Kubenz, V., & Kiwan, D. (2021). *The impact of the COVID-19 pandemic on disabled people in low- and middle-income countries: A literature review*. Disability Under Siege. https://disabilityundersiege.org/wp-content/uploads/2021/03/Impact-of-COVID-19-on-disabled-people-literature-review.pdf.

Office for National Statistics. 2021. *Updated estimates of coronavirus (COVID-19) related deaths by disability status, England: 24 January to 20 November 2020*. https://www.ons.gov.uk/peoplepopulationandcommunity/birthsdeathsandmarriages/deaths/articles/coronaviruscovid19relateddeathsbydisabilitystatusenglandandwales/24januaryto20november2020.

Postlethwaite, V. (2020). *Inspiring a generation(?): Interconnecting discourses between governing actors, policy, and legacy around London 2012* (Doctoral dissertation, University of Worcester).

Pourkiani, M., Afrouzeh, A., Boroumand, M., & Soheili, S. (2022). The impact of the global "imPOSSIBLE" program on the Iranian students' change of attitude toward inclusive sport. *Research on Education Sport*, *8*(20), 172–147. https://doi.org/10.22089/res.2020.9169.1918.

Pring, J. (2013). London 2012 Paralympics boss will lead on disability for EHRC. *Disability News Service*. https://www.disabilitynewsservice.com/london-2012-paralympics-boss-will-lead-on-disability-for-ehrc/.

Ryan, F. (2020). *Crippled: Austerity and the demonization of disabled people*. Verso.

Scope. (n.d.). *Social model of disability*. https://www.scope.org.uk/about-us/social-model-of-disability/.

5 HAS THE LONDON 2012 VOLUNTEERING PROGRAMME ENGENDERED A SUSTAINABLE AND WIDER VOLUNTEERING LEGACY IN THE UK?

Niki Koutrou and Mike Duignan

AIM

The aim of this chapter is to provide context and the key learnings and short-comings from the London 2012 Olympic Games and the focus on delivering a legacy of community volunteering inspired and supported by the event.

DOI: 10.4324/9781003488729-7

LEARNING OBJECTIVES

LEARNING OBJECTIVES

1. To emphasize the need for event organizers to establish clear legacy objectives from the bidding process that will be followed through across an event's lifecycle.
2. To demonstrate that legacy does not take place on its own but needs to be leveraged through appropriate strategies, initiatives, institutional arrangements, and partnerships between event organizers, host city authorities, and the community.
3. To delineate the shortcomings of London 2012's volunteer legacy.

Theoretical focus and significance

Due to space limitations, this chapter does not prioritize any specific theory. However, it is developed with appropriate consideration of relevant theoretical frameworks such as the Legacy Cube (Preuss, 2007) and the concept of Leveraging Legacies (Grix, 2014). The chapter highlights the impact of volunteering on the broader community, the challenges faced, and the strategies required to effectively mobilize skilled volunteers for sustained community support beyond the event.

A particular focus is given to a case study of the London 2012 volunteer programme, examining its impact on the broader community, the challenges encountered, and the strategies needed for sustained support beyond mega-sport events. This discussion addresses the ongoing need for holistic legacy plans developed from the bidding stage, leveraged throughout an event's lifecycle, and continuing after the event concludes. The chapter offers valuable insights for fostering sustained community engagement, skill development, and human capital growth while addressing challenges related to volunteer mobilization and support.

Legacy does not occur spontaneously (Grix, 2014). All legacies must be actively leveraged, and planning for a physical activity, sport, health, and volunteering legacy should be part of an integrated strategy. This strategy should include community and educational programmes, coaching opportunities, and well-planned, accessible facilities that address existing needs; therefore, to leverage sporting events for a volunteering legacy, it is essential to understand the mechanisms involved (Veal et al., 2012). By examining the outcomes of volunteering at the London 2012 Games, organizations and stakeholders can draw valuable lessons for effectively mobilizing and maintaining skilled volunteers for future events and sustained community support (LOCOG, 2009; Dickson & Benson, 2013; Koutrou, 2021). Additionally, the chapter provides critical knowledge on addressing the challenges in mobilizing skilled volunteers and the strategies required for sustained community support, offering guidance for similar issues in the future (Koutrou, 2021).

Practical focus and significance

Effective legacy planning requires setting clear targets and ensuring that the event volunteer programme aligns with the long-term development goals of the host city and country. This alignment is crucial for delivering a lasting community legacy by encouraging and supporting diverse individuals to participate in and benefit from event volunteering.

London 2012 was the first mega-event explicitly designed to enhance the volunteer culture in the UK. Despite its shortcomings, it provides a valuable case study for future mega-sport event organizers, especially when a volunteer legacy is a priority. However, as evidenced by Birmingham 2022 Commonwealth Games (Chen et al., 2023), these lessons are still not consistently applied.

Key practical points highlighted in this chapter focus on the recruitment and experience of the 'Games Makers', their skill development, and the challenges encountered in harnessing the volunteering legacy for sustained community support. It emphasizes the demographic representation of the volunteers, the skills and competencies they developed, and the obstacles in maximizing the volunteering legacy for long-term community engagement. These practical aspects are intricately linked to the theoretical focus on fostering sustained community support and leveraging the legacy of mega-sport events, such as the London 2012 Games, for future volunteer engagement.

TOPIC – HAS THE LONDON 2012 VOLUNTEERING PROGRAMME ENGENDERED A SUSTAINABLE AND WIDER VOLUNTEERING LEGACY IN THE UK?

In recent years, the UK government has prioritized hosting major and mega-events to maximize broader economic and social benefits for the country. Volunteering plays an integral role in these events, reducing the financial burden on organizing committees and making the event more accessible and inclusive by engaging local citizens in its delivery. As such, mega-event organizers, governments, supporters, and other stakeholders claim that event volunteering acts as a catalyst, inspiring individuals through a 'festival effect' to engage in volunteering beyond the event, thereby fostering a community legacy (Weed et al., 2012). The London 2012

Organising Committee (LOCOG, 2009) set a precedent by explicitly aiming to enhance the country's volunteer culture and develop a community of volunteers post-event. Lord Sebastian Coe, the Chair of LOCOG, emphasized the critical role of the Games in inspiring community engagement, and envisioned the event as an opportunity to captivate and unite a diverse range of individuals and communities towards the long-term development of the host city and country. Legacy narratives were central to the planning and execution of these Games, aligning closely with the strategic aims of the International Olympic Committee (IOC) and its Olympic Agenda 2020 (House of Lords, 2013). The emphasis on a legacy of volunteering, albeit ambiguous, laid the groundwork for engaging with the existing volunteering infrastructure in the country, extending the impact of volunteering at the Games to local communities, businesses, and institutions, and providing a pathway to skills development and full-time employment (Lockstone-Binney et al., 2016).

London 2012 Volunteer Programme

As London prepared to host the 2012 Olympic Games, 250,000 individuals registered their interest in volunteering, with 70,000 eventually selected as official 'Games Makers'. Of these, a significant 40% were volunteering for the first time. It was anticipated that these volunteers would reflect the diversity of the United Kingdom. Official data suggests that volunteers primarily came from London (34%), the South-East (21%), and the East of England (13%), with Scotland and Wales each contributing 2%. The majority were 'White-British' (80%) and employed full time (50%), and 4% self-identified as having a disability (Dickson & Benson, 2013). Motivated by national and community pride, a love of sport, and career aspirations, Games Makers took on diverse roles ranging from event services and stewarding to performing at ceremonies, supporting athletes and guests, and issuing accreditations (Dickson & Benson, 2013; Koutrou & Pappous, 2016). Volunteers received official merchandise, uniforms, and sometimes complimentary tickets to the Games, and developed skills such as resilience, interpersonal interaction, and communication (Dickson & Benson, 2013; Koutrou & Pappous, 2016). These skills were expected to translate into sustained community volunteering efforts. Four years after the event, some Games Makers affirmed that the skills gained from their London 2012 volunteering were relevant to their professional and community volunteering activities (Koutrou, 2021).

Leveraging Legacy and Learnings from London 2012

Scholars contend that if an event's volunteer programme is to inspire and sustain volunteering, it needs to be leveraged through careful planning across all stages of the event's lifecycle, including the transition phase (Hayday et al., 2019; Hughes, 2013; Koutrou et al., 2016). In the aftermath of the 2012 Olympics, a surge in voluntarism was observed, with volunteering rates rising from 65% in 2010 to 71% in 2012, attributed to the 'inspiration effect' of mega-sport events (Weed et al., 2012). Despite the initial enthusiasm, by 2021 a decline in volunteering rates in England was evident, raising questions about the sustained impact of the Games on volunteering (Statista, 2024). It is argued that the 'inspiration effect' created by the London Olympics was primarily ad hoc, driven by positive memories and nostalgia rather than coordinated efforts by LOCOG, the UK government, and local stakeholders to build on the Games' momentum and leverage the volunteer legacy (Koutrou et al., 2016).

A survey of London 2012 Games Makers in 2016 revealed that, out of 77 respondents, 44 had volunteered post-2012 for other community organizations or sporting events. However, others were discouraged by their London 2012 experience, feeling like 'another pair of hands' without genuine efforts by LOCOG to allocate suitable roles or invest in training that met their unique needs and aspirations. Many were unaware of Join In, the official legacy organization founded by the Department of Culture, Media and Sport in May 2012, which aimed to connect Games Makers with local sports clubs, events, and community activities to sustain the volunteer legacy (Koutrou et al., 2016).

The Olympics predominantly appealed to certain segments of the UK population, underrepresenting ethnic minorities, people with disabilities, the unemployed, and those from lower-income brackets (Dickson & Benson, 2013). Despite initiatives like the Personal Best programme to encourage broader participation, these efforts had limited impact during and after the event, suggesting a misalignment between London 2012's legacy aspirations and the actual volunteer recruitment strategy. No specific skills development programmes facilitated the transition to employment or further volunteering post-event. LOCOG's governance plans, prioritizing role allocation and recruitment for event delivery over legacy realization, further contributed to this issue (Nichols & Ralston, 2015). The late launch of Join In and its lack of sustainable post-Games strategies, coupled with funding cessation two years after the Olympics, hindered plans for a lasting volunteer legacy (Koutrou et al., 2016; Nichols & Ralston, 2015). While some positive initiatives continued, such as the Team London Ambassadors programme, they were not consistent nationwide.

Conclusion

Despite shortcomings in the London 2012 volunteer legacy strategy, it serves as an instructive case for future event organizers aiming to maximize community impact and growth through volunteer programmes. While the 2012 Games heightened interest and awareness of volunteering, organizers, the government, and local stakeholders fell short in leveraging and sustaining this momentum. Without aligning event objectives with the host community's long-term development plans, the excitement generated will dissipate post-event. Establishing clear plans for legacy realization, funding, and support from the outset is crucial. Sporting events can attract a broader spectrum of individuals, so local organizations should offer tailored and flexible opportunities to engage a diverse range of people. Inclusive and holistic volunteer recruitment requires commitment, partnerships, and consultations between event organizers and the local volunteer sector to fulfil the event's volunteer legacy.

Managerial implications

Managers should prioritize understanding the factors influencing sport event volunteerism, such as shifting societal trends and evolving volunteer expectations, and develop clear volunteer management strategies that align with the current landscape. This involves creating supportive structures for volunteers, addressing their motivations and expectations, and fostering a balanced approach that emphasizes both personal rewards for volunteers and the sustained community impact of their contributions. Event organizers should make concerted efforts to diversify recruitment and match volunteer roles with individual skills and profiles where possible. Collaboration and partnerships between the event's volunteer programme stakeholders and the broader volunteer infrastructure in the country are also crucial for creating sustainable volunteer legacies.

Policy implications

If establishing a volunteering legacy is a priority for hosting a major or mega-sport event, policy makers should incorporate legacy considerations from the initial planning stages through to event delivery. This should include meaningful engagement and collaboration with local volunteering infrastructures and community groups. The focus should not be on merely filling gaps in volunteer roles. Instead, event organizers and policy makers should strive to make volunteering inclusive and accessible, ensuring that diverse segments of the population benefit. Resources should be channelled towards equipping individuals with the skills and capacities to continue volunteering after the event and to transition to paid employment if necessary.

Research implications

Future research should examine the extent to which volunteer legacy outcomes have been achieved in various mega- and major sport events. This includes exploring best practices and case studies of effective planning and leveraging of legacies throughout an event's lifecycle, alongside engagement and close collaboration with the volunteer infrastructure in the host city and country.

Additionally, it is important to study the role of prior planning and feasibility in achieving successful and sustainable legacies in mega-sport events. Investigating the factors that shape volunteer experiences and future intentions, developing a conceptualization of key legacy areas, and proposing future research themes for emerging nations and mega-sport events are also essential areas of focus.

Finally, research on volunteer legacies should move beyond cross-sectional designs to more robust, longitudinal studies that measure changes in volunteering efforts before and after the Games. One-off studies do not adequately support a legacy agenda. Longitudinal studies with pre- and post-event measurements, or more comprehensive case study designs, are crucial for a thorough understanding of the implications and impacts of volunteer legacies in mega-sport events.

QUIZ QUESTIONS

1. How many people are currently volunteering in the UK? Was the impact of London 2012 on volunteering sustained?
2. How could the volunteer enthusiasm arising from the event have been sustained?
3. What could Birmingham 2022 have done differently to enhance the diversity of its volunteer cohort to ensure a sustained volunteer legacy?

DEBATE QUESTIONS

1. To what extent did the London 2012 Olympics succeed in generating a long-term volunteering legacy in the UK? This question could provoke discussion on the lasting impact of the Olympics on volunteer rates and patterns in the country, and whether the event effectively inspired sustained volunteering efforts beyond the Games.

2. Should event organizers prioritize strategies to engage a more diverse range of individuals in volunteer work, and how can this be achieved effectively? This question could lead to a debate on the challenges and best practices for recruiting and retaining volunteers from different backgrounds, including those from ethnic minorities, people with disabilities, and individuals from lower-income brackets.
3. What are the key factors that contribute to the success or failure of volunteer legacy strategies following major sporting events? This question could encourage a discussion about the critical elements necessary for leveraging volunteer enthusiasm and sustaining momentum beyond the conclusion of mega-events like the Olympics.
4. What role should the government, local volunteer sector, and community leaders play in fostering a meaningful and a sustainable volunteer legacy following major and mega-event hosting? This question could spark debate on the responsibilities and collaboration required among different stakeholders to ensure the successful realization of volunteer legacies and community impact.
5. In light of the London 2012 volunteer legacy experience, what lessons can be learned and applied to future event planning to maximize the potential of official volunteer programmes for tangible community growth? This question could lead to a discussion on the implications of the London 2012 volunteer legacy for future event organizers and the development of best practices to harness the full potential of volunteer programmes.

REFERENCES

Chen, S., Veldhuijzen van Zanten, J., Quinton, M., Lee, M., Ali, T., Heyes, A., … & Karamani, M. (2023). Perceptions of the Birmingham 2022 Commonwealth Games: Legacies for individuals and communities from disadvantaged backgrounds. University of Birmingham report.

Dickson, T. J., & Benson, A. M. (2013). London 2012 games makers: Towards redefining legacy. In *Meta-evaluation of the impacts and legacy of the London 2012 Olympic Games and Paralympic Games: Related research*. UK Department for Culture Media and Sport https://www.researchgate.net/publication/250310094_London_2012_Games_Makers_London_2012_Games_Makers_Towards_Redefining_Legacy.

Grix, J. (Ed.). (2014). *Leveraging legacies from sports mega-events: Concepts and cases*. Springer.

Hayday, E. J., Pappous, A., & Koutrou, N. (2019). The role of voluntary sport organisations in leveraging the London 2012 sport participation legacy. *Leisure Studies*, *38*(6), 746–761.

House of Lords (2013). Select Committee on Olympic and Paralympic Legacy Report of session 2013–14 keeping the flame alive: The Olympic and Paralympic legacy. Available at: https://publications.parliament.uk/pa/ld201314/ldselect/ldolympic/78/78.pdf.

Hughes, K. (2013, May 19) Sport mega-events and a legacy of increased sport participation: An Olympic promise or an Olympic dream? Leeds Metropolitan University.

Koutrou, N. (2021). Enhancing volunteer skills through mega sport events: Evidence from London 2012 Olympic Games. In K. Holmes, L. Lockstone-Binney, K. A. Smith, & R. Shipway (Eds.), *The Routledge handbook of volunteering in events, sport and tourism* (pp. 161–173). Routledge.

Koutrou, N., & Pappous, A. S. (2016). Towards an Olympic volunteering legacy: Motivating volunteers to serve and remain – a case study of London 2012 Olympic Games volunteers. *Voluntary Sector Review*, 7(3), 269–291. https://doi.org/10.1332/096278916X14767760874050.

Koutrou N, Pappous A, Johnson A. (2016) Post-event volunteering legacy: Did the London 2012 Games induce a sustainable volunteer engagement? *Sustainability*, *8*(12), 1221. https://doi.org/10.3390/su8121221.

Lockstone-Binney, L., Holmes, K., Shipway, R., & Smith, K. A. (2016). *Evaluating the volunteering infrastructure legacy of the Olympic Games: Sydney 2000 and London 2012.* International Olympic Committee Olympic Studies Centre Final Report.

LOCOG. (2009). Get involved: The volunteer programme – London 2012. The official site of the London 2012 Olympic and Paralympic Games. http://www.london2012.com/get-involved/volunteering/thevolunteer-programme.php.

Nichols, G., & Ralston, R. (2015). The legacy costs of delivering the 2012 Olympic and Paralympic Games through regulatory capitalism. *Leisure Studies*, *34*(4), 389–404.

Preuss, H. 2007. The conceptualisation and measurement of mega sport event legacies. *Journal of Sport and Tourism*, *12*, 207–227.

Statista (2024). Share of the population who participate in voluntary activities in England from 2013/14 to 2021/22, by frequency. https://www.statista.com/statistics/292884/volunteering-in-england/.

Veal, A. J., Toohey, K. & Frawley, S. (2012). The sport participation legacy of the Sydney 2000 Olympic Games and other international sporting events hosted in Australia. *Journal of Policy Research in Tourism, Leisure and Events*, *4*(2), 1–30. doi:10.1080/19407963.2012.662619.

Weed, M., Coren, E., Fiore, J., Mansfield, L., Wellard, I., Chatziefstathiou, D., & Dowse, S. (2009). *A systematic review of the evidence base for developing a physical activity and health legacy from the London 2012 Olympic and Paralympic Games.* Centre for Sport, Physical Education & Activity Research (Spear).

Weed, M., Coren, E., Fiore, J., Wellard, I., Mansfield, L., Chatziefstathiou, D., & Dowse, S. (2012). Developing a physical activity legacy from the London 2012 Olympic and Paralympic Games: A policy-led systematic review. *Perspectives in Public Health*, *132*(2), 75–80.

6 A CRITICAL REVIEW OF THE PARALYMPIC GAMES' POTENTIAL TO INCREASE DISABLED PEOPLE'S SPORT PARTICIPATION

Chris Brown

AIM

To evaluate the evidence for, and potential of, the Paralympic Games in increasing disabled people's sport participation.

DOI: 10.4324/9781003488729-8

LEARNING OBJECTIVES

1. To consider the evidence base for increased sport participation.
2. To evaluate the role of the Paralympic Games' in facilitating increased sport participation.
3. To assess the compatibility between the legitimization of the Paralympic Games as a sporting event and the goal of the International Paralympic Committee in advancing social change for disabled people.

Theoretical focus and significance

The focus here is on the demonstration effect and festival effect concepts in understanding sport participation and the Paralympic Games. A consideration of leveraging sport mega events supports the critique of the Paralympic Games' sport participation legacies, a critique of contemporary evidence in exploring the potential for the Paralympic Games in increasing sport participation. There is a paucity of evidence for this topic area, while the Paralympics are often neglected as a frame of enquiry for sport mega-event legacies.

Practical focus and significance

There is limited evidence to support the argument that the Paralympics can increase grassroots sport participation. The Paralympics may have a catalysing effect for some individuals but is not the solution for sustainable population-level changes. The Paralympics should be one component of a range of initiatives to support disabled people's sport participation. There are 1.5 billion disabled people globally, and they are more likely to be inactive and suffer poor health compared to non-disabled people (Ginis et al., 2021). It is therefore important to critically consider the efficacy of the Paralympics in reducing inactivity as a policy objective.

TOPIC – A CRITICAL REVIEW OF THE PARALYMPIC GAMES' POTENTIAL TO INCREASE DISABLED PEOPLE'S SPORT PARTICIPATION

The potential of the Paralympic Games, often known as the Paralympics, to engender increased participation in sport by disabled people has been a source of debate. Proponents view the Paralympics as a platform to raise awareness and visibility of disability, arguing that the Paralympics demonstrate the potential of disabled people through the extraordinary sporting feats of Paralympians (Craven, 2016). Critics, however, posit that the Paralympics produce no meaningful impact on disabled people's sport participation (Howe & Silva, 2018), and may potentially be counterproductive for advancing disability rights (Peers, 2012). The narrow range of impairments included in the Paralympics, coupled with ignorance of the barriers and inequality that exist for disabled people in society, may mean the event is in fact disempowering for this cohort (Purdue & Howe, 2012). This chapter considers the potential of the Paralympics to increase sport participation of disabled people, drawing on the London 2012 Paralympics as a case study.

Limited impact of sport mega events on sport participation

Mixed evidence exists for the link between a sports mega event (SME) and sport participation. Most data that exist is focused on the Olympic Games. The Paralympics, on the other hand, has been under-researched in comparison (Pappous & Brown, 2018). A common theme in the literature is the paucity of quality research into SMEs and sport participation (Annear et al., 2022; Bauman et al., 2021; Mahtani et al., 2013). Longitudinal studies are rare (Annear et al., 2019), and it is difficult to produce causal links between SMEs and sport participation (Chen et al., 2024).

Systematic reviews investigating population changes in sport and physical activity participation because of the Olympics Games tend to report limited to no positive impact (Annear et al., 2019; Annear et al., 2022; Lion et al., 2023; Mahtani et al., 2013). However some studies have found short-term positive impacts on sport participation (Kokolakakis et al., 2019) as well as potentially long-term effects (Aizawa et al., 2018). Some scholars have reported the potential for people to be inspired by elite sport (Chen et al., 2024; Souza & Brittain, 2022), commonly referred to as the 'demonstration effect' (Weed et al., 2015), and by the experience of the event in the host nation (Chen et al., 2024), known as the 'festival effect' (Weed et al., 2015). A study by Kim et al. (2024) found live spectating of the 2018 PyeongChang Winter Paralympics in South Korea by individuals with physical impairments led to a desire to participate in sport, but whether these individuals converted that interest into sport participation is unclear. Annear et al. (2019) argue the demonstration effect has limited utility for increasing sport participation, but that the festival effect may be more promising.

The importance of leveraging

An important consideration is the intention of the host nation. Sport participation from SMEs is more likely to occur if the host actively aims to increase participation because of the event (Mölenberg et al., 2020). This is known as leveraging. The Paralympics is not a silver bullet for sport participation (Brittain et al., 2022;

Brown & Pappous, 2021; de Souza & Brittain, 2022). Instead, hosts should leverage the Paralympics to produce sustainable sport participation benefits (Brown & Pappous, 2022). Leveraging implies planned strategic initiatives to increase sport participation linked to the Paralympics (Chalip et al., 2017). The Paralympics would therefore be one aspect of a nation's sport participation efforts (Brown & Pappous, 2018; Dickson et al., 2021) – a cherry on top of the cake, not the cake itself.

Is the Paralympics (dis)empowering for disabled people?

The Paralympics may not increase sport participation due to its disempowering nature (Braye et al., 2013). Relying on the Paralympics is misplaced because it obfuscates the lived experience of disability because of its limited inclusion of impairments compared to the wider population (Howe & Silva, 2018; Purdue & Howe, 2012). Moreover, focusing on the Paralympics ignores the requirement for a strong sporting infrastructure to support disabled people (Howe & Silva, 2018) as well as wider individual and external barriers to participation (Darcy et al., 2017). Painting Paralympians as 'superhumans' can be problematic due to reinforcement of negative stereotypes and a focus on individuals 'overcoming' their impairment to be a 'success' (Silva & Howe, 2012). For others, however, success in elite sport and the positioning of Paralympians as superhumans are important in advancing disability sport (Nagata et al., 2023; Souza & Brittain, 2022). For example, member states in the Association of Southeast Asian Nations (ASEAN) exploit elite sport success to raise the profile of disability sport and motivate funders (Nagata et al., 2023).

Questions have been raised as to whether the Paralympics can maintain a balance between advancing disability rights for all and producing a quality elite sport event. Some scholars argue that the increasing 'cyborgification' of athletes in the Paralympics – the use of technology to aid performance (e.g. prosthetic blades, sport wheelchair racers, etc.) – is a response to the interests of a non-disabled audience (Howe, 2011; Howe & Silva, 2017). This marginalizes athletes with severe impairments, reducing the potential for the Paralympics to be relevant to a wide disability audience and to communicate the reality of disability to the general public (Howe, 2011).

London 2012 Paralympics: a missed opportunity?

London 2012 was considered the first Paralympics to place increasing sport participation front and centre (Pappous & Brown, 2018). Despite this, a specific Paralympic legacy plan was only unveiled two years before the event (Weed, 2013). Evidence suggests that inspiration from the London 2012 Paralympics existed. For example, some children with physical impairments viewed the Paralympics as inspirational (Coates & Vickerman, 2016). Moreover, Brown and

Pappous (2018) found evidence for increased demand for some sports following the 2012 Paralympics. Sport participation peaked one year after the event in 2013 but declined by the time of the Rio 2016 Paralympics in Brazil, albeit remaining slightly higher than pre-Games levels (Brown & Pappous, 2018).

Sustaining sport participation proved difficult for several reasons. A prominent factor was a lack of pre-Paralympic leveraging by sports organizations to adequately prepare for heightened demand for participation (Brown & Pappous, 2018; Brown & Pappous, 2022). Negative media characterizations of disabled people created extreme depictions of them as either superhumans or welfare benefit cheats, resulting in unrealistic representations of disability (Crow, 2014). Additionally, austerity measures by the UK government at the time, and a culture of cracking down on supposed benefit cheats, created a fearful mindset among some disabled people worried about having their benefits taken away if seen to be active (Brown & Pappous, 2018; Johnson & Spring, 2018).

The Paralympics is not the solution but may be a catalyst for sport participation

The Paralympics has the potential to spur some disabled people to increase their frequency and/or intensity of sport participation. But it is not *the* solution. It is a resource that can be used as part of a wider array of sport participation initiatives (Amagasa et al., 2022). It may appeal to individuals who are already interested in sport, but is unlikely to move the dial for inactive individuals (Brown & Pappous, 2021) and on a population-wide level (Lion et al., 2023).

Managerial implications

The Paralympics needs to be leveraged to support potential inspiration generated from the event and sporting achievements of Paralympians. Addressing wider social, economic, and individual determinants of sport participation is likely to be more influential in encouraging inactive individuals to become active and to create sustainable sport participation.

Policy implications

The Paralympics is not a silver bullet for sport participation, and is unlikely to empower inactive disabled people to increase their sport participation. Physical activity and public health interventions targeted at inactive disabled people, rather than an elite sport event such as the Paralympics, may be more cost-effective (Weed, 2016).

Research implications

There is a need for higher-quality evidence on the Paralympic Games and sport participation. Longitudinal studies to track changes over time are required, as well as more studies investigating the utility of the festival effect and the demonstration effect.

QUIZ QUESTIONS

1. What is meant by the demonstration effect?
2. What is meant by the cyborgification of athletes?
3. What were some of the reasons offered by Brown and Pappous (2018) for the decline in sport participation after the 2012 London Paralympics?

DEBATE QUESTIONS

1. Why can it be problematic to produce causal links between the Paralympics and grassroots sport participation?
2. How does the context surrounding the event (e.g. wider economic conditions, political change, etc.) influence the sport participation potential of the Paralympics?
3. To what extent is the Paralympics a source of empowerment for disabled people?
4. How effective can the Paralympics be in advancing disability rights?
5. To what extent can the Paralympics influence the sport participation behaviour of inactive disabled people?

Table 6.1 Alignment to United Nations Sustainable Development Goals

Goal	How
Good Health and Well-Being Reduced Inequalities	The chapter considers the potential for the Paralympics to increase sport participation and physical activity of disabled people. Disabled people often participate in sport and physical activity less than non-disabled people, and may also have poorer health. By focusing on disabled people as the population of interest, this chapter provides a perspective on how sport participation is influenced by the Paralympics.

REFERENCES

Aizawa, K., Wu, J., Inoue, Y., & Sato, M. (2018). Long-term impact of the Tokyo 1964 Olympic Games on sport participation: A cohort analysis. *Sport Management Review*, *21*(1), 86–97. https://doi.org/10.1016/j.smr.2017.05.001.

Amagasa, S., Kamada, M., Bauman, A. E., Miyachi, M., & Inoue, S. (2022). Evaluation of pre-Games effects of the Tokyo 2020 Olympic Games on Japanese population-level physical activity: A time-series analysis. *International Journal of Behavioral Nutrition and Physical Activity*, *19*, 96. https://doi.org/10.1186/s12966-022-01332-x.

Annear, M., Sato, S., Kidokoro, T., & Shimizu, Y. (2022). Can international sports mega events be considered physical activity interventions? A systematic review and quality assessment of large-scale population studies. *Sport in Society*, *25*(4), 712–729. https://doi.org/10.1080/17430437.2021.1957834.

Annear, M. J., Shimizu, Y., & Kidokoro, T. (2019). Sports mega-event legacies and adult physical activity: A systematic literature review and research agenda. *European Journal of Sport Science*, *19*(5), 671–685. https://doi.org/10.1080/17461391.2018.1554002.

Bauman, A. E., Kamada, M., Reis, R. S., Troiano, R. P., Ding, D., Milton, K., Murphy, N., & Hallal, P. C. (2021). An evidence-based assessment of the impact of the Olympic Games on population levels of physical activity. *Lancet*, *398*(10298), 456–464. https://doi.org/10.1016/S0140-6736(21)01165-X.

Braye, S., Dixon, K., & Gibbons, T. (2013). 'A mockery of equality': An exploratory investigation into disabled activists' views of the Paralympic Games. *Disability & Society*, *28*(7), 984–996. https://doi.org/10.1080/09687599.2012.748648.

Brittain, I. S., Duignan, M., & Postlethwaite, V. (2022, July 27). London 2012's legacy boosted Paralympic sport, but disabled people's lives have worsened. *The Conversation*. https://theconversation.com/london-2012s-legacy-boosted-paralympic-sport-but-disabled-peoples-lives-have-worsened-187298.

Brown, C., & Pappous, A. S. (2018). 'The legacy element … it just felt more woolly': Exploring the reasons for the decline in people with disabilities' sport participation in England 5 years after the London 2012 Paralympic Games. *Journal of Sport and Social Issues*, *42*(5), 343–368. https://doi.org/10.1177/0193723518781237.

Brown, C., & Pappous, A. S. (2021). Are mega-events a solution to address physical inactivity? Interrogating the London 2012 Paralympic sport participation legacies among people with disabilities. *European Journal for Sport and Society*, *18*(1), 18–43. https://doi.org/10.1080/16138171.2020.1792112.

Brown, C., & Pappous, A. S. (2022). Leveraging the London 2012 Paralympic Games to increase sports participation: The role of voluntary sports clubs. *Managing Sport and Leisure*, *29*(5), 813–829. https://doi.org/10.1080/23750472.2022.2105253.

Chalip, L., Green, B. C., Taks, M., & Misener, L. (2017). Creating sport participation from sport events: Making it happen. *International Journal of Sport Policy and Politics*, *9*(2), 257–276. https://doi.org/10.1080/19406940.2016.1257496.

Chen, S., Lang, X., Hu, X. R., & Xing, X. (2024). Long-term sport participation after the Olympic Games: From 'inspirational feelings' to 'inspirational effects'. *Sport in Society*, *27*(4), 555–577. https://doi.org/10.1080/17430437.2023.2297369.

Coates, J., & Vickerman, P. B. (2016). Paralympic legacy: Exploring the impact of the games on the perceptions of young people with disabilities. *Adapted Physical Activity Quarterly*, *33*(4), 338–357. https://doi.org/10.1123/APAQ.2014-0237.

Craven, P. (2016). The Paralympic Games and the promotion of the rights of persons with disabilities. *UN Chronicle*, *53*(2). https://www.un.org/en/chronicle/article/paralympic-games-and-promotion-rights-persons-disabilities.

Crow, L. (2016). Scroungers and superhumans: Images of disability from the summer of 2012: A visual inquiry. *Journal of Visual Culture*, *13*(2), 168–181. https://doi.org/10.1177/1470412914529109.

Darcy, S., Lock, D., & Taylor, T. (2017). Enabling inclusive sport participation: Effects of disability and support needs on constraints to sport participation. *Leisure Sciences*, *39*(1), 20–41. https://doi.org/10.1080/01490400.2016.1151842.

de Souza, D. L., & Brittain, I. (2022). The Rio 2016 Paralympic Games: The visibility of people with disabilities in Brazil as a possible legacy. *Communication & Sport*, *10*(2), 334–353. https://doi.org/10.1177/2167479520942739.

Dickson, T. J., Darcy, S., & Walker, C. (2021). A case of leveraging a mega-sport event for a sport participation and sport tourism legacy: A prospective longitudinal case study of Whistler Adaptive Sports. *Sustainability*, *13*(1), 170. https://doi.org/10.3390/su13010170.

Ginis, K. A. M., van der Ploeg, H. P., Foster, C., Lai, B., McBride, C. B., Ng, K., Pratt, M., Shirazipour, C. H., Smith, B., Vásquez, P. M., & Heath, G. W. (2021). Participation of people living with disabilities in physical activity: A global perspective. *Lancet*, *398*(10298), 443–455. https://doi.org/10.1016/S0140-6736(21)01164-8.

Howe, P. D. (2011). Cyborg and supercrip: The Paralympics technology and the (dis)empowerment of disabled athletes. *Sociology*, *45*(5), 868–882. https://doi.org/10.1177/0038038511413421.

Howe, P. D., & Silva, C. F. (2017). The cyborgification of Paralympic sport. *Movement & Sport Sciences*, *97*, 17–25. https://doi.org/10.1051/sm/2017014.

Howe, P. D., & Silva, C. F. (2018). The fiddle of using the Paralympic Games as a vehicle for expanding [dis]ability sport participation. *Sport in Society*, *21*(1), 125–136. https://doi.org/10.1080/17430437.2016.1225885.

Johnson, E., & Spring, E. (2018). *The activity trap: Disabled people's fear of being active.* https://www.activityalliance.org.uk/how-we-help/research/the-activity-trap.

Kim, H., Lee, C., Kim, K. T., & Kim, J. (2024). Paralympic legacy as seen through the lenses of spectators with physical disabilities: A case of the PyeongChang Paralympic Games. *Annals of Leisure Research*, *27*(2), 293–312. https://doi.org/10.1080/11745398.2022.2132521.

Kokolakakis, T., Lera-López, F., & Ramchandani, G. (2019). Did London 2012 deliver a sports participation legacy? *Sport Management Review*, *22*(2), 276–287. https://doi.org/10.1016/j.smr.2018.04.004.

Lion, A., Vuillemin, A., Léon, F., Delagardelle, C., & van Hoye, A. (2023). Effect of elite sport on physical activity practice in the general population: A systematic review. *Journal of Physical Activity and Health*, *20*(1), 77–93. https://doi.org/10.1123/jpah.2022-0123.

Mahtani, K. R., Protheroe, J., Slight, S. P., Demarzo, M. M. P., Blakeman, T., Barton, C. A., Brijnath, B., & Roberts, N. (2013). Can the London 2012 Olympics 'inspire a generation' to do more physical or sporting activities? An overview of systematic reviews. *BMJ Open*, *3*, e002058. https://doi.org/10.1136/bmjopen-2012-002058.

Mölenberg, F., de Waart, F., Burdorf, A., & van Lenthe, F. J. (2020). Hosting elite sport events to target recreational sport participation: An interrupted time series analysis. *International Journal of Sport Policy and Politics*, *12*(4), 531–543. https://doi.org/10.1080/19406940.2020.1839530.

Nagata, S., Bloyce, D., Sato, T., & Okade, Y. (2023). It's about inspiring the greater community to continue supporting this sector: Elite sport success as a main policy objective for disability sport promotion in ASEAN member states. *International Journal of Sport Policy and Politics*, *15*(4), 655–670. https://doi.org/10.1080/19406940.2023.2236635.

Pappous, A. S., & Brown, C. (2018). Paralympic legacies: A critical perspective. In I. Brittain & A. Beacom (Eds.), *The Palgrave handbook of Paralympic studies* (pp. 647–664). Palgrave Macmillan. https://doi.org/10.1057/978-1-137-47901-3.

Peers, D. (2012). Patients, athletes, freaks: Paralympism and the reproduction of disability. *Journal of Sport and Social Issues*, *36*(3), 295–316. https://doi.org/10.1177/0193723512442201.

Purdue, D. E. J., & Howe, P. D. (2012). Empower, inspire, achieve: (Dis)empowerment and the Paralympic Games. *Disability & Society*, *27*(7), 903–916. https://doi.org/10.1080/09687599.2012.695576.

Silva, C. F., & Howe, P. D. (2012). The (in)validity of supercrip representation of Paralympian athletes. *Journal of Sport and Social Issues*, *36*(2), 174–194. https://doi.org/10.1177/0193723511433865.

Souza, D. L., & Brittain, I. (2022). The Rio 2016 Paralympic Games: Inspiration as a possible legacy for disabled Brazilians. *European Journal for Sport and Society*, *19*(1), 78–93. https://doi.org/10.1080/16138171.2021.1879363.

Weed, M. (2013). London 2012 legacy strategy: Did it deliver? In V. Girginov (Ed.), *The handbook of the London 2012 Olympic and Paralympic Games, Volume One: Celebrating the Games* (pp. 281–294). Routledge.

Weed, M. (2016). Should we privilege sport for health? The comparative effectiveness of UK government investment in sport as a public health intervention. *International Journal of Sport Policy and Politics*, *8*(4), 559–576. https://doi.org/10.1080/19406940.2016.1235600.

Weed, M., Coren, E., Fiore, J., Wellard, I., Chatziefstathiou, D., Mansfield, L., & Dowse, S. (2015). The Olympic Games and raising sport participation: A systematic review of evidence and an interrogation of policy for a demonstration effect. *European Sport Management Quarterly*, *15*(2), 195–226. https://doi.org/10.1080/16184742.2014.998695.

7 HOW DOES HOSTING THE OLYMPICS BENEFIT LOCAL COMMUNITIES?

An examination of Tokyo 2020

Judith Mair and Mike Duignan

AIM

To discuss the concept of mega event legacy and identify and document some of the short-term and longer-term negative social impacts of the Tokyo Olympic Games on the residents of the host city.

DOI: 10.4324/9781003488729-9

LEARNING OBJECTIVES

LEARNING OBJECTIVES

1. Understand the concept of mega event legacy.
2. Identify a range of long-term social impacts of mega events on the residents of the host city/country.
3. Consider the options for mega event organisers to maximize the legacy benefits for local residents and communities.

Theoretical focus and significance

To interrogate and differentiate the meanings of mega event social impacts and legacies, this chapter will focus on how such events alter the constitution and representation of community and culture in the host destination. The Olympic Games, in particular, have often faced criticism for their negative impacts and legacies. This criticism arises either from a lack of meaningful legacy planning or from the failure of promised legacies to materialize, often leaving behind disused infrastructure, white elephants, and debt as the only reminders of hosting the Games. This chapter aims to understand why legacies, even those that are meticulously planned, may still fail.

Practical focus and significance

This chapter aims to identify the elements of long-term negative social impacts of mega events on host communities and societies, while proposing potential strategies to mitigate these impacts and improve mega event legacies. This investigation is crucial because the Olympic Games continue to impose significant financial and social costs on host destinations. A critical examination of legacy potential is therefore essential to encourage future bids for hosting these mega events and to ensure that enhanced benefits accrue to local residents and communities.

TOPIC – HOW DOES HOSTING THE OLYMPICS BENEFIT LOCAL COMMUNITIES? AN EXAMINATION OF TOKYO 2020

Over the past 20 years, the concept of legacy has become increasingly central to any campaign to host the Olympic Games. As World Athletics president and former chairman of the London 2012 Organising Committee Sebastian Coe stated in 2006, legacy constitutes nine-tenths of what hosting the Olympics is about (Culf, 2006). He emphasized that "It is the local people who should stand to gain most from the Games" (Select Committee on Olympic and Paralympic Legacy, 2014).

Dubbed the 'Legacy Games', London 2012 aimed to project a new and positive future for the city, a vision satirized on television by the BBC's mockumentary *Twenty Twelve*. Framing the Olympics as a long-term investment in a future destination helps justify the costs, aiming to convince local populations that the Games will bring net benefits compared to investing in sectors such as health and education. These benefits may include improved access to education and skills development, enhanced social cohesion, civic pride, social capital, health and well-being through increased sports participation, and greater inclusion and diversity (Mair et al., 2023).

However, the final expenditure on the Tokyo Olympics was $12.9 billion, 20% more than initial estimates, with an additional $9.8 billion spent on other Games-related projects (Sankar, 2022). As the Tokyo 2020 Games concluded, the pressing question for many, especially local residents, is: Was it worth it?

Tourism development

Shinzo Abe, Japan's prime minister when Tokyo won the bid for the 2020 Games, stated that it was a key opportunity to open up Japanese culture and people to the world (McCurry, 2013). The Tokyo Olympic Committee emphasized bringing international visitors to Japan as a central legacy goal, arguing that interactions between visitors and local communities – cultural producers, small businesses – were unique selling points for Tokyo as a tourism destination (Tokyo Vision for Arts and Culture, n.d.). However, displacing existing residents and businesses undermines this justification.

Despite this, significant urban development projects in Tokyo replaced diverse and authentic Japanese backstreets. Research by Suzuki et al. (2018) showed that older neighbourhoods were feeling the squeeze before Tokyo 2020. By 2015, the Shinagawa area of Musashi-Koyama – a vibrant maze of small eateries, tapas restaurants, and bars – had become a ghost town (Ito, 2015). Tokyo parks saw increased policing, and many shops closed due to rising property prices and rents (Olympics Watch, 2020).

The corporate colonization of local business precincts reflects a broader concern highlighted by Olympic tourism scholars: host cities becoming clone towns and urban 'blandscapes', with small businesses replaced by global and national chains (Duignan, 2019). This undermines the diverse and unique cultural offerings promised in Olympic hosting campaigns, ultimately hampering long-term tourism competitiveness and alienating local communities.

Local fallout

A review by Duignan and Talbot (2021) shows that local communities around Olympic sites are directly affected leading up to the Games. For example, the construction of the new National Stadium in Shinjuku for Tokyo 2020 saw elderly tenants evicted and homeless people displaced in alarming numbers (Suzuki et al., 2018). This pattern of displacement, disruption, and gentrification is consistent with every successful Olympic bid. Barcelona saw a 130% increase in property prices five years before the Games (Mannan, 2013), and Sydney experienced an 11% rise in house prices compared to the rest of Australia ahead of the 2000 Summer Olympics (London Assembly, 2007).

Low-income residents are often replaced by upwardly mobile individuals as new apartment blocks are erected, while rising commercial rents force small businesses to close, replaced by high-end stores and coffee-shop chains (Duignan, 2019). These effects persist long after the Games end. Post-event gentrification is so common that it is referred to as the 'Olympic effect' (Rose & Spiegel, 2009). For those facing eviction, the reality is bleak, highlighting an indifference towards protecting local business communities and diverse urban high streets. Research shows that these communities struggle to survive and are barely recognized as key contributors to local and national economies (Duignan, 2019).

Cities evolve over decades due to social and economic policies. However, the Olympics accelerate gentrification that would otherwise occur more gradually. This is often due to targeted regeneration schemes such as the creation of Meiji Park for Tokyo 2020 (Japan Property Central, 2019) or the Porto Maravilha cultural quarter in Rio de Janeiro (World Bank Group, n.d.). Event-induced touristification of urban spaces exacerbates gentrification (Bruttomesso, 2018; Sequera & Nofre, 2020).

Following Paris 2024, future Olympic host cities, including Los Angeles (2028) and Brisbane (2032), must strive to limit negative social impacts. Displacing local people and businesses may not be an immediate political or economic priority, but the unique local culture produced by vibrant communities is what attracts visitors in the long term.

Managerial implications

Mega event organizers (often governments or statutory bodies) should collaborate and co-design with local residents and communities to ensure that the event, and its planned legacies, are desired and supported. They should also make sure that funding for legacy is ring-fenced long in advance of the event to avoid legacy failure due to budget cuts.

Policy implications

Similar to the managerial implications, governments should ensure that they cooperate fully with local residents, community associations, and interested stakeholders.

Research implications

Further research on the long-term outcomes of planned mega event legacies is needed in order both to assess how well past legacies are progressing (if at all) and to develop stronger foundations for planning future successful legacies.

QUIZ QUESTIONS

1. According to Lord Coe, who should gain most from hosting an Olympic Games?
2. Identify a selection of possible benefits for local residents and communities from hosting the Olympic Games.
3. Identify some of the hallmark characteristics associated with gentrification.

DEBATE QUESTIONS

1. Discuss the effects of hosting the Olympic Games on residents of the host city. Consider positive and negative effects as well as short- and long-term effects.
2. Consider ways for host cities to mitigate some of the negative effects of hosting an Olympic Games and improve outcomes for local residents and communities.

Table 7.1 Alignment to United Nations Sustainable Development Goals

Goal	How
Decent Work and Economic Growth	Mega events can bring many opportunities for economic growth to a host city. However, often the employment opportunities associated with them are limited, temporary, or in low-skill positions.
Industry, Innovation and Infrastructure	Mega events often create new infrastructure, so any new infrastructure created needs to have a clear post-event use and funding model to ensure its sustainability.
Sustainable Cities and Communities	Mega events have the potential to transform cities, but this should only happen where it will benefit the local communities and residents in the long term.

REFERENCES

Bruttomesso, E. (2018). Making sense of the square: Facing the touristification of public space through playful protest in Barcelona. *Tourist Studies*, *18*(4), 467–485. https://doi.org/10.1177/1468797618775219.

Culf, A. (2006, May 4). Legacy is central to 2012 says Coe. *The Guardian*. https://www.theguardian.com/sport/2006/may/04/Olympics2012.politics.

Duignan, M. B., & Talbot, A. (2021) *Tokyo Olympics: How hosting the Games disrupts local lives and livelihoods*. The Conversation. https://theconversation.com/tokyo-olympics-how-hosting-the-games-disrupts-local-lives-and-livelihoods-162893.

Duignan, M. B. (2019). London's local Olympic legacy: Small business displacement, 'clone town' effect and the production of 'urban blandscapes'. *Journal of Place Management and Development*, *12*(2), 42–163. https://doi.org/10.1108/JPMD-05-2018-0033.

Ito, M. (2015, November 7). Heart of darkness: Nostalgic Tokyo disappearing amid construction boom. *Japan Times*. https://www.japantimes.co.jp/life/2015/11/07/lifestyle/heart-darkness-nostalgic-tokyo-disappearing-amid-construction-boom/.

Japan Property Central (2019, May 20). *Redevelopment details for Meiji Jingu Stadium district*. https://japanpropertycentral.com/2019/05/redevelopment-details-for-meiji-jingu-stadium-district/.

London Assembly (2007). *A lasting legacy for London? Assessing the legacy of the Olympic Games and Paralympic Games*. Greater London Authority. https://www.london.gov.uk/sites/default/files/gla_migrate_files_destination/archives/assembly-reports-econsd-lasting-legacy-uel-research.pdf.

Mair, J., Chien, P. M., Kelly, S. J., & Derrington, S. (2023). Social impacts of mega-events: A systematic narrative review and research agenda. *Journal of Sustainable Tourism*, *31*(2), 538–560. https://doi.org/10.1080/09669582.2020.1870989.

Mannan. T. (2013, September 4). Hosting the Olympics: A win for the housing market? *Your Money*. https://www.yourmoney.com/investing/hosting-the-olympics-a-win-for-the-housing-market/.

McCurry, J. (2013, September 8). Tokyo 2020 Olympics: Hugs, tears and shouts of 'banzai' greet news of victory. *The Guardian*. https://www.theguardian.com/sport/2013/sep/08/tokyo-2020-olympics-jubilation-relief.

Olympics Watch (2020). *Tokyo 2020*. https://olympicswatch.org/tokyo-2020/.

Rose, A. K. & Spiegel, M. M. (2009). The Olympic effect. National Bureau of Economic Research Working paper 14854. https://www.nber.org/papers/w14854.

Sankar, V. (2022). *Hosting Tokyo 2020 cost $12.9 billion, 20 per cent more than initial calculations*. Inside the Games. https://www.insidethegames.biz/articles/1131922/tokyo-costs.

Select Committee on Olympic and Paralympic Legacy (2014). *Keeping the flame alive: The Olympic and Paralympic legacy*. House of Lords. https://publications.parliament.uk/pa/ld201314/ldselect/ldolympic/78/78.pdf.

Sequera, J., & Nofre, J. (2020). Touristification, transnational gentrification and urban change in Lisbon: The neighbourhood of Alfama. *Urban Studies*, *57*(15), 3169–3189. https://doi.org/10.1177/0042098019883734.

Suzuki, N., Ogawa, T. & Inaba, N. (2018). The right to adequate housing: Evictions of the homeless and the elderly caused by the 2020 Summer Olympics in Tokyo. *Leisure Studies*, *37*(1), 89–96. https://doi.org/10.1080/02614367.2017.1355408.

Tokyo Vision for Arts and Culture (n.d.). *Culture and the vision for Tokyo*. https://www.seikatubunka.metro.tokyo.lg.jp/en/document/vision_english02.pdf.

World Bank Group (n.d.). *Porto Maravilha case study: Urban regeneration*. https://www.thegpsc.org/sites/gpsc/files/2._porto_maravilha.pdf.

SECTION

2 TRANSFORMING PLACES

8 DOES CARNIVAL STILL COME FIRST IN RIO EVEN WHEN THE OLYMPICS COME TO TOWN?

Karen Davies

AIM

To compare and contrast the impacts of the Rio Carnival – a hallmark event rich in history and culture staged every year in Rio de Janeiro, Brazil – and the Olympic Games, a mega-event hosted there in 2016.

DOI: 10.4324/9781003488729-11

LEARNING OBJECTIVES

LEARNING OBJECTIVES

1. To explore the social, cultural and economic impacts of hallmark events such as the Rio Carnival and mega-events such as the Olympic Games on a city and its residents.
2. To examine the similarities and differences between hallmark cultural events and mega-sporting events in terms of impact and legacy.

Theoretical focus and significance

This chapter focuses on the social, cultural and economic impacts and legacies, both positive and negative, of cultural hallmark and mega-sporting events in a specific location. It aims to contribute to the ongoing debate on the long- and short-term social, cultural and economic impacts of mega-sporting events compared to those of hallmark cultural events on a city, region or nation.

Practical focus and significance

The chapter aims to indicate areas for ongoing scrutiny to ensure ethical approaches to long-term impacts and legacies from both mega-sporting and hallmark cultural events are followed by policy makers. It provides a comparative case study to highlight the differences in social, cultural and economic impacts between cultural hallmark events and one-off mega-sporting events.

TOPIC – DOES CARNIVAL STILL COME FIRST IN RIO EVEN WHEN THE OLYMPICS COME TO TOWN?

The Rio Carnival in Brazil involves five days of revelry, and is a global phenomenon that attracts international media attention and more than a million visitors and participants each year. It captures a sense of South American culture with exotic, creative flair, and projects this to an enormous audience from around the world through images of flamboyant dancers, costumes/headdresses and colourful floats. The event also embodies Brazilian culture through its vibrant collection of human art installations, and fits firmly within the category of 'hallmark cultural event' in that it has "become synonymous with the name of the place and gain[s] widespread recognition" (Bowdin et al., 2024, p. 27).

Carnivals take place in many locations throughout the world, and most have their origins in cultural and religious traditions and rituals. Indeed, the word 'carnival' comes from the Latin *carne-vale* (flesh farewell), originally marking a period of feasting and revelry before the fasting of Lent (Turner, 1983). But the modern version of the carnival raises questions related to forces of globalisation and commodification, and has arguably become a mere spectacle staged for the consumption of tourists, as discussed by Andrews and Leopold (2013). Some would argue that the event in Rio has become a spectacle bereft of meaning; but in fact it is still a fundamental element of both the cultural character and the economic survival of the people who live there, not least those from disadvantaged parts of the city.

Rio's Carnival generates in the region of 11 billion Brazilian reais (approximately US$3.7 billion), three-quarters of which comes from tourism alone (Brazilian-American Chamber of Commerce, 2018). Over 200 samba schools take part in the parades and spend up to the equivalent of £3 million on preparations; 10 million people took part in the street parades in 2020, and more than 200,000 spectators attended in 2022 (López, 2021; López, 2023). In 2022, 15,200 temporary jobs were created by the carnival (López, 2023), and this was set to rise by another 50,000 in 2024 due to the investment of 62.5 million reais (£10m; $12.5m) by the state government (Brown, 2024).

In 2016 Rio staged the Olympic Games, a mega-sporting event that, with effective management, was set to secure a high return on investment alongside the Carnival. According to Faria and Pereira (2023, p. 28), "the Olympic Games had a significant impact on the Brazilian economy, both in the short term, during the event, and in the long term, through the legacy left in infrastructure, job creation, tourism and mobility works". However, their survey of residents also highlighted that there was concern about excessive costs and a lack of transparency and accountability. It is notable that 53% of participants believed that the costs incurred by the Games were not justified by the benefits brought to the city, and that investment in the event had increased the burden on Brazilian debt.

Mega-events are ambulatory occasions that "are so large that they affect whole communities and reverberate in the global media [and] are usually developed through competitive bidding" (Bowdin et al., 2024, p. 26). Despite their potential for increasing economic development, notoriously they have also been surrounded by much controversy, especially in terms of accountability and questions around the real 'winners' and 'losers'. Often public funding is sacrificed to host mega-events; and increased taxes and spending cuts to other areas are often not taken into account when calculating the financial benefits. Furthermore, whereas a major proportion of money invested comes from the public purse, much of the profit received does not go back to the public, but rather to shareholders and investors (Zimbalist, 2015).

According to the UK Department for Culture, Media and Sport (2010), social and cultural benefits are also achievable from staging these events through

Figure 8.1 Rio de Janeiro, Favela des Plaisirs (Flickr, 2024).

sound ethical investments in education, sports participation and community engagement, as per London 2012's Legacy Policy. But all too often these provisions are short term, and there are also huge social disadvantages, with little or no consideration for the needs of local communities in the host city (Lee Ludvigsen et al., 2022).

One example of negative social impacts can be seen in the *favelas*, which have become a major part of Brazilian culture. *Favelas* are informal urban settlements that typically house a city's poorest residents (such as in Rio). However, while they are often associated with social and health issues such as violence and teenage pregnancy (Penglase, 2014), they are also people's homes. Many of Rio's samba schools – which prepare the floats for the Carnival parades – are based in these areas: the celebrations are woven into their economic and cultural fabric. Part of the programme to prepare for the Olympics was to 'clean up' or 'pacify' the *favelas* to make the city safe for tourists. With a greater police presence, forced evictions and questionable pacification tactics (Talbot, 2016; Rocha, 2023), this policy has the potential to stifle creativity and freedom of expression, quashing the counterculture that gives Rio its unique character.

The year 2016 in Rio serves as a good example of how two very different types of event, although similar in scale and media exposure, produced varying long-term legacies and impacts on host communities and the city as a whole. Carnival arguably offers more to local people than any mega-event ever could through a sense of ownership and shared values. In essence, the playful cultural activities that it involves reflect community culture, provide freedom of expression, promote inclusion and bolster the creative industries. Carnival is Rio: it has been part of the city's cultural life since the 1700s. While hosting the Olympic Games gave Brazil and Rio the opportunity to invest in new infrastructure, improve the country's economy and gain political status, it can be argued that Carnival is much more important to the long-term cultural and spiritual survival of the city and the nation.

The comparison of the events held in Rio in 2016 provides an interesting case study on the various considerations required by policy makers, organisers and stakeholders to ensure positive short- and long-term impacts from staging large-scale events, both cultural and sporting. Economic benefits should be allocated fairly, and local communities should be considered throughout the process. The sort-termism of mega-sporting events sometimes means that these ethical objectives are not met due to issues with governance (Lee Ludvigsen et al., 2022). Hallmark cultural events such as the Rio Carnival are in danger of over-commercialisation, and therefore need careful managing to ensure that cultural authenticity and tradition are not lost; and, when a mega-event comes to town, the beneficiaries of those events should not be forgotten or pushed to one side.

Managerial implications

Consideration of how to manage the impact on local residents and communities in a city of hosting one-time mega-sporting events in comparison to cultural hallmark events should be encouraged.

Policy implications

These are to highlight how to balance the social and cultural elements of large-scale events with their economic impacts and ensure ethical approaches to impact and legacy management.

Research implications

This chapter highlights the potential for investigation and comparison between the management of impacts of two very different types of large-scale event (cultural and sporting) in a case study location.

QUIZ QUESTIONS

1. Identify the differences between a hallmark event and a mega event.
2. What are the social impacts of the Rio Carnival and the Olympic Games? How do they differ?
3. Why do mega events often fail to have as many positive impacts as planned?

DEBATE QUESTIONS

1. In your opinion, which event is more beneficial in terms of long-term impacts for the people and city of Rio? Why?
2. Do you think that clearing out the *favelas* was good for the city of Rio? Think about the answer from a number of different stakeholder and policy perspectives.
3. Should Brazil host other mega events? Discuss reasons for and against.

Table 8.1 Alignment to United Nations Sustainable Development Goals

Goal	How
Decent Work and Economic Growth	By exploring the opportunities that large-scale event projects can provide in a city
Industry, Innovation and Infrastructure	By considering introducing innovative large-scale event projects and their infrastructure developments for positive impacts for all stakeholders
Sustainable Cities and Communities	By comparing how managing the impacts of cultural hallmark events and one-off mega-sporting events can help sustain cities and communities, both economically and culturally

REFERENCES

Andrews, H., & Leopold, T. (2013). *Events and the social sciences.* Abingdon: Routledge.

Bowdin, G., Allen, J., Harris, R., Jago, L., O'Toole, W., & McDonnell, I. (2024). *Events management* (4th Ed.). Abingdon: Routledge.

Brazilian-American Chamber of Commerce. (2018). *Rio 2016 Carnival impact.* https://brazilcham.com/category/brazil-business/.

Brown, S. (2024, February 13). *Rio de Janeiro is betting on Carnival for 'cooler' parties – and a better Brazil.* BBC Worklife. https://www.bbc.com/worklife/article/20240212-rio-de-janeiro-brazil-carnival-investment.

Department for Culture, Media and Sport (2010, December). *Plans for the legacy from the 2012 Olympic and Paralympic Games*. https://assets.publishing.service.gov.uk/media/5a74f325e5274a3cb28687cc/201210_Legacy_Publication.pdf.

Faria, M. J. da S., & Pereira, B. L. G. A. (2023). The impact on the Brazilian economy of the Olympic Games in Rio de Janeiro in 2016. *International Journal of Professional Business Review*, *8*(11), 1–38. https://doi.org/10.26668/businessreview/2023.v8i11.3886.

Lee Ludvigsen, J. A., Rookwood, J., & Parnell, D. (2022). The sport mega-events of the 2020s: Governance, impacts and controversies. *Sport in Society*, *24*(4), 704–711. https://doi.org/10.1080/17430437.2022.2026086.

López, A. M. (2021, September 15). Carnival in Rio de Janeiro: Number of attendees 2017–2020. Statista. https://www-statista-com/statistics/977628/number-participants-carnival-brazil-rio-de-janeiro/.

Lopez, A.M. (2023, February 14). Carnival in Brazil: Number of seasonal jobs created 2013–2023. Statista. https://www.statista.com/statistics/977084/number-temporary-jobs-created-carnival-brazil/.

Penglase, R. B. (2014). *Living with insecurity in a Brazilian favela: Urban violence and daily life*. New Brunswick, NJ: Rutgers University Press.

Rocha, C. M. (2023). Rio 2016 Olympic legacy for residents of favelas: Revisiting the case of Vila Autódromo five years later. *Social Sciences*, *12*(3), 166. https://doi.org/10.3390/socsci12030166.

Talbot, A. (2016, January 12). Vila Autódromo: The favela fighting back against Rio's Olympic development. *The Conversation*. https://theconversation.com/vila-autodromo-the-favela-fighting-back-against-rios-olympic-development-52393.

Turner, V. (1983). Carnival in Rio: Dionysian drama in an industrializing society. In F. E. Manning (Ed.), *The celebration of society: Perspectives on contemporary cultural performance* (pp. 103–124). Bowling Green, OH: Bowling Green University Popular Press.

Zimbalist, A. (2015). *Circus Maximus: The economic gamble behind hosting the Olympics and the World Cup*. Washington, DC: The Brookings Institution.

9 CREATING QUEER SPACES

Small-town Prides grow in numbers and popularity

Beck Banks

AIM

The chapter aims to show the challenges and, ultimately, the power of small-town and rural Pride celebrations.

DOI: 10.4324/9781003488729-12

LEARNING OBJECTIVES

1. People will understand that Pride celebrations are happening in small towns and rural areas.
2. These Prides are popular and help the communities they serve.
3. The smaller Prides create a needed space that larger city Prides take for granted.

Theoretical focus and significance

Small towns and rural locations are often ignored in discussions about LGBTQ populations. The queer rurality theory shows how often this happens and puts it in conversation with the emerging, smaller Prides. Despite the consistent narrative of LGBTQ communities only belonging in metropolitan areas, they are everywhere, and these regional Prides celebrate and serve them.

Practical focus and significance

Prides are proliferating across the United States and in unexpected locations. Those Prides have a strong and positive impact on the queer people residing in those areas. This chapter highlights non-metropolitan Prides, which are important to often overlooked queer residents throughout the US. These events bring public support – despite some initial issues.

TOPIC – CREATING QUEER SPACES: SMALL-TOWN PRIDES GROW IN NUMBERS AND POPULARITY

Too often, LGBTQ people in rural places and small towns are left out of discussions about queer life and culture. Despite this, Pride celebrations continue to spread throughout these overlooked pockets of the United States. While sometimes met with resistance, the impact of these events cannot be understated.

It's easy to conflate metropolitan areas with queerness. Even as a trans person from Central Appalachia and a communications professor who studies transgender rurality and regionality, I manage to mix the two more than I want. The melding of queer and the city reduces the lives of too many people. I know I was doing that the day I traveled to Pikeville Pride in Eastern Kentucky.

On the trip there, I tried to talk myself out of the visit. To be clear, I respect what Pride entails – a commemoration of an uprising against a police raid that took place at the Stonewall Tavern in June 1969. The raid enforced laws that prevented queer people from gathering. Perhaps more now than in recent years,

Pride is returning to its uprising roots and its 1980s' AIDS/HIV activism as, according to the American Civil Liberties Union (ACLU, 2024), the country has seen a record-breaking 515 anti-LGBTQ bills six months into 2024.

That said, when I attended Pikeville Pride in 2019, its second year, I thought I was attending a highly commercialized Pride – the one I knew in big cities.

I was not.

Pikeville Pride

I had heard about one or two Prides that had encountered issues with white nationalists before attending Pikeville in October 2019. However I didn't know about the scope of these encounters or that it was close to a regular threat for the Prides getting started in Central Appalachia.

Pikeville's population is approximately 7,750, nestled in the mountains of Kentucky. Close to 400 people attended its first Pride in 2018 (Pikeville Pride, 2024). The next year, the event saw over 500 people in attendance; and, Covid quarantine years aside, the event continues to grow.

Pikeville Pride took place directly in its downtown area. The central square contained nonprofit organizations, activist booths, and a central stage with a rotation of bluegrass and drag queen performances. Not far from the stage, a sheltered picnic area provided free rainbow cake, two-liter soda, and plenty of pizza. There was no lack of opportunities for involvement. This Pride wasn't designed for one type of queer person; it was meant for all of them.

Figure 9.1 Chalk and the sidewalks were available for people to write messages such as the ones shown at Pikeville Pride in fall 2019. Author own image.

Pikeville Pride founder Tonya Jones says her involvement in Pride was not a reaction to a white nationalist rally that took place in Pikeville in 2017, but other founders do say that's the reason they started it (Pikeville Pride, 2024). Jones says her primary motivation was to make the town more welcoming and inclusive. In its first year, Jones saw two protesters in attendance. About two hours away in Tennessee, Johnson City experienced more protesters at its first TriPride event, launched the same year as Pikeville Pride. The event encompasses East Tennessee's Tri-Cities area – Bristol, Johnson City, and Kingsport. White nationalists threatened the event but, ultimately, only 20 protesters attended. By the next year, that number dropped to 10–12 protesters who stayed in a designated area, according to Jason Willis, founder and former president of TriPride. Due to the threats and attendance of white nationalists (Baker, 2018), state and federal law enforcement showed up in droves at the first TriPride. About 200 police officers worked at the event, and a helicopter circled it. Because of the threat, people attended in solidarity as well as to celebrate this first Pride with crowds upwards of 10,000 (Prehne, 2018).

As of 2024, current TriPride president Justin Hall recalls two emails from upset religious people, and those weren't angry emails. The larger political backlash against LGBTQ people highlights the need for TriPride and other such organizations, he says. Both TriPride and Pikeville Pride continue to grow. According to Hall, TriPride is the largest annual event in the Tri-Cities area; and according to Jones, Pikeville Pride is the second largest annual event in Pikeville, behind the long-standing Hillbilly Days festival, and is hoping to expand its programming. TriPride is already on that path, with regular gatherings and guiding local organizations to help provide even more opportunities, such as regular LGBTQ teen meetings, clothing thrifts, and food drives.

Both Jones and Hall note that these Prides have created more organization and support. Other Prides started in smaller towns near them, such as Ashland and Morehead in Kentucky and Breaks in Virginia. Jones says that people wear Pikeville Pride t-shirts around town and compliment her when she shows up in stories about the organization: "In the past, people would have been afraid to talk about these things."

Pride festivals in Appalachia are an important trend in small towns and rural America. Others have been held in a wide range of places, such as Window Rock (Arizona), Starkville (Mississippi), and Stockholm (Wisconsin).

The impact of smaller Prides

Prides outside of major metropolitan areas are as important – if not more important – than the ones in major cities as they serve people who need more resources and support. Anthropologist Kath Weston (1995) established the idea of "the gay imaginary," which looks at how queer people are searching for others like them. This search can result in moving to larger cities, making the journey to a gay bar, or other quests for community. It's an imagined community people have well before they have a real one. There is often an idea that other queer people will be like them; it's just a matter of finding them. The realities of this quest can be disappointing.

Similarly, gender studies and English professor Jack Halberstam (2005) uses the term "metronormativity" to expand on this idea. Metronormativity favors the city over the country. It links a journey from small town to big city as a rite of passage, a narrative not unlike puberty.

Essentially, large cities are considered queer spaces, while every other place is not. Queer rural life, according to scholar Scott Herring, goes unnoted; but when it does appear it is to be rejected or pitied. According to Herring (2010, p. 5), "the rural (take your pick: Idaho, North Carolina, small-town America, hick) is shelved, disavowed, denied, and discarded in favor of metropolitan sexual cultures such as New York City, San Francisco, or Buffalo. In each, the rural becomes a slur, one that has proliferated into an admittedly rich idiom."

That sentiment is reflected in screen culture. Queer characters on television are rarely from smaller towns or rural places. Some are characters who left such places – like Titus Andromedon from Chickasaw County, Mississippi, in *Unbreakable Kimmy Schmidt* or *Search Party*'s Elliott from a fictional holler (hollow) in West Virginia. Whether the person left or stayed, the queer character is one that is out of place. Often, that is part of the joke.

Belonging matters. Jones understands the importance of Pride, having seen what Pikeville Pride did for her wife of 27 years (as quoted in Banks, 2021):

> She never felt comfortable here until Pride. She never felt she could be open. We foster children too, and a lot of these kids are in foster care because of coming out. We want to show them that they can have a family, and it doesn't have to be a blood connection.

Policy implications

The chapter shows the positive impacts of Pride on residents and the economy in a particular place in the United States. There is a path for more of these events throughout the country.

Research implications

Small-town and rural queer life needs more examination. These Prides provide a strong entry to further research and understanding of how to help support the LGBTQ population.

QUIZ QUESTIONS

1. How does Pride benefit LGBTQ populations outside of major cities?
2. What is the gay imaginary?

DEBATE QUESTIONS

1. When you think of small-town or rural queer life, what comes to mind?
2. What screen portrayals have you seen of rural queer life? Is there a common theme to those depictions?
3. How would you deal with white nationalists threatening an event?

Table 9.1 Alignment to United Nations Sustainable Development Goals

Goal	How
No Poverty	These Prides are an economic boon to more remote areas.
Good Health and Well-Being	The events promote good health and well-being for LGBTQ residents and others.
Quality Education	Education and community outreach are present at these Prides.
Gender Equality	Gender equality is a component of these events, especially trans-related.
Decent Work and Economic Growth	These Prides are an economic boon to more remote areas.
Industry, Innovation and Infrastructure	Due to their outreach, many of these Prides play a role in innovation and support their region's infrastructure.
Reduced Inequalities	This is a primary goal of these events.
Peace, Justice and Strong Institutions	Smaller regional Prides support peace, justice, and stronger institutions.
Partnerships for the Goals	Many of these Prides use partnerships for the annual event and throughout the year.

REFERENCES

ACLU. (2024, May 30). *Mapping attacks on LGBTQ rights in U.S. state legislatures in 2024*. https://www.aclu.org/legislative-attacks-on-lgbtq-rights-2024.

Baker, N. (2018, August 22). White nationalist group moves planned rally to Elizabethton, will have presence at Johnson City pride event. *Johnson City Press*. https://www.johnsoncitypress.com/news/update-white-nationalist-group-moves-planned-rally-to-elizabethton-will-have-presence-at-johnson-city/article_6465e85a-3361-569a-9ff4-f393cdb9ff9c.html.

Banks, B. (2021, November 3). Small-town Pride celebrations emerge – and show that LGBTQ life in America is flourishing outside of cities. *The Conversation*. https://theconversation.com/small-town-pride-celebrations-emerge-and-show-that-lgbtq-life-in-america-is-flourishing-outside-of-cities-165518.

Halberstam, J. (2005). *In a queer time and place: Transgender bodies, subcultural lives*. New York University Press.

Herring, S. (2010). *Another country: Queer anti-urbanism*. New York University Press.

Pikeville Pride. (2024, May 30). *Pikeville Pride 2020*. https://pikeville-pride.square.site/.

Prehne, C. (2018, Sept. 15). Tri-Cities first LGBT pride parade and festival draws thousand. *WCYB*. https://wcyb.com/news/tennessee-news/tri-cities-first-lgbt-pride-parade-and-festival-draws-thousands.

Weston, K. (1995). Get thee to a big city: Sexual imaginary and the great gay migration. *GLQ: A Journal of Lesbian and Gay Studies*, *2*(3), 253–277.

10 OLYMPICS FOR WHOM? Winners and losers of mega-events

Adam Talbot

AIM

To explore the way impacts of hosting mega-events are unevenly distributed across host cities, often accruing benefits to the already well off and harming the marginalized.

DOI: 10.4324/9781003488729-13

LEARNING OBJECTIVES

LEARNING OBJECTIVES

1. To understand the uneven distribution of event impacts.
2. To evaluate the Olympic Games from the perspective of the right to the city.

Theoretical focus and significance

The right to the city is a fairly nebulous concept that broadly refers to ensuring that cities are developed to support those who inhabit them, as opposed to more transient visitors. The right to the city has been embraced by urban social movements throughout the world; and, in the context of mega-events, it provides a useful way of linking diverse social issues through a single lens, ultimately uniting opposition.

Practical focus and significance

The chapter examines how the multi-faceted impacts of hosting mega-events are distributed across the host city. To understand the way this distribution of impacts serves to reinforce inequality instead of addressing it, as most hosts claim.

TOPIC – OLYMPICS FOR WHOM? WINNERS AND LOSERS OF MEGA-EVENTS

The Summer Olympic Games is among the most-watched media events in the world. Occurring on a four-year cycle, hosting the event usually brings wide-ranging transformations to the urban environment where it takes place. From the construction of new stadia and transport infrastructure to the impacts on public finances and security, these impacts are often claimed as positives by organizers but criticized as damaging by protestors. So who is right?

This chapter will explore four examples from four Summer Olympics, making the case that benefits from hosting the Olympic Games tend to accrue to the already privileged, whereas damaging impacts tend to fall on the most marginalized. We can understand this phenomenon based on the French social theorist Henri Lefebvre's concept of the right to the city. Heavily picked up by urban social movements, the right to the city is defined by David Harvey (2008) as "far more than the individual liberty to access urban resources: it is a right to change ourselves by changing the city" (p. 23). In particular, the right to the city emphasizes the role of residents and inhabitants in driving the development of urban space to suit their needs, as opposed to the needs of a transnational capitalist class.

For the 2012 Olympic Games in London, several new stadiums were constructed, particularly concentrated in the East End of the city, a traditionally poorer area which was intended to be regenerated through hosting the event. This included the main Olympic stadium, now occupied by West Ham United football club, and the aquatics centre, which now serves the local community. The Queen Elizabeth Olympic Park, home to both of these facilities, now serves as a hub of the East End, alongside the adjacent Westfield shopping centre.

However, these developments had a significant impact on the local population. For example, the Clays Lane housing estate, which previously stood on the site, was demolished and the residents rehoused to make space for these stadiums. The loss of natural spaces such as the Hackney Marshes impacted local wildlife as well as leisure space for residents. Most notably though, the rapid rise in housing costs in the area has led to significant gentrification as poorer residents are forced to move further away from jobs and other urban amenities, changing the character of the neighbourhood. Hosting the Games to develop the East End therefore actually ended up further marginalizing many of the residents who were most in need of support (Watt, 2013).

In 2016, Rio de Janeiro in Brazil invested billions of dollars in public transport infrastructure, developing new bus rapid transit and metro lines, such as the line linking the wealthy South Zone neighbourhood of Ipanema to the wealthy gated communities of Barra da Tijuca where the main Olympic park was located. While the majority of beneficiaries of this new line are already wealthy residents, it also serves Rocinha, Brazil's largest *favela* community.

The bus rapid transit lines, largely focused in the sparsely populated West Zone of the city, were one of the major drivers of the 22,059 families evicted from their homes in preparation for the mega-event. While these lines undoubtedly serve a relatively poorer segment of Rio's population, some stretches are underused as they connect parts of the city that only needed to be connected during the event, not during everyday life. To make this worse, as a result of economic crises in the years before the Games, many regular bus routes were cut, meaning that, despite billions of dollars of investment in urban mobility, average commute times actually increased after the Games (Pereira, 2018).

The Tokyo Olympic Games, originally scheduled for 2020 but postponed by a year due to the Covid-19 pandemic, were hailed in Japan for their potential to kickstart an economy that has struggled with sluggish growth since the 1980s. According to a Bank of Japan report (Osada et al., 2016), the return on investment was expected to come through an increase in foreign tourism and construction linked to the event. In particular, by targeting an increase in North American and European tourists, the Games were intended to leave a lasting legacy to the

Figure 10.1 A house is demolished in Rio's Vila Autódromo *favela*. The graffiti reads "We are going to stay." Photo by Adam Talbot, March 2016.

Japanese economy. However, the implementation of tourism development initiatives was concentrated in the already saturated tourist areas of Tokyo, Kyoto and Osaka, and lacked deep engagement with stakeholders in the tourism industry.

To be sure, Covid-19 had a severe impact on Tokyo's plans, forcing more spending and significantly limiting the number of Olympic visitors. However, the broader pattern of Olympic economics shows that Tokyo cannot blame its economic woes on the pandemic. The sheer cost of hosting the Games in the 21st century means any economic benefits that developments linked to the event may bring are often outweighed by the costs of the event (Zimbalist, 2015).

Finally, the Paris 2024 Games sat within a wider development project referred to as 'Grand Paris', which was particularly focused on integrating the north-eastern arrondissements and Seine-Saint-Denis, a separate municipality that lies immediately to the north-east of Paris and is among the most deprived areas of France. Alongside numerous urban development projects, including new metro lines and the creation of the athlete's village, new security infrastructure was developed, theoretically enabling an effective tourism legacy for the Games as potential visitors could feel safer.

However, this stimulated criticism from privacy groups, particularly around the use of facial recognition and other artificial intelligence (AI) technology in Games security which would then be used for policing the domestic population. Such concerns were particularly heightened due to the racial biases associated with these technologies, particularly as they would be deployed in largely

Figure 10.2 Graffiti on an Olympic advertisement denounces the Games as an accelerator of pillaging. Photo by Adam Talbot, May 2022.

non-white areas of the city (La Quadrature du Net, 2020). These kinds of security issues have long been deliberate legacies from hosting the Games; and, as Coaffee (2024) argues, they are becoming increasingly embedded in the fabric of Paris itself.

Ultimately, every Olympic Games produces winners and losers in host cities, as well as on the track. In general, positive impacts tend to affect the already well off and facilitate access for tourists while exacerbating inequalities by negatively impacting marginalized groups. Seen through the lens of the right to the city, we can see how the Olympic Games tend to serve a transnational capitalist class at the expense of those who inhabit host cities. As such, there is a need to explore new models of hosting that do not infringe on the rights of host populations.

Policy implications

We need to engage much more deeply and more effectively with host communities, particularly marginalized groups in host communities, to ensure that mega-events actually address inequalities in host cities.

Research implications

Research is necessary to see whether reforms to the Olympic Games, such as Agenda 2020 or the new bidding process, make a meaningful change to the dynamic of winners and losers outlined here.

QUIZ QUESTIONS

1. What is gentrification and how do mega-events stimulate this?
2. Why is new security spending not necessarily a good thing for residents of host cities?
3. How can we explain the failure of legacy projects despite significant investment?

DEBATE QUESTIONS

1. How can we ensure spending on public transport results in effective legacy post-Games?
2. Is it the fault of the International Olympic Committee or the host city if the delivery of the Games exacerbates inequality?
3. Are damaging legacies inevitable?

Table 10.1 Alignment to United Nations Sustainable Development Goals

Goal	How
Reduced Inequalities	The chapter explored how the Olympic Games actually exacerbate inequalities – challenging the narrative that the Games are good for development
Sustainable Cities and Communities	The chapter focused on how the Olympics can do more to increase (social) sustainability in cities, and the right to the city provides a framework for thinking about this

REFERENCES

Coaffee, J. (2024). Evolving security motifs, Olympic spectacle and urban planning legacy: From militarization to security-by-design. *Planning Perspectives*, *39*(3), 637–657. https://doi.org/10.1080/02665433.2024.2322002.

Harvey, D. (2008). The right to the city. *New Left Review*, *53*(Sept/Oct), 23–40.

La Quadrature du Net (2020, June 22). *Racisme policier: Les géants du net font mine d'arretêr la reconnaissance faciale* [*Police racism: Net giants pretend to stop facial recognition*]. https://www.laquadrature.net/2020/06/22/racisme-policier-les-geants-du-net-font-mine-darreter-la-reconnaissance-faciale/.

Osada, M., Ojima, M., Kurachi, Y., Miura, K., & Kawamoto, T. (2016). *Economic impact of the Tokyo 2020 Olympic Games*. Bank of Japan Reports and Research Papers. https://www.boj.or.jp/en/research/brp/ron_2016/ron160121b.htm.

Pereira, R. H. M. (2018). Transport legacy of mega-events and the redistribution of accessibility to urban destinations. *Cities*, *81*, 45–60. https://doi.org/10.1016/j.cities.2018.03.013

Watt, P. (2013). 'It's not for us': Regeneration, the 2012 Olympics and the gentrification of East London. *City*, *17*(1), 99–118. https://doi.org/10.1080/13604813.2012.754190.

Zimbalist, A. (2015). *Circus Maximus: The economic gamble behind hosting the Olympics and the World Cup*. Brookings Institution Press.

11 WHO BENEFITS WHEN A CITY HOSTS THE WORLD CUP?

David Roberts

AIM

The aim of this chapter is to inform readers about the most common impacts on cities that come with hosting an event like the World Cup, and to provide an alternative vision for planning such events.

DOI: 10.4324/9781003488729-14

LEARNING OBJECTIVES

1. Discuss the motivating factors that lead cities to want to host mega-events like the FIFA Men's World Cup.
2. Elucidate some of the common consequences of hosting such events.
3. Point to alternative ideas on what to prioritize in mega-event event planning.

Theoretical focus and significance

The theoretical focus of this chapter is what it means to be a world-class city in an unequal world, and how the hosting of mega-events such as the World Cup contribute to exacerbating existing urban inequalities. The theoretical significance of this chapter is identifying the ways in which hosting the World Cup exacerbates inequalities while pointing to the possibility of an alternative approach.

Practical focus and significance

World Cups, Olympics, and other mega-events happen regularly, and have become intimately tied to the urban strategies of many cities across the world. Planning for these events can provide a window into urban priorities of key decision makers. The hosting of such events requires a significant amount of resources – financial, time, focus – and has long-term consequences for a city's budget, planning priorities, and policing orientation, among many other things.

TOPIC – WHO BENEFITS WHEN A CITY HOSTS THE WORLD CUP?

With a viewership of 3.5 billion people in 2018, few events capture the world's attention like the FIFA Men's World Cup (Inside FIFA 2018). While the vast majority of consumers of the World Cup, as with many other sports mega-events, watch the event remotely through television and the internet, the impacts on cities that host such events are significant and long-lasting – and generally exacerbate existing inequalities while placing additional pressures on urban life. And yet cities around the world continue to seek out opportunities to host these events.

Why do cities want to host mega-events?

Advocates of events often point to the potential for economic windfalls from hosting them. However, claims of short-term economic gains in host cities and countries are disingenuous at best as host cities and countries consistently incur significant debt related to the cost of hosting (Brownsell 2022). With events such as the World Cup and the Olympics, much of the profit is extracted by the governing bodies, in this case FIFA or the International Olympic Committee (Simmons & Deutscher 2012).

Promises of economic windfalls are often based on the hope that successfully hosting an event like the World Cup or Olympics will appreciably improve a city's brand image, which will then translate to increases in tourism and business investment into the future. But, as I have argued elsewhere, "even this justification, at least from an economic point of view, relies on some pretty fuzzy math and long-term forecasting that rarely gets audited" (Roberts 2022, citing Horne 2007). This is not to discount the power of a positive urban brand on the economic vitality of a place, but rather to point to the shaky foundation upon which many claims regarding the potential for improving a city's economy through a strategy of hosting mega-events lie.

While hosting a mega-event is clearly connected to an urban branding strategy, the desire of cities to market themselves to the world as good places to visit, move to, or do business in is not unique to host cities of such events. Harvey (1989), along with many other scholars, has documented a clear shift in urban orientation from what has been described as managerial – or the provision of services and programmes to improve the quality of life of current urban residents – to an increasingly entrepreneurial orientation designed to attract tourists, new residents, and corporate investment and to brand a city as "world-class".

A "world-class city" for whom?

Unfortunately, these entrepreneurial pursuits generally share a narrow perspective of what it means to be a "world-class city". During the 2010 FIFA Men's World Cup in South Africa, Streetnet International – a South African-based organization advocating for street vendors – ran a campaign, "World Class Cities for All", pointing to this pattern. As the website argued:

> It has become a boringly predictable reality that, when a country prepares to host a high-profile international event, the country and its local government authorities prepare to create "World Class Cities" of a particular type, i.e. "World Class Cities" which:

- will attract foreign investment;
- have modern up-to-date infrastructure;

- have no visible signs of urban decay;
- have smooth traffic flows;
- have no visible poor people or social problems. (Streetnet International n.d.)

In essence, a "world-class city" is one that caters to the wants of middle- and upper-class tourists and urban residents through targeted investments in particular forms of infrastructure and the policing out or covering up of poverty, social inequality, or any number of things that may not fit the desired brand image of the entrepreneurial city. While there may be local innovations to the way a city approaches its duties as host of an event like the World Cup, these are variations on the theme articulated by Streetnet International.

An all-too-common mechanism to achieve this type of "world-class city" is through increased policing by hiring or calling on additional officers, the military (McMichael 2012), or private security (Muñana 2024) and deploying additional surveillance measures (Sugden 2012). Police, private security, and the military are often also given additional powers to police *undesirable* activities and individuals – often through public nuisance ordinances. While the framing of these laws focuses on nuisance behaviours, they are often used to police vulnerable urban populations – such as youth, the precariously housed or unhoused, racialized individuals, and street vendors, among others (Roberts 2010).

Beyond policing, the pursuit of this type of world-class city leads to urban investment choices that privilege tourist infrastructure and tourist-oriented areas of the city, creating an uneven landscape of investment and under-investment, and often exacerbating existing socio-spatial inequalities in host cities (Gaffney 2010). The fact that such large numbers of the audience for such events are experiencing them through the medium of television only further facilitates this unevenness given how much of a host city remains off-camera (Sadler & Haskins 2005).

An alternative approach?

In framing its campaign as "World Class Cities for All", Streetnet challenged event planners, host city governments, urban citizens, and consumers of these events to imagine an alternative approach to hosting them – and defining what it means to be a "world-class city". For Streetnet, this starts with protecting the rights of some of the city's most vulnerable – in this case, street vendors – as a core principle for hosting a mega-event. At least in terms of new rhetoric, FIFA appears to be listening as it announced "Human Rights – Key Focus for FIFA World Cup 2026™" (Inside FIFA 2022).

However the shift from the status quo of these events – which exacerbates inequalities and leaves cities in significant debt while catering to the wants of the well off in society – requires much more than lofty rhetoric or claims that human

Figure 11.1 World Class Cities for All campaign. Author own image.

rights are now a focus. The beauty of the "World Class Cities for All" campaign is that it is a call to action – not just about how to better host a mega-event, but how to imagine more just, sustainable, liveable futures for all urban residents as integral to what it means to be a "world-class city". This requires leveraging investments – in mega-events or other infrastructure – towards these ends.

Managerial implications

The managerial implications are for municipal governments, planners, and mega-event hosts to move beyond rhetorical commitments to human rights when hosting such events to leveraging the investment in these events towards urban social development.

Policy implications

Much could be done to improve transparency, commitment to human rights, and other elements of hosting mega-events.

Research implications

Research should continue to focus on the relationship between hosting mega-events and other trends in urbanization. Additionally, it should continue to document the ways in which these events exacerbate inequalities despite rhetorical commitments to human rights.

QUIZ QUESTIONS

1. What are elements of a typical approach to being a world-class city?
2. What is a common argument used to justify the hosting of a mega-event?
3. What is an entrepreneurial city?

DEBATE QUESTIONS

1. Should cities pursue hosting mega-events like the World Cup?
2. How can the hosting of the World Cup be improved using an equity lens?
3. Do mega-events positively contribute to urban development?

Table 11.1 Alignment to United Nations Sustainable Development Goals

Goal	How
No Poverty	Hosting mega-events generally exacerbates inequalities; this chapter articulates the possibility of an alternative approach
Good Health and Well-Being	An alternative approach to hosting mega-events could help reduce inequality and thus promote better health
Decent Work and Economic Growth	Highlighting an alternative approach to hosting mega-events
Industry, Innovation and Infrastructure	The chapter addresses the equity issues related to infrastructure investment
Reduced Inequalities	This is the focus of the chapter
Sustainable Cities and Communities	The chapter proposes an alternative approach

REFERENCES

Brownsell, J. (2022, November 17). *Do host countries make money from the World Cup?* Al Jazeera. Retrieved April 30, 2024, from https://www.aljazeera.com/sports/2022/11/17/do-host-countries-make-money-from-the-world-cup.

Gaffney, C. (2010). Mega-events and socio-spatial dynamics in Rio de Janeiro, 1919–2016. *Journal of Latin American Geography*, *9*(1), 7–29.

Harvey, D. (1989). From managerialism to entrepreneurialism: The transformation in urban governance in late capitalism. *Geografiska Annaler: Series B, Human Geography*, *71*(1), 3–17.

Horne, J. (2007). The four 'knowns' of sports mega-events. *Leisure Studies*, *26*(1), 81–96.

Inside FIFA (2018, December 21). *More than half the world watched record-breaking 2018 World Cup*. Retrieved April 30, 2024, from https://inside.fifa.com/tournaments/mens/worldcup/2018russia/media-releases/more-than-half-the-world-watched-record-breaking-2018-world-cup.

Inside FIFA (2022, July 20). *Human rights – Key focus for FIFA World Cup 2026*. Retrieved April 30, 2024, from https://inside.fifa.com/social-impact/human-rights/news/human-rights-key-focus-for-fifa-world-cup-2026-tm.

McMichael, C. (2012). "Hosting the world": The 2010 World Cup and the new military urbanism. *City*, *16*(5), 519–534.

Muñana, G. (2023, November 25). *£320 million for private security in Paris 2024*. Inside the Games blog. Retrieved April 30, 2024, from https://www.insidethegames.biz/articles/1142660/320-million-private-security-paris-2024.

Roberts, D. (2010). Durban's future? Rebranding through the production/policing of event-specific spaces at the 2010 World Cup. *Sport in Society*, *13*(10), 1486–1497.

Roberts, D. (2022, November 29). *When hosting mega-events like FIFA, cities market themselves at the expense of the most vulnerable*. The Conversation. Retrieved April 30, 2024, from https://theconversation.com/when-hosting-mega-events-like-fifa-cities-market-themselves-at-the-expense-of-the-most-vulnerable-195069.

Sadler, W. J., & Haskins, E. V. (2005). Metonymy and the metropolis: Television show settings and the image of New York City. *Journal of Communication Inquiry*, *29*(3), 195–216.

Simmons, R., & Deutscher, C. (2012). The economics of the World Cup. In L. H. Kahane & S. Shmanske (Eds.), *The Oxford handbook of sports economics: The economics of sports, volume 1* (pp. 449–469). Oxford Academic.

Streetnet International (n.d.). *World Class Cities for All*. Retrieved April 30, 2024, from https://streetnet.org.za/document/world-class-cities-for-all/.

Sugden, J. (2012). Watched by the Games: Surveillance and security at the Olympics. *International Review for the Sociology of Sport*, *47*(3), 414–429.

12 HOW HOSTING THE OLYMPICS CAN LEAD TO DISPLACEMENT

Adam Talbot and Mike Duignan

AIM

To explore the links between processes of displacement and the organization of mega-events in urban environments.

DOI: 10.4324/9781003488729-15

LEARNING OBJECTIVES

LEARNING OBJECTIVES

1. To critically evaluate the impact of mega-events on displacement in host cities.
2. To explore David Harvey's concept of accumulation by dispossession in the context of mega-events.

Theoretical focus and significance

The theoretical focus of this chapter is on accumulation by dispossession, a process that continually concentrates power and wealth in increasingly fewer hands. The challenges posed by accumulation by dispossession for achieving positive societal transformation through events are severe and necessitate a rethinking of our current economic approaches.

Practical focus and significance

Mega-events often drive displacement in host cities, ultimately resulting in increased inequality and leaving a negative legacy.

TOPIC – HOW HOSTING THE OLYMPICS CAN LEAD TO DISPLACEMENT

This chapter explores the links between mega-events and various forms of displacement, with a focus on the Olympic Games due to their significant impact on urban environments. Although these displacement processes are common to all mega-events to varying degrees, the Olympics tend to have the largest effect due to their scale and concentrated geographical footprint.

The Marxist geographer David Harvey (2003) introduced the term 'accumulation by dispossession' to describe a shift in the dynamics of capitalism in urban contexts since the 1970s. Unlike traditional wealth accumulation, which relies on capitalists paying labourers for their productive value, this process derives value from the increasing attractiveness of urban space. Consequently, changing the ownership of urban spaces serves to concentrate capital and political power in the hands of a few.

In the context of the Olympics, the most obvious form of accumulation by dispossession is the direct eviction of residents to make way for stadiums and other event infrastructure. Evictions have been a persistent consequence of hosting the Olympic Games, as integral to the event as medals and podiums. A report by the Centre for Housing Rights and Evictions (2007) documented 720,000 forced evictions in Seoul 1988; the displacement of low-income earners in Barcelona 1992; 9,000 arrests of homeless individuals and 30,000 displacements in Atlanta 1996; hundreds of displacements in Athens 2004; and an estimated 1.5 million displacements in Beijing 2008. Since that report, there have been over 1,000 evictions linked to London 2012, particularly around the Clays Lane Housing Estate (Bernstock 2013). In Rio de Janeiro, 77,209 people were evicted from *favelas* ahead of the 2016 Olympics (Comitê Popular da Copa e Olimpíada 2015), and hundreds were evicted in Tokyo prior to the 2020 Summer Games (Suzuki et al. 2018). Evictions have also occurred in preparation for the Paris 2024 and Los Angeles (2028) Olympics, though accurate figures are not yet available.

These evictions, although varied in their legal contexts, consistently disrupt lives and community connections for the sake of a temporary sports event. For instance, in Rio de Janeiro, numerous evictions also occurred in *favelas* in the lead-up to the 2014 FIFA World Cup. The Brazilian civil society group Comitê Popular da Copa e Olimpíada (2015) argues that, including legacy projects like the Bus Rapid Transit system, the number of evicted households rises to 4,120, with a further 17,939 evictions due to real estate speculation spurred by the events. Magalhães (2019) supports this, suggesting that *favela* evictions became public policy during Rio's mega-event years. Faulhaber and Azevedo (2015) note that these evictions typically moved residents from central and southern zones to the far west of the city, far from amenities and economic opportunities.

The process of eviction itself also generates harm. Residents often receive little to no warning or compensation, along with disruptive actions such as unremoved rubble and cut utilities. Raquel Rolnik (2015), former UN Special Rapporteur for the right to adequate housing, argues that these conditions, combined with a lack of public debate and individual negotiation tactics, violate the right to housing.

Beyond forced evictions, gentrification is another subtle but pervasive form of displacement associated with mega-events. Gentrification, where neighbourhood improvements lead to higher housing costs, forces poorer residents to relocate. This is a classic case of Harvey's accumulation by dispossession as land values and rental incomes increase by displacing existing residents.

Mega-events contribute significantly to gentrification. For example, while the causes of gentrification in London are multifaceted, the 2012 Olympics exacerbated existing problems in UK housing policy (Corcillo and Watt 2022). Similar patterns are seen globally: in Rio, improved security in *favelas* like Santa Marta and Vidigal during 'pacification' led to gentrification (Gaffney 2016); and in Los Angeles, new stadiums in lower-income neighbourhoods such as Inglewood have increased housing costs, benefiting landowners and exemplifying accumulation by dispossession (Robertson 2022).

Since the 1980s, when the Olympics and other mega-events fully embraced commercialization and capitalist principles, these events have been used to serve capital interests in host cities. This process often makes host cities less equal, contradicting claims that such events support marginalized populations. This chapter seeks to understand how and why even well-planned legacies can fail, examining the broader implications of mega-events on urban environments and local communities.

Policy implications

We need to give much more consideration not just to areas of cities that are targeted for event-led regeneration, but also to the people who live there, ensuring that benefits accrue to existing residents instead of already wealthy landowners.

QUIZ QUESTIONS

1. How is accumulation by dispossession different from traditional accumulation processes?
2. What is the difference between eviction and gentrification?
3. Why do local businesses not benefit from mega-events?

DEBATE QUESTIONS

1. How would the Olympic Games need to change to address the problem of accumulation by dispossession?
2. How would our economic system need to change to address the problem of accumulation by dispossession – and how can mega-events lead that change?
3. What practical steps can be taken to reduce or eliminate displacement processes at mega-events?

Table 12.1 Alignment to United Nations Sustainable Development Goals

Goal	How
Sustainable Cities and Communities	Ultimately, the issue of accumulation by dispossession makes our cities and communities less sustainable, so addressing this issue with help address this SDG

REFERENCES

Bernstock, P. (2013). Tensions and contradictions in London's inclusive housing legacy. *International Journal of Urban Sustainable Development*, 5(2), 154–171. https://doi.org/10.1080/19463138.2013.847839.

Centre on Housing Rights and Evictions. (2007). *Fair play for housing rights: Mega-events, Olympic Games and housing rights*. Geneva International Academic Network. https://www.ruig-gian.org/ressources/Report%20Fair%20Play%20FINAL%20FINAL%20070531.pdf.

Comitê Popular da Copa e Olimpíadas. (2015). *Rio 2016 Olympics: The exclusion games: Mega-events and human rights violations in Rio de Janeiro dossier*. https://comitepopulario.files.wordpress.com/2016/03/dossiecomiterio2015_eng1.pdf.

Corcillo, P. and Watt, P. (2022). Social mixing or mixophobia in regenerating East London? 'Affordable housing', gentrification, stigmatisation and the post-Olympics East Village. *People, Place & Policy Online*, *16*(3), 236–254. https://doi.org/10.3351/ppp.2022.8325576466.

Faulhaber, L. and Azevedo, L. (2015). *SMH 2016: Remoções no Rio de Janeiro Olímpico [SMH 2016: Removals in Olympic Rio de Janeiro]*. Mórula Editorial.

Gaffney, C. (2016). Gentrifications in pre-Olympic Rio de Janeiro. *Urban Geography*, *37*(8), 1132–1153. https://doi.org/10.1080/02723638.2015.1096115.

Harvey, D. (2003). *The new imperialism*. Oxford University Press.

Magalhães, A. A. (2019). *Remoções de favelas no Rio de Janeiro: Entre formas de controle e resistências [Evictions of favelas in Rio de Janeiro: Between forms of control and resistance]*. Appris Editora.

Robertson, C. (2022). 'Built to host'? Built for whom? The LA2028 Olympics and urban exclusions. In Hanakata, N. C., Bignami, F., and Cuppini, N. (Eds.), *Mega events, urban transformations and social citizenships: A multi-disciplinary analysis for an epistemological foresight* (pp. 215–228). Routledge. https://doi.org/10.4324/9780367625726.

Rolnik, R. (2015). *Guerra dos lugares: A colonização da terra e da moradia na era das finanças [War of places: The colonization of land and housing in the era of finance]*. Boitempo.

Susuki, N., Ogawa, T. and Inaba, N. (2018). The right to adequate housing: Evictions of the homeless and the elderly caused by the 2020 Summer Olympics in Tokyo. *Leisure Studies*, *37*(1), 89–96. https://doi.org/10.1080/02614367.2017.1355408.

13 MARGINALIZATION, DISPLACEMENT, AND EXCLUSION IN MONTREAL'S CULTURAL ECONOMY

Piyusha Chatterjee

AIM

The aim of this chapter is to foreground, through an oral historical approach, the experiences of long-time buskers in a city undergoing post-industrial transformation and witnessing the growth of a cultural economy.

DOI: 10.4324/9781003488729-16

LEARNING OBJECTIVES

1. To recognize the diversity of experiences within cultural economies.
2. To become aware of the challenges posed by outdoor festivals and events for local buskers.
3. To analyse effects of a top-down approach to planning and regulatory practices on the ground.

Theoretical focus and significance

This chapter focuses on the role of festivals in the cultural economy. Through the use of oral history methodology, it takes a bottom-up approach to understanding the diversity of the impact of post-industrial transformation on people. The significance is to elaborate on the complexity of experiences in post-industrial cities and develop an understanding of labour in the cultural economy. It also draws attention to surveillance experienced by marginalized groups and their displacement from public spaces.

Practical focus and significance

The practical focus is on the design and regulation of urban spaces in cultural economies that work to exclude marginalized groups from accessing economic opportunities and maintaining social bonds. The significance of this is to create awareness about the diversity of experiences and impact of top-down planning and regulatory measures on marginalized groups in cultural economies.

TOPIC – MARGINALIZATION, DISPLACEMENT, AND EXCLUSION IN MONTREAL'S CULTURAL ECONOMY

The practice of busking – which the *Oxford English Dictionary* (n.d.) defines as "performing music or some other entertainment in a public place … for monetary donations" – has a long but discontinuous tradition in western cities (Cohen & Greenwood, 1981). Buskers keep appearing, disappearing and reappearing on city streets through history. Stereotyped, stigmatized and often criminalized in 19th- and early 20th-century industrial cities for their poverty, itinerancy and transient occupation of public space (Zucchi, 1992; Smith 1996; Hawkins, 2012; Watt, 2018, 2019; Owens, 2018; Whiteoak, 2018), buskers have become more tolerated, and even welcomed, in post-industrial cities. Street music and performances are seen as adding colour to otherwise mundane urban spaces and giving them a sense of vibrancy (Doughty & Lagerqvist, 2016), which has led to their inclusion and proliferation in the cultural economy.

Despite the commercialization of busking as an urban cultural practice through open-air festivals and outdoor cultural events, buskers hold a subversive political potential because of practices that challenge power and the top-down planning and management of urban public space (Ferrell, 2001; Seldin, 2020). Jostling for "temporary ownership of liminal space ... indicates [their] low status" (Bywater, 2007, p. 118). Buskers draw on or appropriate public spaces and infrastructure – even if briefly – to entertain people and make some money. As an informal way of earning a living, networking for economic opportunities and building social bonds, busking blurs the lines between work, leisure and begging. It is precarious work that is either illegal and unregulated or poorly regulated and poorly remunerated.

This acceptance of busking in the cultural economy is making visible new social fragmentations. While busking festivals around the world are attracting internationally mobile and highly stylized performers to cities, those buskers who are socially or economically marginalized and lack mobility due to a range of factors – such as race, gender, ethnic and class identity, citizenship status, etc. – find themselves displaced from their usual pitches or devoid of prospects within the cultural economy. The discourse on safety and security encourages surveillance and manual, technological and digital interventions, further contributing to their removal from city centres and sites of economic opportunity.

Through oral history interviews, this chapter explores the tensions around the place of buskers in the political economy of the post-industrial city through a case study of Place Jacques-Cartier, a public square in Old Montreal, Canada. Since the 1960s, a progressive deindustrialization of Montreal (High 2022) has led the city to be rebranded as a cultural metropolis and an economy driven by industries such as tourism, music, design and circus (Sirois, 2021; Leslie & Rantisi, 2011, 2006; Paul, 2004; Levine, 2003). Busking has become popular in those parts of the city that draw large numbers of commuters and tourists. The interviews with buskers were analysed against a study of local regulations related to busking.

Busking in Old Montreal

Street entertainers are not new to Old Montreal. As a public market located close to the port, Place Jacques-Cartier attracted itinerant musicians and other street entertainers, such as acrobats and animal exhibitors, in the late 19th and early 20th century. Now part of the heritage district of Old Montreal, buskers flock to the square, particularly in the summer season, to etch out a living by street-entertaining. With a new functioning port located further up the Saint Lawrence

River, the old port of Montreal has also been turned into a zone for leisure and entertainment.

Old Montreal is one of the few places where busking is viable in the summer. The underground subway (Metro) is another popular busking site for musicians. Other forms of street entertainer, such as human statues, balloon-sculptors and jugglers, are not allowed in the subway. Over the years, both top-down and bottom-up practices have regulated buskers and their pitches in Old Montreal. In 2019, when the oral history interviews were conducted, the borough of Old Montreal had an annual official season, and buskers were expected to renew their licences every year to play music or perform in the square. A number of self-governing practices were also present among buskers, such as the daily drawing of lots at noon to decide the day's line-up of performers. Anyone arriving after the draw was offered a spot at the end of the queue. The queue repeated itself until the end of the day and a new draw conducted the next day. The interviews also revealed friendships that had evolved over the years. Buskers shared ideas, borrowed tricks and swapped busking times and spots as per their convenience.

Marginalization and displacement at the square

Place Jacques-Cartier has several officially approved busking spots (Ville-Marie, 2024). In the summer of 2019, buskers had decided to stay off the pitch in Old Montreal to protest against the introduction of an online lottery system by the borough administration (see mapvillemarie.com). Apart from being forced to access a digital platform to find a pitch, buskers were at the mercy of an algorithm to assign times, frequency and spots for busking on the square, which took no account of weather conditions and other factors important to buskers. Interviewee Suzanna Martinez, a flamenco dancer who had emigrated from Mexico, explained that, under the new system, if it rained during their assigned time, a busker could go without making any money. It therefore took away a busker's agency in deciding when and where to perform to get a 'good hat'. "With these rules," Martinez said, "my life will be difficult."

The online lottery had added a new layer of precarity in her life. She frequented Old Port area until buskers were banned from there. Under the new rules, buskers needed contracts to perform in the old port. Some noise complaints made against buskers were really the fault of the festivals that used large stage speakers pointed towards the city, Martinez explained in the interview conducted in French. Martinez also spoke at length about how local buskers were mistreated by the city while visiting artists were encouraged to busk at the square.

In his interview, Eric Girard, a sword juggler and fire-breather, reflected on Place Jacques-Cartier's history as a site where itinerant entertainers had always flocked. "We have always been here," he said, referring to the square's history as a public market next to a port that attracted itinerant musicians and visiting circus artists and jugglers. With the latest regulations and the emergence of spaces such as Quartier des spectacles and other open-air venues, Girard also felt the city was "getting rid of the proper busker" as events such as the Jazz Fest organized and hired their own street performers. "There's always a festival, or something. And when there's nothing, they'll put like a wall or something," Girard said about Quartiers des spectacles. The Rue des artistes – a narrow lane off Place Jacques-Cartier that had housed street artists for decades – has also disappeared. Now caricaturists and portrait painters jostle for space with other buskers on the square.

According to interviewee Peter Snow, "Real street performing is – go stand in the corner right there, now, and I do a little something and I get a little bit of money." A magician and an escape artist, in 2019 Snow had been street-performing in Montreal for over thirty years; but the festivals, which involved "big money" and where buskers made "five times more" than him, don't accept him, explaining that he and others are "considered a bit wild, okay, and they want safe people".

At the start of the pandemic, Snow decided not to return to busking in Old Montreal. With the new regulations in place, Girard had also been looking for opportunities elsewhere. As for Martinez, she had limited mobility: during the week she spent her time in a suburban town of Montreal where her daughter went to school; and at weekends she and her daughter took the train to the city to join her husband, a caricaturist at the square, "to be a family". Being on the square at weekends allowed her the opportunity to make some money as well; however the lottery system threatened to upset this carefully organized routine.

Managerial implications

These include considering a bottom-up approach to managing public spaces in cultural economies and understanding the needs of different stakeholders in urban space, such as those who are economically and socially marginalized.

Policy implications

Policy makers should better understand the need to develop bottom-up approaches to building inclusive cities.

Research implications

Localized studies should be carried out on the impact of the cultural economy on various actors, including those who are among the most vulnerable and marginalized in urban space.

QUIZ QUESTIONS

1. What is busking?
2. What factors contribute to the marginalization and displacement of buskers in the cultural economy?
3. How does this chapter inform and/or expand your understanding of the following terms: cultural economy, flexible labour, the Global North?

DEBATE QUESTIONS

1. Is a cultural economy more desirable than an industrial economy? Give reasons why or why not.
2. What is flexible labour? Is it good or bad?
3. What makes a city inclusive? Can you think of examples of places and practices that are welcoming of marginalized social groups?
4. Can corporates develop public spaces that do not displace marginalized groups? If so, how?

Table 13.1 Alignment to United Nations Sustainable Development Goals

Goal	How
No Poverty	The chapter shines a light on how cultural economies are contributing to economic marginalization and what needs to be done in order to create inclusive cities.
Decent Work and Economic Growth	Buskers find dignity in their work: they see busking as an activity that allows them to avoid poverty and offers opportunities to find economic and social networks that are important for their well-being.
Reduced Inequalities	The chapter highlights the importance of thinking through regulations on urban spaces with all stakeholders, including those who may occupy public space only transiently.
Sustainable Cities and Communities	All the above-mentioned points contribute to developing an understanding of what economically and socially sustainable cities and communities might look like in the near future.

REFERENCES

Bywater, M. (2007). "Performing Spaces: Street Music and Public Territory." *Twentieth-Century Music* 3:1, 97–120. doi:10.1017/S1478572207000345.

Cohen, D. & Greenwood, B. (1981). *The Buskers: A History of Street Entertainment.* David & Charles.

Doughty, K. & Lagerqvist, M. (2016). "The ethical potential of sound in public space: Migrant pan flute music and its potential to create moments of conviviality in a 'failed' public square." *Emotion, Space, and Society* 20, 58–67.

Ferrell, J. (2001). *Tearing Down the Streets: Adventures in Urban Anarchy*. Palgrave Macmillan.

Hawkins, R. (2012). "'Industry Cannot Go On without the Production of Some Noise': New York City's Street Music Ban and the Sound of Work in the New Deal Era." *Journal of Social History* 46:1, 106–23. https://doi.org/10.1093/jsh/shs025.

High, S. (2022). *Deindustrializing Montreal: Entangled Histories of Race, Residence and Class.* McGill-Queen's University Press.

Leslie, D. & Rantisi, N. M. (2006). "Governing the Design Economy in Montréal, Canada." *Urban Affairs Review* 41:3, 309–37. doi:10.1177/1078087405281107.

Leslie, D. & Rantisi, N. M. (2011). "Creativity and Place in the Evolution of a Cultural Industry: The Case of Cirque du Soleil." *Urban Studies* 48:9, 1771–87.

Levine, M. V. (2006). "Tourism-based Development and the Fiscal Crisis of the City: The Case of Montréal." *Canadian Journal of Urban Research* 12:1, 102–23.

Owens, S. (2018). "'Unmistakeable Sauerkrauts': Local perceptions of itinerant German musicians in New Zealand, 1850–1920." *Nineteenth-Century Music Review* 15:1, 37–49. doi:10.1017/S1479409817000076.

Oxford English Dictionary (n.d.). "Busking, Sense 2." https://doi.org/10.1093/OED/2936944058.

Paul, D. E. (2004). "World Cities as Hegemonic Projects: The Politics of Global Imagineering in Montreal." *Political Geography* 23, 571–96.

Seldin, C. (2020). "The Voices of Berlin: Busking in a 'Creative' City." *Culture Unbound* 12(2), 233–55.

Sirois, G. (2021). "Design: An Emergent Area of Cultural Policy in Montreal." *Journal of Arts Management, Law, and Society* 51:4, 238–50. doi:10.1080/10632921.2021.1918596.

Smith, M. (1996). "Traditions, stereotypes, and tactics: A history of musical buskers in Toronto." *Canadian Journal of Traditional Music* 24, 6–22.

Ville-Marie (Montréal). (2024). *Guide des artistes de rue*. https://portail-m4s.s3.montreal.ca/pdf/vdemtl_amuseursmusiciens_de_rue_depliant_2024w_0.pdf.

Watt, P. (2018). "Street Music in London in the Nineteenth Century: 'Evidence' from Charles Dickens, Charles Babbage and Lucy Broadwood." *Nineteenth-Century Music Review* 15:1, 9–22. doi:10.1017/S1479409817000040

Watt, P. (2019). "Buskers and Busking in Australia in the Nineteenth Century." *Musicology Australia* 41:1, 22–35. doi:10.1080/08145857.2019.1621437.

Whiteoak, J. (2018). "What Were the So-Called 'German bands' of Pre-World War I Australian Street Life?" *Nineteenth-Century Music Review* 15, 51–65. doi:10.1017/S1479409817000088.

Zucchi, J. E. (1992). *The Little Slaves of the Harp: Italian Child Musicians in Nineteenth-Century Paris, London, and New York.* McGill-Queen's University Press.

SECTION

3 TRANSFORMING EXPERIENCES

14 THE ROAR OF THE CROWD

How fans create electric atmospheres

Tim Hill, Robin Canniford, Giana Eckhardt, and Stephen Murphy

AIM

To give insight into the underlying forms of social interactions that give events their unique and memorable energy and emotion.

DOI: 10.4324/9781003488729-18

LEARNING OBJECTIVES

LEARNING OBJECTIVES

1. To explain how atmosphere is co-created between organizers and fans before, during, and after an event.
2. To explain what organizers can do to improve and intensify the atmosphere.

Theoretical focus and significance

The theoretical focus of this chapter is atmosphere and how it is created in mega-events. Understanding how atmosphere is created in these events is difficult because they are complex. However, our research highlights the key ingredients that give places an electric ambiance.

Practical focus and significance

The practical focus of this chapter is on how organizers and fans co-create atmosphere, which requires both organizers and fans to play a part. The practical significance of the chapter is that, as economies recover from the COVID-19 pandemic, it is more important than ever to understand and explain what makes mega-events special and unique.

TOPIC – THE ROAR OF THE CROWD: HOW FANS CREATE ELECTRIC ATMOSPHERES

The ban on spectators at the 2020 Olympic Games in Tokyo (delayed until 2021 due to the pandemic) resulted in stadiums full of empty seats and eerie silences. Simulated crowds, ambient noise soundtracks and big screen programming, usually used to elicit crowd participation, did little for the atmosphere beyond highlighting its absence. With crowds returning for the 2024 Games in Paris, event organizers are working hard to bring the Olympic buzz back. Our ethnographic research into Anfield stadium, the home of English Premier League football club Liverpool (Hill et al. 2022), shows how powerful atmospheres are created when a crowd's behaviour and emotions align in a social gathering (Collins 2004). Crowds that share a common focus and respond to events with similar expressions of contagious excitement create economic value for the organizations staging the events, and pleasure for fans. Venues that do this well gradually become known for their unique atmosphere, which then leads people to return on a regular basis to relive those magical experiences (Borghini et al. 2021).

Yet creating the right kind of atmosphere at mega-events remains difficult for sports stadiums, festival venues, and cities in general. The challenge facing Paris was to make it possible for visiting supporters and the city's inhabitants to come together to create an electric atmosphere that people would remember. Creating an atmosphere when the eyes of world are watching is an important strategic objective for host nations looking to boost tourism, attract investment and foster civic pride.

How can organisers ensure that the right kind of atmosphere is created over the course of the Games?

Our study of Premier League football crowds suggests that atmosphere is a shared creation between firms and fans, before, during and after an event (Steadman et al. 2021). For example, fans regularly prepare the 'ingredients' of atmosphere in anticipation. By chanting, singing songs and waving flags, they create symbols of community, which are later used as shared points of focus and revelry. And, just as sports teams and musicians warm up before a match or performance, atmosphere is created by smaller groups of fans hours before an event. Bars, restaurants and public transport are brought to life by fans rehearsing songs and gestures that will later unite thousands of people. At the venue, these smaller groups then need to be unified into a crowd. This is where formal rituals that focus the crowd's attention are useful. For example, the New Zealand All Blacks' rugby team haka (Māori ceremonial war dance) and Liverpool FC's anthem 'You'll Never Walk Alone' both illustrate the power of formalized rituals to evoke shared emotion as an event begins.

Atmospheres are difficult to manage and rarely emerge spontaneously. Instead, it is through individual fans mentally preparing for and engaging with other fans that crowds become capable of responding as one – as if they are emotionally 'in sync' with one another (Goulding et al. 2009).

Not all atmospheres should be the same however. For example, galleries, museums and shopping centres tend not to involve shared emotions among large groups. Instead they rely on multi-sensory cues such as sounds (music) and smell to stimulate visitors' feelings and emotions, where the creation of spectacle is paramount.

In contrast, with music and sports, fans often want to create atmospheres themselves, and attempts to 'pump in' an atmosphere can be counterproductive. In the Premier League, for instance, bright lights, pyrotechnics and loud music are distracting, and drown out the sights and sounds of crowd revelry such as singing and chanting. Let fans create the atmosphere; do not try to force it on them.

The return of crowds for the Paris Olympics brought enormous financial potential for businesses; but, as is often the case with mega-events, the people of the host city and the legacy that they are left to deal with are often sources of conflict that can prevent the right type of atmosphere from being created.

To manage this dilemma properly, our research suggests that event organizers should acknowledge and harness the power of a host city's inhabitants as well as visiting fans to influence the success of an atmospheric event. Recognizing that atmosphere is an outcome of social interactions between a variety of stakeholders is crucial to this success. Unless diverse interests are acknowledged and catered for, the social atmospheres at events such as the Olympic Games will suffer.

Fan zones

Constructive and open dialogue between a city's inhabitants, visiting fans and event organizers is vital to encourage the social practices that contribute to atmospheres. Understanding and managing differences in what stakeholders want from an event will alleviate tensions that could otherwise get in the way of social atmospheres. For example, the introduction of safe-standing areas in some Premier League venues represents a positive instance where fans' requests to stand more closely together have been heard. Atmospheres are likely to benefit as a result.

Fans are the lifeblood of atmosphere, so organizers should find ways of encouraging these groups to return time and time again. Providing these invaluable fans with unique opportunities and privileges is one way to ensure they remain loyal. Olympic organizers should use social media platforms to communicate the Game's rich traditions, contributing to atmosphere and aiding participation by a host city's inhabitants, which could number millions.

Finally, event organizers should develop partnerships with local venues such as cafes, pubs and bars to make sure that fans have space to warm up before events, initiating the creation of atmosphere even before the doors of stadiums have opened. Of course, the need to balance environmental and safety concerns with the opportunity to create atmospheric events will remain an ongoing challenge. But the possibility of sharing emotions with others will be a powerful draw to events that provide the electric atmosphere so many of us crave.

Managerial implications

Managers need to consider whether elaborate productions involving loud music, light shows and firework displays detract from rather than enhance an event's atmosphere. They also need to consider the mood and energy fans bring to the venue or event, and how best to ensure that fans are suitably prepared and energized to help co-create atmosphere.

Policy implications

Staging mega-events requires buy-in from local citizens and residents. Understanding how fans like to socialize before an event will also require local bars, cafes and public spaces to agree to accommodate them.

Research implications

There is a need to examine how atmosphere is successfully staged and presented across broadcast media.

QUIZ QUESTIONS

1. Who is responsible for the creation of atmosphere?
2. Where does atmosphere begin?
3. How is atmosphere created?

DEBATE QUESTIONS

1. Are all atmospheres such as those created in mega-events similar?
2. How do the atmospheres in places like luxury retail stores differ from the ones created at mega-events?
3. Can atmosphere ever be under total control?

Table 14.1 Alignment to United Nations Sustainable Development Goals

Goal	How
Good Health and Well-Being	Shared emotional experiences with strangers are vital for civic life. This chapter explains how these emotions are created.

REFERENCES

Borghini, Stefania, John F. Sherry, and Annamma Joy. 2021. "Attachment to and Detachment from Favorite Stores: An Affordance Theory Perspective." *Journal of Consumer Research* 47(6):890–913.

Collins, Randall. 2004. *Interaction Ritual Chains*. Princeton, NJ: Princeton University Press.

Goulding, Christina, Avi Shankar, Richard Elliott, and Robin Canniford. 2009. "The Marketplace Management of Illicit Pleasure." *Journal of Consumer Research* 35(5):759–71. doi:10.1086/592946.

Hill, Tim, Robin Canniford, and Giana M. Eckhardt. 2022. "The Roar of the Crowd: How Interaction Ritual Chains Create Social Atmospheres." *Journal of Marketing* 86(3):121–39.

Steadman, Chloe, Gareth Roberts, Dominic Medway, Steve Millington, and Louise Platt. 2021. "(Re)Thinking Place Atmospheres in Marketing Theory." *Marketing Theory* 21(1):135–54.

15 COULD VIRTUAL REALITY CHANGE GIGS FOREVER?

Trudy Barber

AIM

To examine the potential impact of emerging technologies on live music entertainment events.

DOI: 10.4324/9781003488729-19

LEARNING OBJECTIVES

LEARNING OBJECTIVES

1. To contest the impact of emerging technologies on live music events.
2. To explore the future of audience engagement and experience with music events.
3. To develop an understanding of avatar performance.

Theoretical focus and significance

The theoretical focus of this chapter is to consider audience experience through the use of technologies such as virtual reality (VR) and artificial intelligence (AI) by exploring theoretical approaches to notions of 'the uncanny valley' and digital culture. The theoretical significance of this chapter is to introduce the impact of emerging technologies such as AI on live entertainment.

Practical focus and significance

The practical focus of this chapter is to instigate debate surrounding immersion, audience experience, and artificial intelligence. It practical significance is to develop awareness of the contemporary nature of AI and the development of avatars.

TOPIC – COULD VIRTUAL REALITY CHANGE GIGS FOREVER?

ABBA, the pop sensation well known for their Eurovision win in 1974, are back. In 2018 the Swedish superstars toured with a curious performance they called a new 'virtual and live experience' in partnership with Spice Girls' manager, Simon Fuller. What this extravaganza entailed promised to capitalise on our 'new technological world', making use of artificial intelligence combined with virtual reality. So, does this herald a new era for experiencing live music, and does it mean that the classic gig is a thing of the past?

Of course, the use of emerging technologies for entertainment is nothing new. Musicians, movie technicians and performance designers have all attempted to harness the technology of the day in order to create something new with their music and performances. Accomplished cinematographer Morton Heilig (1926–1997) is often called the father of virtual reality due to his fabulous 'Sensorama' machine of the late 1950s to the early 1970s. Heilig created an immersive entertainment device through which viewers could experience a specially made 3D movie – complete with sounds and smells. He also invented something he called the 'Thrillerama Theatre Experience', which mixed 3D images, projections and live stage action.

However, although Heilig's place in the development of VR has been somewhat contested, he is renowned for his inventiveness and passion in mid twentieth-century media and popular culture. This is well recognised, as Gutierrez (2023, p. 89) who argued that 'Heilig's interest in simulator technologies aligned with a mid-twentieth-century culture of mass media sensory experimentation that saw the advent of large-scale, widescreen projection systems, commercially viable 3D film, multichannel sound, and the simulated scents of "AromaRama"'.

Billy Idol, rockabilly punk of the late 1980s and early 1990s, brought together early concepts of VR, cyberspace and digital culture with his music and performances on MTV. Idol used computer animation and stop-frame animation inspired by the cult Japanese cyberpunk film *Tetsuo* (Tsukamoto, 1989) to supplement his music and create a new cross-genre experience – as seen in his classic music video *Shock to the System* (Leonard, 1993).

VR today

Of course, virtual reality technologies have advanced quite a bit since these early experiments. Back in the early 1990s, VR was awkward and prohibitively expensive. Headsets were very large and heavy, and showed very basic computer graphic imagery that had picture lag – when you moved your head, the image in the headset would struggle to keep up. This unfortunately contributed to the sensation of 'cybersickness', one of the physical responses to being in virtual reality due to what has been described as circular and linear vection – that is, accompanied by image speed (Chardonnet et al., 2021).

The latest digital holographic and augmented reality (AR) technologies could prevent such individual responses and be used as a way of engaging the immersive social aspect of attending live music events. This has already been attempted with Michael Jackson, who appeared to perform on stage at the 2014 Billboard Music Awards as a hologram after his death – although some audience members found this a little creepy and disturbing. This is due to what has been described as the 'uncanny valley', effect where the photorealism of computer graphics or human interaction and presentation of a robot, for example, causes a sense of unease (Mori, 1970).

The Icelandic pop icon Björk has produced her own digital works using immersive VR. Her private theatrical experience at London's Somerset House provided a more intimate approach for her audience. Accordingly, 'Björk believes that by offering a private theatrical experience, VR provides a unique way to connect with her audiences' (Somerset House, 2016).

So what did we see from ABBA?

The group certainly attempted something similar to the time-bending properties of the Jackson hologram experience. For example, they could be seen to be playing alongside younger versions of themselves in holographic form (known as 'ABBAtars'), thus forming an eight-piece band. The context of this event has been discussed at length by Matthews and Nairn (2023, pp. 288–289), who state:

> It is because what ABBA has created is both standardized and unique that we are particularly interested in how audiences responded to the announcement of the concert and the meanings that were made for this experiential and subjective creative product before people had had the chance to consume it. In essence, we were interested in their reactions, given that the ABBAtar approach is novel and had not been previously tried.

Alternatively, in the future, one could possibly foresee an overlay of augmented reality through a phone app that transforms performers on stage into earlier playback versions of themselves. And, even if all members of a band could not perform together in physical reality, holographic projections of their networked selves as VR meta-human avatars could provide a telepresent simulation of them actually being together on stage. The 'experience' will also involve the use of artificial intelligence, which could mean that the various technologies will be able to react quickly to feedback from the audience and between band members (both real and virtual) on stage.

Social experience

However the success of this new generation of gigs will largely come down to whether they make full use of social media and artificial intelligence, the rise of which means that audiences expect to be able to engage with and share their experiences immediately. The more this is enabled, the better for the performer. Networked VR experiences would allow fans to engage with and be immersed in global social media entertainment extravaganzas while not necessarily leaving their homes. Performances could be streamed live online through VR or mobile phone technology (such as Samsung Gear) using 3D photography, immersive quadraphonic sound and other novel sonic architecture.

Of course, the enabling of a networked and wired audience that could have access to augmented reality and VR, and have an appreciation of 3D holography, would be a massive technological, financial, sociological and logistical challenge. And then there is the actual sound of the band. The digital subtleties of multiple projections of sound and live music together would need to be assimilated. And noisy, enthusiastic fans, who may well want to sing along, would complicate this further. But, in time, it is hoped that such issues will be mastered.

So will future gigs still take place in bars and arenas, but be accompanied by holograms on stage and crowds in VR headsets? Or will the audience wave their smart phones as they do today – but this time gazing, *Pokémon Go* style, at a supernatural incarnation of their idol on stage along with the real one? Or will all gigs be truly virtual, allowing viewers in headsets at home to match up their favourite bandmembers on a virtual stage and feel part of a social experience, either real or technologically manufactured? Having personally experienced an immersive 3D gig in VR at home using Oculus Quest, the Foo Fighters – along with their sadly deceased drummer – played a fabulous set (Meta Quest, 2022). The experience gave the appearance of the viewer being in a TV studio, and part of the band's recording and filming session. The experience was mesmerising and extraordinarily very intimate.

The reality will likely be some formulation of all of these speculative futures. But, whatever form they take, live technological music experiences are certain to be just as exciting as they have always been; but in turn they will also give an historical aura to 'analogue' gigs such as the complex and theatrical Prog Rock extravaganzas of the past. In this light, it was announced at the time of writing that the outrageous Glam Rock band Kiss (who also started in the 1970s) is going entirely digital with avatars of themselves along with developing VR immersive performances (WGN, 2023). It would appear that the social experience using these immersive technological methods and artificial intelligence will certainly allow for the audience, as Kiss has always stated, 'to rock and roll all night, and party every day'.

QUIZ QUESTIONS

1. What is the 'uncanny valley'?
2. How does virtual reality impact live music experience?
3. What is a networked audience?

DEBATE QUESTIONS

1. Are artificial intelligent avatars of a band as good as the live musicians?
2. Would you pay more to see a live band or a virtual one?
3. Are virtual music experiences better for the planet?
4. Should a dead musician (for example, Michael Jackson) be revived as an avatar for entertainment?

REFERENCES

Chardonnet, J.R., Mirzaei, M.A., & Merienne, F. (2021). Influence of navigation parameters on cybersickness in virtual reality. *Virtual Reality*, *25*, 565–574. https://doi.org/10.1007/s10055-020-00474-2.

Gutierrez, N. (2023). The ballad of Morton Heilig: On VR's mythic past. *JCMS: Journal of Cinema and Media Studies*, *62*(3), 86–106.

Leonard, Brett, Dir. (1993). Billy Idol 'Shock to the System'. YouTube https://www.youtube.com/watch?v=lx2fZU5USus.

Matthews, J., & Nairn, A. (2023). Holographic ABBA: Examining fan responses to ABBA's virtual 'live' concert. *Popular Music and Society*, *46*(3), 282–303. https://doi.org/10.1080/03007766.2023.2208048.

Meta Quest. (2022, February 7). Catch Foo Fighters in VR: Horizon venues concert to air February 13 after the big game. https://www.meta.com/en-gb/blog/quest/catch-foo-fighters-in-vr-horizon-venues-concert-to-air-february-13-after-the-big-game/.

Mori, M. (1970). The uncanny valley. *Energy*, *7*, 33–35.

Somerset House (2016). Bjork digital. https://www.somersethouse.org.uk/whats-on/bjork-digital.

Tsukamoto, Shinya, Dir. (1989). *Tetsuo: The Iron Man*. Kaijyu Theatre, Japan.

WGN News: (2023, December). KISS says farewell to live touring, set to be first US band to go virtual with digital avatars. https://www.youtube.com/watch?v=ci7q9FbXDQM.

16 LOOKING BEYOND THE SCREEN
Smartphone effects on festival engagement

Christine Van Winkle

AIM

The aim of the chapter is to explore how mobile devices (phones, tablets) impact festival experiences, and to provide practical strategies for managing phone usage to enhance communal engagement. This chapter will prompt readers to reflect on their own digital habits in social settings.

DOI: 10.4324/9781003488729-20

LEARNING OBJECTIVES

LEARNING OBJECTIVES

1. Analysing the impact of technology on social interaction.
2. Developing strategies for mindful technology use.
3. Making informed decisions about technology use.

Theoretical focus and significance

This chapter aims to enhance understanding of how and why people use mobile devices when participating in festivals. The chapter will apply a well-established framework known as the Unified Theory of the Acceptance and Use of Technology 2 (UTAUT2), and will tailor the theory to better reflect the festival environment. Finally, the effect of device use on attendee satisfaction will be explored. The adoption of mobile technology occurred at an unprecedented rate, and rapidly transformed global communication, culture, and commerce within a few decades. Understanding how this mass mobile adoption and use affects all aspects of our lives, including leisure, will allow us to make informed choices about the role we want these devices to play in our lives.

Practical focus and significance

This chapter explores factors influencing mobile technology use at festivals and the effects of using different types of mobile technology on satisfaction with festivals. By knowing which factors affect use, practitioners can design experiences where technology enhances the festival experience and does not interfere with attendees' experiences.

TOPIC – LOOKING BEYOND THE SCREEN: SMARTPHONE EFFECTS ON FESTIVAL ENGAGEMENT

Festivals are lively celebrations that break the monotony of everyday life. They bring people together, offering opportunities for fun and connection with others from different backgrounds. Whether dancing to live music, trying new food from vendors, or simply enjoying shared moments with friends and family, these gatherings are an important part of our social lives.

Figure 16.1 Family photo. Author own image.

In today's digital world, wherever we go we tend to bring along our mobile devices. It is common to see people clutching their smartphones, whether at home, work or leisure. As phones facilitate communication and entertainment, it is no surprise they are a part of our festival experience. However, we often overlook how they affect our interactions and enjoyment of these events. The findings of researchers who have been studying our experiences with mobile devices while attending festivals (e.g. Van Winkle, 2019) should give us pause to think about how we use technology in these settings.

To inform our understanding, Van Winkle et al. (2019) explored factors that affect mobile device use at festivals. This research was informed by the UTAUT2, which suggests that various factors affect our intention to adopt and use technology. The authors found that the use of mobile devices at festivals was influenced by performance expectancy, hedonic motivation, habit and age. Since Van Winkle et al.'s 2019 study, Khan et al. (2022) have proposed UTAUT3, taking into account personal innovativeness as a factor influencing technology adoption and use. This concept adds an important factor that may influence mobile use and how this use affects our experiences.

One important finding from past research is how our daily phone habits spill over into festival time (Geissinger & Laurell, 2020; Van Winkle et al., 2019). Whether checking work emails, scrolling through social media or answering texts, our digital routines can prevent us from fully immersing ourselves in the festival atmosphere.

Figure 16.2 Person on mobile device. Author own image.

Interestingly, people react differently to having their phones at festivals. Some disconnect, leaving their phones behind to fully engage in the moment. For them, being free from digital distractions enhances their festival experience and helps them connect better with others. On the other hand, some people feel anxious about being without their phones. So, even as they are enjoying a festival, they are constantly torn between the real world around them and the digital world on their screens. They worry about missing out on capturing memories or staying in touch with friends (Price, 2018). For some people, having their smartphone facilitates their participation and enhances inclusion. Notably, women reported feeling safer in public spaces when they had their phones with them (Lenhart, 2010).

Interviews with festival-goers reveal how social influences affect phone usage. When everyone around them is glued to their phone, individuals often feel pressured to do the same, even if they would rather be fully present. This mirror effect is powerful; but not all phone use at festivals is bad. Using your phone to check schedules, find your way around, or coordinate with friends can enhance your experience (Wilmer et al., 2017). It's when we mindlessly scroll through apps that we lose out on the true connection events offer.

In another study, Van Winkle et al. (2018) found that using a mobile device for aspects related to the festival (capturing memories with photos or videos, checking the festival programme or site map and related activities) positively affected satisfaction, whereas using the device for other tasks (checking emails, viewing texts or websites unrelated to the event) negatively influenced their satisfaction. Dodds et al. (2020) observed that event attendees are becoming more distracted by technology, which detracts from the experience.

Exploring the connection between mobile device use and event satisfaction further, Van Winkle et al. (2018) found that memorable experiences completely mediated the effect of festival-related mobile device use on satisfaction. When people use their mobile to engage with the festival, they create memorable experiences related to the festival, which, in turn, affects their satisfaction.

Given the research findings, should we rethink our relationship with our phones? While they have benefits, we must be aware of the downsides of relying too much on them. It's about finding a balance between staying connected digitally and being present in the moment.

From a festival organizer's perspective, it is essential to weigh the cost and benefits of encouraging or discouraging mobile device use. Mobile phones enable attendees to share their experiences with others and facilitate inclusion (Hudson et al., 2013). Social media, often accessed through mobile devices, has become a key platform for promoting and communicating with audiences. While Park et al. (2021) noted the benefits of promoting events through Facebook, they also recognized the distraction it could cause for attendees during their event experience.

For attendees gearing up for festivals, there are practical steps to manage phone use. From turning off notifications to setting aside phone-free times, there are ways to minimize distractions and fully enjoy the experience. However, using your phone to check the festival programme and meet up with friends makes for a smoother experience.

Ultimately, we must decide how to engage with technology at festivals. Rather than mindlessly allowing our daily habits to spill over into our leisure time, we should be mindful of our habits and prioritize meaningful interactions and having memorable experiences. This approach would allow us to make the most of these communal celebrations without being tethered to our screens. Festival organizers can also consider how to encourage use to enhance the attendee experience and discourage use that detracts from the experience.

Managerial implications

Managers should recognize that mobile device use during leisure experiences is not benign. Depending on the technology used during leisure, satisfaction can be enhanced or harmed by using mobile phones during the experience.

Policy implications

Festivals may want to adopt policies about engaging audiences using mobile technology. These policies should focus on use that engages audience members in the festival experience, rather than use that takes people out of the experience.

Research implications

The Unified Theory of Acceptance and Use of Technology 2 (UTAUT2) should be explored in diverse leisure and tourism contexts to better explain the unique factors in these settings that influence mobile technology use. Exploration of device use in creating memorable experiences that contribute to a satisfying experience should be undertaken in a range of event, leisure and tourism settings to better understand the universality of this phenomenon.

QUIZ QUESTIONS

1. How does 'memorable experience' affect the relationship between mobile device use and satisfaction?
2. What aspects of the UTAUT2 model affect mobile use in the festival context?
3. What strategies could event organizers use to encourage mobile use related to the event and discourage use unrelated to the event?

DEBATE QUESTIONS

1. To what extent should event organizers try to discourage mobile device use at their events?
2. Given how common mobile devices are, is it still useful to explore their adoption and use in specific contexts?
3. Should festival and event organizers continue to invest limited human and financial resources in developing online content for use during events given how using mobile devices can affect our experiences?

Table 16.1 Alignment to United Nations Sustainable Development Goals

Goal	How
Industry, Innovation and Infrastructure	As the event and entertainment arm of the tourism industry adopts technology, it is essential to explore how this impacts the experiences of event and entertainment attendees.

REFERENCES

Dodds, R., Novotny, M., & Harper, S. (2020). Shaping our perception of reality: Sustainability communication by Canadian festivals. *International Journal of Event and Festival Management*, *11*(4), 473–492.

Geissinger, A., & Laurell, C. (2020). Multibrand events and social media engagement: Concentration or spillover? *Event Management*, *24*(2–3), 253–262.

Hudson, H. E. (2013). *From rural village to global village: Telecommunications for development in the information age*. Routledge.

Khan, F. M., Singh, N., Gupta, Y., Kaur, J., Banik, S., & Gupta, S. (2022). A meta-analysis of mobile learning adoption in higher education based on unified theory of acceptance and use of technology 3 (UTAUT3). *Vision*, 09722629221101159.

Lenhart, A. (2010, September 2). *Cell phones and American adults. Part three: Adult attitudes towards the cell phone*. Pew Research Center. https://www.pewresearch.org/internet/2010/09/02/part-three-adult-attitudes-towards-the-cell-phone/.

Park, S., Park, K., Park, J. Y., & Back, R. M. (2021). Social media analytics in event marketing: Engaging marathon fans in Facebook communities. *Event Management*, *25*(4), 329–345.

Price, C. (2018). *How to break up with your phone: The 30-day plan to take back your life*. Ten Speed Press.

Van Winkle, C. (2019, June 6). Don't let your phone interrupt the good vibe of a summer music festival. The Conversation. https://theconversation.com/dont-let-your-phone-interrupt-the-good-vibe-of-a-summer-music-festival-116946.

Van Winkle, C. M., Bueddefeld, J. N., Halpenny, E. A., & MacKay, K. J. (2019). The unified theory of acceptance and use of technology 2: Understanding mobile device use at festivals. *Leisure Studies*, *38*(5), 634–650.

Van Winkle, C., Bueddefeld, J., Halpenny, E., & MacKay, K. (2018). Going mobile: Outcomes of device use during a festival experience. *Travel and Tourism Research Association Conference Proceedings*.

Wilmer, H. H., Sherman, L. E., & Chein, J. M. (2017). Smartphones and cognition: A review of research exploring the links between mobile technology habits and cognitive functioning. *Frontiers in Psychology*, *8*, 605.

17 THE NEED FOR LIVE EVENT SECURITY RISK MANAGEMENT PRACTICES IN A POST-COVID-19 WORLD

Sean Spence

AIM

This chapter aims to inform the reader as to why policy changes are needed within the live events industry in order to make them safer from a security risk management perspective.

DOI: 10.4324/9781003488729-21

LEARNING OBJECTIVES

1. Inform the reader that the lack of professionalism within the live events industry is a security risk for event operations.
2. Inform the reader that the lack of government regulation over the live events industry is a security risk for events operations.
3. Inform the reader that the lack of adequate public–private intelligence partnerships severely limits industry practitioners' ability to effectively protect their events from security risks and leaves employees and attendees extremely vulnerable.

Theoretical focus and significance

The theoretical focus of this chapter involves examining the importance of having sound security risk management processes in place across the live events industry. The theoretical significance of this chapter is highlighting how important it is in a post-pandemic world for industry stakeholders to put risk management policies in place to better protect the events sector from a wide range of security risks given evolving global threats and increased uncertainties.

Practical focus and significance

The practical focus of this chapter is to convey that the theoretical challenges are multi-faceted and that solutions will involve the input of many different stakeholders. The practical significance of this chapter is demonstrated by the negative impacts of recent global incidents at various live events where security risks not mitigated have resulted in mass causalities and members of the general public being victimized.

LEARNING OBJECTIVES

TOPIC – THE NEED FOR LIVE EVENT SECURITY RISK MANAGEMENT PRACTICES IN A POST-COVID-19 WORLD

In the spring of 2017, the international media and the entire social media ecosystem were captivated by the fiasco surrounding the Fyre Festival, eloquently dubbed "the greatest party that never happened" (Smith, 2019). Since then, several movies and dozens of articles have recounted the story of the most hyped festival in history that never happened. The main event promoter, fraudster and con artist Billy McFarland, sold thousands of young people around the world on the dream of a luxurious, VIP festival on an exclusive Caribbean island that never existed. The fact that these stranded, frustrated and defrauded festival attendees did not resort to widespread rioting and violence is yet another miracle and another near miss within the event world. The Fyre Festival is a cautionary tale of the exposure to criminal and security issues that attendees of live events can face in what is largely an unregulated sector globally.

Live events can be described as social constructs where attendees attach meaning to their experiences (Getz & Page, 2016). The entertainment, excitement and positive emotions that participants experience by actively engaging in the events sector are usually greatly overshadowed and far removed from the inherent safety and security risks often deeply embedded within these same events. While live events are inherently full of physical security risks, it is not the job of the general public to conduct a risk analysis of every event they choose to attend. Threats such as active shooters, acts of terrorism, crowd surging, theft of property, sexual harassment and physical assaults are all examples of intentional social dangers to which event-goers are exposed. High-density crowded spaces such as live sporting events, outdoor music festivals and large-scale concerts are attractive targets for threat actors, and as such leave individuals highly vulnerable to injury or even death (Homeland Security, 2018).

Figure 17.1 Example of a high-density music concert (Pixabay)

It is natural for people to assume that businesses and service providers have their best interests at heart as consumers. Within a capitalist economy, the prevailing assumption is that businesses operate as ongoing financial concerns with long-term time horizons where repeat customers and reputation are essential ingredients for success. However, within the live events industry, many organizers often operate on a tight budget or under a not-for-profit model, and even as a one-off event never to be repeated. These dynamics sometimes lead decision-makers to cut financial corners and not invest as much, if at all, in security risk management practices, which can often lead to disastrous results.

The last few decades have reminded us just how deadly events can be when proper risk management measures are not in place. In 2010, the Love Parade music festival in Germany saw 21 people die after being crushed in the crowd, and over 500 people sustaining injuries. Organizers were blamed for being negligent in failing to understand the need to anticipate and control for factors related to crowd dynamics (Pretorius et al., 2013). In 2017, an Islamic extremist suicide bomber killed 23 people and wounded 1,017 others at an Ariana Grande concert at the Manchester Arena in the UK. The subsequent public inquiry revealed that the arena management had an inadequate security risk assessment related to terrorism and took a complacent approach to implementing security countermeasures that were recommended (House of Commons, 2021). Lastly, in November 2021, ten people died from crowd-crushing injuries and dozens more were injured at the Astroworld music festival in Houston, USA. Similar to the Love Parade, the organizers' event security risk assessment failed to account for the dangers of crowd dynamics and created a concert space that made attendees physically vulnerable to being crushed (Flores & Rappard, 2021).

There are three main problems plaguing the events management field that are contributing to the continued emergence of security risks within the events

Figure 17.2 Manchester Arena, site of the 2017 bombing (Wikipedia Commons)

sector. Firstly, there is a lack of professionalism among the event practitioner community (Silvers et al., 2005). Unlike doctors, lawyers and engineers who have regulatory bodies that grant certification and can discipline their members for wrongdoings, there is no such equivalent organization for event organizers. While some organizations exist to serve various categories of event (e.g. the International Live Events Association or Meeting Professionals International), they are all voluntary – meaning that aspiring practitioners are not required to be members of such groups in order to organize any private or public event. Sadly, convicted criminals like Billy McFarland looking to scam attendees and potential sponsors could easily organize an event in most countries tomorrow with few to no restrictions. In fact, McFarland was reported to be looking to organize another remote island party event fresh from his release from prison (Traylor, 2023). Neither public officials nor members of the general public are conducting background checks on organizers as a condition of event approval or consideration of participation in such events.

The second issue within the live events sector relates to a lack of industry or government regulation over the community and its practitioners. This has a significant impact on whether or not security risk management principles are incorporated in the creation of public events. Various countries have different degrees of regulation and interest in this area. The COVID-19 pandemic exposed how little public officials were prepared to regulate an entire sector with no prior considerations or consultation in place (Harris et al., 2021).

One study sought to compare the regulatory regimes of public events in Canadian and Australian jurisdictions. Surprisingly, even though Canada had more gun violence, fewer counter-terrorism capabilities and weaker national security laws than Australia, Australian jurisdictions had stronger regulations for its live event sector than Canada (Spence, 2024). For example, large Australian cities require organizers to submit applications on average six months before the scheduled date of the event. In Canada, the average was less than four months, suggesting less due diligence in examining risks within live events. Australian authorities also tend to stress risk management features in their event application forms (e.g. proactive measures), while the Canadian application process stresses emergency response.

In the UK, lessons learned from the 2017 Manchester Arena bombing provided the impetus for victims and survivors of the attack to advocate for increased protection of public spaces from terrorism via proposed legislation known as Martyn's Law (Home Office, 2024). This legislation would require all public spaces and venues with capacities of over 100 persons to have a "standard tier" protection concept; and those with capacities of over 800 would be required to implement an "enhanced tier" of counter-terrorism measures. Many stakeholders and industry practitioners have praised these new regulations as long overdue. However, some UK Members of Parliament were holding up passage of the legislation as they felt the current regulations disproportionately place undue hardship on small businesses and non-profit organizations hosting events (BBC, 2024).

The third obstacle hindering proper security risk management at live events is the lack of public–private partnerships and critical intelligence sharing between government security agencies and event organizers. After the terrorist attacks of September 11, 2001, many Western governments realized the importance of open transparency and the sharing of intelligence with private sector partners, who often own and operate most of society's critical industries, such as banking, energy and transportation (Alcaraz & Zeadally, 2015). However, in some countries, many of those formal relationships and protocols have not been properly distributed across the wider business economy, particularly within the live events industry (Bronskill, 2024). This problem is further exacerbated when government intelligence agencies fail altogether to detect terrorists' intentions to attack soft targets at live events. Most recently, these glaring failures were highlighted by the Hamas attacks on October 7, 2023, at the Supernova music festival in Israel, where over 300 people were murdered (Dover, 2023); and on March 22, 2024, ISIS-K terrorists attacked a Moscow concert venue, killing over 130 people despite alleged warnings from US intelligence officials on the likelihood of a possible attack (Sonne, 2024). In both instances, event organizers were at the mercy of failed government anti-terrorism countermeasures and, as a result, attendees were left extremely vulnerable and on their own to defend themselves.

Ultimately, if we expect live event spaces to be efficient and effective at protecting employees and attendees from security risks in the future, these three key policy deficiencies will need to be addressed by government, academia, and industry practitioners in a significant manner to close existing gaps.

Figure 17.3 A memorial to victims of violence (Pixabay)

Managerial implications

The managerial implications of this chapter are that practitioners within the field of event management should be knowledgeable about their operating environment and understand the needs of various stakeholders to mitigate security risks as a fundamental requirement for operational success. A key to this success is for event practitioners as well as security providers to be proficient at conducting security risk analysis that encompasses both the assessment of security risks for each live event and selecting appropriate treatment strategies. Understanding the myriad of security risks that can negatively impact event objectives comes from gaining practical operational experience as well as receiving valuable intelligence from public officials. In this capacity, managers within the public safety domain also have an important role to play in the security of the live events sector.

Firstly, public licensing officials who review and ultimately approve public events occurring in their jurisdiction must develop the competencies needed to properly review event security risk management plans to evaluate their rigour in order to safeguard the general public's security interests. Secondly, intelligence officials must strive to develop better relationships with event organizers of all sizes so that there is equity in the distribution of intelligence and widespread coverage of overall community security. Thirdly, public sector security managers need to devise a model that enables actionable intelligence to be shared directly with key designated private sector stakeholders, but at the same time does not compromise integrity or cause the unnecessary leak of such intelligence to authorized users.

Policy implications

The policy implications of this chapter are:

- For event practitioners to learn, develop and implement security risk management principles as part of their professional duties and place them within their wider risk assessment responsibilities.
- For public officials to create new policies on how they vet, review and approve public events in order to better protect members of the public and maintain the trust that society has in the operators of live events.

- For government officials to better detect threats to live events and come up with tangible ways to develop meaningful relationships with the organizers and better communicate security risks to stakeholders.

Research implications

The research implications of this chapter involve studying how best to implement baseline industry standards in terms of security risk management, and what roles the different stakeholders can play in further advancing the effective treatment of security risks.

QUIZ QUESTIONS

1. What role do public officials play in reviewing and approving public events with regard to public safety?
2. What key lessons have been learned from recent terrorist attacks at live events around the world?
3. Name three challenges facing the live events industry that have a direct impact on the safety and security of public events.

DEBATE QUESTIONS

1. How much intelligence (classified or unclassified) should government officials share with event practitioners who do not hold security clearances? What would be some risks in sharing such intelligence?
2. How can security risk management principles be adequately applied uniformly across an event sector that has many different operators with varying degrees of available resources (e.g. money, time, education, professional experience, etc.)?
3. One of the obstacles to implementing Martyn's Law in the United Kingdom is the fear that it will create undue hardship for small businesses operating small-scale events (e.g. non-profit events, religious events, etc.). What solutions or exceptions might government officials propose to reduce such a risk?

Table 17.1 Alignment to United Nations Sustainable Development Goals

Goal	How
Sustainable Cities and Communities	This chapter promotes safer communities by advocating for strong private–public partnerships in securing community events and making them more resilient. It also advocates for increased inclusivity, recognizing that the protection of community events requires many voices and viewpoints from a variety of stakeholders.
Peace, Justice and Strong Institutions	This chapter promotes stronger relationships with private event operators and public officials to effectively increase the general public's confidence in community security and safety for the enjoyment of leisure activities.

REFERENCES

Alcaraz, C., Zeadally, S. (2015). Critical infrastructure protection: Requirements and challenges for the 21st century. *International Journal of Critical Infrastructure Protection*, *8*, 53–66,

BBC. (2024, February 5). Martyn's Law: Consultation into anti-terror legislation launched. https://www.bbc.com/news/uk-england-manchester-68208227.

Bronskill, J. (2024, January 19). Companies want Canada's spy agency to share threat intelligence with them. *The Canadian Press*. https://globalnews.ca/news/10237208/csis-threat-intelligence-sharing/.

Dover, R.M. (2023, December 7). Why Israel's intelligence chiefs failed to listen to October 7 warnings – and the lessons to be learned. *The Conversation*. https://theconversation.com/why-israels-intelligence-chiefs-failed-to-listen-to-october-7-warnings-and-the-lessons-to-be-learned-219346.

Flores, R., & Rappard, A.-M. (2021, November 8). *Here's what the operations plan for the Astroworld Festival included and didn't include.* CNN. https://www.cnn.com/2021/11/08/us/astroworld-festival-operations-plan/index.html.

Getz, D., & Page, S.J. (2016). Progress and prospects for event tourism. *Tourism Management*, *52*, 593–631, https://doi.org/10.1016/j.tourman.2015.03.007.

Harris, M., Kreindler, J., El-Osta, A., Esko, T., & Majeed, A. (2021). Safe management of full capacity events in COVID-19 will require mathematical, epidemiological and economic modelling. *Journal of the Royal Society of Medicine*, *114*(6), 283–330. https://journals.sagepub.com/doi/epub/10.1177/01410768211007759.

Home Office. (2024, February 5). *Terrorism (Protection of Premises) Bill – Standard Tier: Government consultation.* UK Government. https://assets.publishing.service.gov.uk/media/65c0dcd3c43191001 41a456e/05.02.24_Martyn_s_Law_Standard_Tier_Consultation_.pdf.

Homeland Security. (2018). U.S. Department of Homeland Security Soft Targets and Crowded Spaces Security Plan Overview.

House of Commons. (2021). *Report of the Public Inquiry into the attack on Manchester Arena on 22nd May 2017: Manchester Arena Inquiry Volume 1: Security for the Arena.* https://assets.publishing.service.gov.uk/media/60cc659fe90e07438f7af765/CCS0321126370-002_MAI_Report_Volume_ONE_WebAccessible.pdf.

Pretorius, M., Gwynne, S., & Galea, E.R. (2013). Large crowd modelling: An analysis of the Duisburg Love Parade disaster. *Fire and Materials*, *39*, 301–322. doi:10.1002/fam.2214.

Silvers, J.R., Bowdin, G.A.J., O'Toole, W.J., & Nelson, K.B. (2005). Towards an International Event Management Body of Knowledge (EMBOK). *Event Management*, *9*(4), 185–198. https://doi.org/10.3727/152599506776771571.

Smith, C. (Dir.). (2019). *FYRE: The Greatest Party that Never Happened.* [Film]. Netflix.

Sonne, P., Schmitt, E., & Schwirtz, M. (2024, March 28). Why Russia's vast security services fell short on deadly attack. *New York Times*. https://www.nytimes.com/2024/03/28/world/europe/russia-concert-attack-security-failures.html.

Spence. S. (2024). *Stakeholders' perceptions of security risks and emergency preparedness in the live events industry.* [Doctoral thesis, University of Portsmouth].

Traylor, J. (2023, January 20). The Fyre Festival fraudster is launching his latest thing, and it looks like a party on an island. *NBC News*. https://www.nbcnews.com/tech/internet/fyre-festival-fraudster-launching-latest-thing-looks-party-island-rcna62564.

18 STRATEGIES FOR EVENT MANAGERS TO SAFEGUARD AGAINST DEADLY CROWDS

Alison Hutton

AIM

The chapter aims to show how event managers can foster cooperative crowding, and how event managers, security personnel, and other key stakeholders can collaborate to promote positive crowd behaviour.

DOI: 10.4324/9781003488729-22

LEARNING OBJECTIVES

1. To understand the tenets of cooperative crowding.
2. To develop ways of creating a shared understanding across professions at events.

Theoretical focus and significance

The theoretical focus is to develop trust and cooperation of key stakeholders across events to improve crowd safety. A mass gathering event is a concentration of people at a specific location, for a specific purpose, over a defined period of time, and in sufficient numbers to potentially strain the planning and response resources of a host community, state and/or nation (Hutton & Brown, 2015). Despite this potential for straining the host community resources, mass gathering events are sought-after and dynamic elements of social existence. Mass gatherings have multiple positive social impacts and health benefits for attendees; the sharing of time, the sense of goodwill, and the *communitas* that organised events engender has been identified as socially vital (Brown et al., 2020; Laing & Mair, 2015). Further, outdoor music festivals and other mass events are impactful on the capacity of social settings (places and people) to be resilient to change (Gibson & Connell, 2015; Gibson et al., 2010).

Practical focus and significance

The aim of this chapter is to explore how specific protocols and principles can be put in place by key stakeholders to support the effective ongoing crowd management of safety at a mass gathering event. Building shared knowledge in regard to crowd safety requires a sense of commitment from all key stakeholders. Building trust in the context of mass gatherings brings forward an opportunity for new crowd management strategies.

TOPIC – STRATEGIES FOR EVENT MANAGERS TO SAFEGUARD AGAINST DEADLY CROWDS

The legacy of Travis Scott

The tragic crowd surge during a performance by US rapper Travis Scott at his Astroworld music festival in Houston on the night of Friday, 5 November 2021 has emerged as one of the most deadly incidents at a music event in recent memory, with fatalities and numerous injuries.

If we reflect on the proceedings that night, trouble was inevitable. The first clue came with thousands of people lining up early and being disruptive. Even before the event started there was a report of 54 people being treated by the medical team, and the police had already noted that the crowd was 'dangerous'. Any event personnel who had shown due diligence would already have known and understood the inherent risks that came with this performer as it was not the first time that controversy had followed him. However it appears that this history had not been taken into consideration and, surprisingly, the legacy surrounding Scott appeared to have been disregarded.

Why is it important to understand your audience?

Understanding your audience and the atmosphere they are likely to foster is crucial as the music genre dictates the demographic and sets expectations for crowd behaviour. If a show is expected to attract a high-energy audience, preparations should be made accordingly. Effective crowd management is proactive, not reactive. Table 18.1 outlines some points to for the host organisation to consider when planning an event, with relevant data obtained through questionnaires.

Table 18.1 Pre-event considerations for host organisations

Core Values What is the key rationale for the event? Who are the event's target audience? What is the basic concept behind the event? (e.g. the programme, what happens) What measurable outcomes are set for the event?
Situational/SWOT (strengths, weaknesses, opportunities, threats) analysis
Event Type
Programme Content (e.g. music, dance) Style (hip hop, death metal) Scale (international act, local act, known/unknown) Active vs passive elements
Duration Day(s)/week(s) Day/night Seasonal Overall event (hours) Each programme element (hours or minutes)
Site Design Indoor/outdoor Shade/shelter Natural structures Existing/built/temporary structures

(Continued)

Table 18.1 (Continued)

Staffing Ratios
Front of house
Catering
Management
Security/police
Police
First aid/medical
Location
Permanent/temporary site
Central Business District (CBD)
Metropolitan/regional/remote

Source: Based on Hutton and Brown (2015, p. 156).

Overall, event managers prioritise crowd safety and comfort, investing in amenities such as 'chill-out spaces', shaded areas and free water. In the case of Astroworld, if key stakeholders such as police, security and event managers had been in agreement as to how to manage the crowd, perhaps this tragedy could have been avoided. In a well-managed event, organisers can cultivate an atmosphere where attendees feel relaxed and connected. Early reports of pushing and shoving at Astroworld should have been enough to alert event mangers, security and police.

Event organisers have various methods at their disposable to pacify intense crowds, even when the performers are high energy. For example, during the 2011 Big Day Out in Australia, event managers used pyrotechnics and ambient music between sets to change up the crowd dynamics. Performers also have the power to cultivate a peaceful atmosphere through their interaction with the audience, exerting a positive influence on the crowd. Lastly, the presence of on-the-ground security is crucial for crowd management and ensuring adequate safety and spacing measures (Robertson et al., 2018).

A venue's layout and design can play a pivotal role, requiring the ability to accommodate expected attendance levels. The Love Parade music festival disaster in Germany in 2010 serves as a stark reminder of the tragic consequences of systematic failures, where communication issues and inadequate entry and exit points resulted in 21 facilities in a tunnel crush.

Working in silos

It is evident from the reports of the Astroworld concert that a siloed approach was taken: there was no agreement on how to manage the crowd; and there seemed to be a disconnect between what was happening on stage and what was going on in the crowd. Even though Scott stopped the show three times in response to crowd behaviour, there was no response by the staff on the stage when audience members reported that people were being crushed. This begs the question

Table 18.2 Coding behaviour in real time

Rank	Colour Code	Assessed Risk
1	Green – watch and wait	Low risk, no action required
3	Yellow – standby	Pending risk, continuous observation, action identified, staff standby
5	Red – act	High risk, immediate action required

Source: Hutton and Brown (2015).

whether the staff were wired up and on the same channel, and whether there was an agreed principle on how to manage the crowd.

In fact, there are several ways organisers and performers on stage can attempt to pacify a crowd – even audiences of high-intensity musical acts. For example, event managers will often turn the lights up or play music with a slower tempo. Lighting conditions and music are both important psychological considerations.

So, what can we do to manage crowds effectively?

Cooperative crowd management refers to the importance of communication and proactive planning to ensure the health and safety of the crowd. For example, identified risk and harm minimisation strategies should be agreed upon and communicated to key organisational and event staff prior to the event (Brown & Hutton (2013). Audience behaviour should be monitored in real time at an event and action taken pre-emptively to reduce the influence of factors (psychosocial or environmental) that may lead to poor crowd behaviour (Hutton & Brown, 2015).

Crowd management plans should include measures to mitigate potential risk (which can be determined through the history of the event, audience demographics, performers, etc.) as well as protocols for medical incidents, evacuation, and testing of communication equipment. Overall, the central tenet is for a cohesive and coordinated approach, including the sharing of information and agreed ways of working together before the start of the event.

Managerial implications

Agreed principles on how to manage crowds:

- Method of communication/signage.
- Method of surveillance and understanding of different crowd behaviours (cooperative, cohesive, etc.), as in Table 18.3.
- Action needed if crowd becomes dysfunctional (lights up, slow songs, light show).

Table 18.3 Crowd behaviours/audience types

Audience type	Characteristics
Ambulatory	Walking, usually calm
Disability/Limited mobility	Individuals have limited or restricted movement; requires additional planning
Cohesive/Spectator	Watching specific activity
Expressive/Revelling	Emotional release (e.g., community fun runs)
Participatory	Involved in actual event (e.g., protests, marches)
Aggressive/Hostile	Initially verbal, prone to lawlessness
Demonstrator	Organised to some degree (e.g., protests, marches)
Escape/Trampling	Danger may be real or imaginary
Dense/Suffocating	Reduction of individual physical movement
Rushing/Looting	Attempt to acquire/obtain/steal (e.g., tickets)
Violent	Attacking/terrorising

Source: Berlonghi (1995).

QUIZ QUESTIONS

1. What were the circumstances surrounding the tragic crowd surge during Travis Scott's performance at the Astroworld Music Festival on 5 November 2021?
2. How did early indicators, such as disruptive behaviour among attendees before the event started, suggest trouble for the event organisers?
3. Why is it important for event personnel to understand the demographics and behavioural expectations of their audience?
4. Describe some proactive measures event managers can take to ensure crowd safety and comfort.
5. How did event organisers handle reports of pushing and shoving during Scott's performance, and what should they have done differently?

DEBATE QUESTIONS

1. Reflecting on the Love Parade disaster in Germany in 2010, what are some systemic issues that can contribute to crowd-related tragedies, and how can they be prevented?
2. In what ways did the reported siloed approach to crowd management contribute to the tragedy at the Astroworld Music Festival, and what measures could have been implemented to prevent it?
3. Provide examples of how performers and event organisers can influence crowd behaviour during high-energy musical acts?

4. Why is it crucial for event staff, including security and stage personnel, to be coordinated and on the same page regarding crowd management protocols?
5. Can adjustments to lighting and music tempo affect crowd dynamics and behaviours?

Table 18.4 Alignment to United Nations Sustainable Development Goals

Goal	How
Good Health and Well-Being	Basic emergency preparedness and evacuation drills/protocols, learning to be safe Developing life skills and resilient practices
Quality Education	Understanding and assessing risks, impacts and vulnerability aspects People-centred mindset Concern for social justice Commitment to human rights
Industry, Innovation and Infrastructure	Application of best practice Planning, monitoring and evaluation skills Appreciation of safe spaces and security Concern for fair and equitable use of resources

REFERENCES

Berlonghi, A (1995) Understanding and planning for different spectator crowds, *Safety Science*, Vol. 18 No. 4, pp. 239–247.

Brown, A. E. Donne, K. Fallon, P. and Sharpley, R. (2020). From headliners to hangovers: Digital media communication in the British rock music festival experience. *Tourist Studies*, Vol. 20 No. 1, pp. 75–95. doi:10.1177/1468797619885954.

Brown, S. and Hutton, A. (2013). Developments in the real-time evaluation of audience behaviour at planned events. *International Journal of Event and Festival Management*, Vol. 4 No. 1, pp. 43–55. doi:10.1108/17582951311307502.

Gibson, C. and Connell, J. (2015). The role of festivals in drought-affected Australian communities. *Event Management*, Vol. 19 No. 4, pp. 445–459.

Gibson, C. Waitt, G. Walmsley, J. and Connell, J. (2010). Cultural festivals and economic development in nonmetropolitan Australia. *Journal of Planning Education and Research*, Vol. 29 No. 3, pp. 280–293. doi:10.1177/0739456x09354382.

Hutton, A. and Brown, S. (2015). Chapter 16: Psychosocial considerations. In World Health Organization (Ed.), *Public health for mass gatherings: Key considerations*. Geneva: WHO.

Laing, J. and Mair, J. (2015). Music festivals and social inclusion: The festival organizers' perspective. *Leisure Sciences*, Vol. 37 No. 3 pp. 1–17. doi:10.1080/01490400.2014.991009.

Robertson, M. Hutton, A. and Brown, S. (2018). Event Design in Outdoor Music Festival Audience Behavior (A Critical Transformative Research Note). *Event Management*, Vol. 22 No. 6, pp. 1073–1081.

SECTION 4 TRANSFORMING IDENTITY AND PERSPECTIVES

19 BLACK PETE
An annual tradition or a national embarrassment?

Coen Heijes and Ayanna Thompson

AIM

To examine the evolving, though ambivalent, Dutch attitudes to Black Pete and argue the need for a larger global reckoning regarding blackface.

DOI: 10.4324/9781003488729-24

LEARNING OBJECTIVES

LEARNING OBJECTIVES

1. Recognize and analyze the debate surrounding Black Pete.
2. Draw comparisons between Black Pete and blackface traditions across the world.
3. Deepen students' critical awareness of the intricate relationship between blackface, systemic racism, and the social-political context.

Theoretical focus and significance

The focus here is the relationship between blackface and the wider social and cultural discourse on racism in society. Amid growing concerns across the globe about racism and xenophobia, an awareness of blackface traditions and what these represent is of increased importance.

Practical focus and significance

The aim is to raise awareness of blackface traditions and their damaging effects, not only as expressions of but also as supporting pillars of systemic racism. It is important to challenge blackface traditions and the underlying racism, thereby reducing xenophobia and inequality in organizations and societies.

TOPIC – BLACK PETE: AN ANNUAL TRADITION OR A NATIONAL EMBARRASSMENT?

As Black Lives Matter protests and social uprisings spread across U.S. cities in the summer of 2020, civil rights icon Reverend Jesse Jackson wrote a personal letter to then Dutch Prime Minister Mark Rutte regarding an annual tradition that many believe to be racist. Every December 5, people across the Netherlands used to paint their faces black and don afro wigs to celebrate the arrival of Black Pete, the blackface servant of St. Nicholas who helps deliver presents.

With conversations about racial justice, systemic racism and prejudice against black people gaining fresh impetus worldwide, Jackson took issue with the Dutch leader's defense of the Black Pete tradition, writing:

> Your Excellency, as the whole world mourns the brutal murder of George Floyd, followed by the worldwide mass protest demonstrations calling for actions to combat racism, I do not think that it was appropriate for you to explain that you understand better the sufferings of Black people … and that you do not consider Black Pete as racist. (Jackson, 2020)

Figure 19.1 Black Pete. Author own image.

As scholars who have extensively researched blackface in the U.S., the Netherlands and worldwide (Heijes, 2020, 2022a, 2022b; Heijes & Thompson, 2020a, 2020b; Thompson, 2011, 2020, 2021), we believe the episode captures the evolving, though ambivalent, Dutch attitudes toward Black Pete, and the need for a larger global reckoning regarding blackface performances in general.

In his letter, Jackson argued that the tradition of Black Pete could not "be separated from the very offensive tradition of blackface", and noted that the Rev. Martin Luther King Jr. recognized that "there are times when it's appropriate to be political, but sometimes it's more important to be prophetic – to just do what's right" (Jackson, 2020).

A growing controversy

The Dutch tradition of the Catholic St. Nicholas dates back to the Middle Ages, while Black Pete has often been associated with Indo-European traditions of devilish characters with a mixture of black masks, horns, faces and clothes who would occasionally accompany a white, gray-haired man bearing gifts. The first illustration of St. Nicholas with a colorfully dressed black servant dates from an 1850 illustrated children's book by Jan Schenkman.

Figure 19.2 St. Nicholas and his servant, 1850. (Open Source Image).

While the tradition of Black Pete may not have been directly related to minstrelsy or slavery, its influence was unmistakable; and in the second half of the 19th century the Dutch character of Black Pete increasingly adopted aspects of minstrelsy performances, which were a popular element of the Dutch theater repertoire at the time.

The blackface performance tradition of Black Pete has come under international scrutiny over the past 10–15 years, with the United Nations also speaking out against the tradition. Backlash against the tradition has seen such U.S.-based companies as Amazon and Facebook no longer allowing depictions of Black Pete on their sites. In the Netherlands, too, the tide seemed to be turning in the wake of the Black Lives Matter protests. Prime Minister Rutte indicated that his views on Black Pete were changing, saying he was aware of the pain these depictions and performances might cause.

In the wake of Black Lives Matter, the Kick Out Black Pete campaign – launched by the eponymous Dutch activist organization founded in 2014 to end any racially offensive representation of the character – has grown in strength in recent years. Libraries across the Netherlands have silently started removing children's books that contain illustrations of Black Pete, arguing the tradition is at odds with public decency. And over the past several years the arrival of St. Nicholas by steamboat, traditionally a few weeks before December 5, has him in most Dutch towns surrounded by so-called "Soot" Petes instead of Black ones. Rather than a completely blackened face, Soot Petes have a face streaked with lines of

Figure 19.3 Black Pete protest. Author own image.

chimney ash – supposedly caused by their climbing through the sooty chimneys to deliver gifts. It is the only variation of Pete that is acceptable to the Kick Out Black Pete organization.

In a final twist, Google has taken the pressure surrounding the tradition a step further by also banning Soot Pete from its advertising, arguing that the alternative compromise, which is still supported by Kick Out Black Pete, is also based on racial stereotypes.

In a representative national poll from November 2022, for the first time a majority considered Soot Pete to be an acceptable alternative to Black Pete, while only a small minority thought that Black Pete would still exist in ten years' time. And in 2024 Kick Out Black Pete announced that it planned to dissolve the organization on 5 December 2025 as it expected to have achieved its goals by then.

However, this is only part of the story. Prime Minister Rutte indicated that a ban on Black Pete should not be a task for central government, arguing that cultural change happens on its own. A national poll in 2023 showed no further increase in support for Soot Pete, and a closer look reveals that only a minority of Dutch nationals consider Black Pete to be a racist phenomenon; instead, they see it as part of their cultural history. The support for Soot Pete replacing Black Pete stems not so much from a desire to be anti-racist as from people "being fed up with the ongoing debate" or "wanting to restore the peace during a children's festivity", as respondents in the national survey stated.

At the same time, the Black Pete discussion is increasingly becoming a part of the "culture wars", in which support for the tradition is greater among voters with lower educational backgrounds and among more right-wing parties. The PVV (a Dutch nationalist and right-wing populist party known for its anti-immigration policy) advocates that Black Pete, as an integral part of the country's tradition, should remain black, as (still) opposed to most other political parties. During the Dutch general elections in November 2023, the PVV became, for the first time in its history, the largest party in parliament. The debate on Black Pete, it seems, is far from over.

A global reckoning

The ambivalence surrounding Black Pete's status in the Netherlands is not an isolated Dutch issue. Rather, it mirrors an international unease about the function and significance of blackface images and performances globally. Although often addressed as a uniquely American performance tradition and problem, blackface performances were exported globally both through blackface performances of Shakespeare's *Othello* and through blackface minstrel shows.

A 2018 Dutch production of *Othello* was only the second in the country's history to feature a black actor in the lead role – the first was the American-born British actor Ira Aldridge's performance in 1863. The 2018 production was well received, and the media hailed the introduction of a black actor and the production's focus on racism – a first in Dutch stagings of the play. Yet one source of inspiration for that performance – Anousha Nzume's book *Hello White People* (2017), which criticized Dutch blackface and focused on racism aimed at black people – was derided by both left- and right-wing media for exaggerating the problem and being a poisonous product of identity politics. The debate surrounding Black Pete seems to support a paradox in Dutch society: the coexistence of institutional racism and xenophobia alongside the (self-)perception of a tolerant society and denial of racial discrimination.

Variations of the debate over blackface in Dutch traditions are playing out across the globe. For example, the use of blackface by contemporary Japanese singers on variety shows has come under scrutiny in recent years. In the United States, television stars such as Tina Fey, Jimmy Fallon, Jimmy Kimmel and Sarah Silverman have all apologized for their use of blackface in the 21st century. Meanwhile, in Russia a pro-Kremlin television show mocked former U.S. President Barack Obama in a sketch featuring blackface.

As Jesse Jackson warned, Black Pete cannot be understood in isolation from the history of blackface. Nor should Black Pete be addressed as an isolated Dutch problem. If we accept Prime Minister Rutte's view that cultural change happens without government intervention, then we believe that the conversations about the history, significance and legacy of blackface performances need to be more robust, more global and more sustained.

Managerial implications

A need to address the presence of blackface traditions both with employees and in products and services that organizations provide to the public.

Policy implications

An increased focus in (profit and non-profit) organizations on the potentially harmful effects of blackface traditions and finding ways to address these.

Research implications

Increased focus on an interdisciplinary approach is needed, with research teams composed of social scientists and humanities scholars considering the entanglement between blackface traditions and wider social-cultural trends.

QUIZ QUESTIONS

1. What are the origins of the Black Pete tradition?
2. How did this tradition change from an "innocent" children's festivity into a controversial debate about systemic racism?
3. How do culture wars figure in this debate?
4. How do public and profit organizations respond to the debate?
5. What are the wider implications of the Black Pete debate for blackface discussions around the world?

DEBATE QUESTIONS

1. Is government intervention necessary in the blackface debate or does cultural change happen on its own?
2. Is it possible for the tradition of Black Pete to return to being an innocent children's festivity?
3. Does white fragility prevent a serious discussion about blackface traditions?
4. Are blackface traditions relatively innocent, and does criticizing them only exacerbate existing divisions in society rather than solve them?
5. To what extent should organizations become actively involved in the debate regarding blackface?

Table 19.1 Alignment to United Nations Sustainable Development Goals

Goal	How
Zero Hunger	As both an expression and a support element of systemic racism, the continuation of blackface traditions helps perpetuate inequality within societies over the whole spectrum of health care, education, job opportunities, justice, social integration, housing and income.

REFERENCES

Heijes, C. (2020). *Shakespeare, blackface and race: Different perspectives.* Cambridge University Press.

Heijes, C. (2022a). Dutch negotiations with otherness in times of crisis. In B. Sokolova & J. Valls-Russell (Eds.), *Shakespeare's others in 21st-century European performance: The Merchant of Venice and Othello* (pp. 171–189). The Arden Shakespeare.

Heijes, C. (2022b). "It is all about passion": Reception of *Othello* amidst an emerging multicultural society. In E. Bandín, F. Rayner & L. Campillo Arnaiz (Eds.), *Othello in European culture* (pp. 153–169). John Benjamins.

Heijes, C. & Thompson, A. (Eds.). (2020a). Shakespeare, blackface and performance: A global perspective [Special issue]. *Multicultural Shakespeare: Translation, Appropriation and Performance, 22.*

Heijes, C. & Thompson, A. (2020b, December 4). In a year of Black Lives Matter protests, Dutch wrestle (again) with the tradition of Black Pete. *The Conversation.* https://theconversation.com/in-a-year-of-black-lives-matter-protests-dutch-wrestle-again-with-the-tradition-of-black-pete-150592.

Jackson, J. L. Sr. (2020b, June 17). Personal letter to Prime Minister Mark Rutte. https://dekanttekening.nl/samenleving/afro-amerikaanse-dominee-jesse-jackson-schrijft-rutte-brief-over-zwarte-piet/.

Nzume, A. (2017). *Hallo witte mensen* [*Hello white people*]. Amsterdam University Press.

Thompson, A. (2011). *Passing strange: Shakespeare, race, and contemporary America.* Oxford University Press.

Thompson, A. (2020). *Blackface.* Bloomsbury Academic.

Thompson, A. (Ed.). (2021). *The Cambridge companion to Shakespeare and race.* Cambridge University Press.

20 CONTRADICTIONS AND COMPLEXITIES

The Sydney Gay and Lesbian Mardi Gras, LGBT tourism events and social reform

Kevin Markwell

AIM

The aim of this chapter is to examine critically the complex and sometimes contradictory relationships between the Sydney Gay and Lesbian Mardi Gras (SGLMG) in Australia, tourism events and social reform.

DOI: 10.4324/9781003488729-25

LEARNING OBJECTIVES

LEARNING OBJECTIVES

1. Appreciate the historical background to the SGLMG parade and its significance to LGBTQI+ communities
2. Understand the ways in which tourism can commercialise and commodify a community-based celebration and, through this process, compromise the scope for political and social reform.

Theoretical focus and significance

This chapter is primarily concerned with the intersections between sexual identities and communities and the tourism economy that play out in the temporary 'LGBT space' created and facilitated by the SGLMG. It also highlights that there are inherent concerns, contradictions and complexities when a community-based event intersects with the commercial imperatives of tourism.

Practical focus and significance

The chapter is concerned with the complexities of running a major event that has emerged from within what was once a marginalised and disenfranchised community and has been incorporated into the tourism economy. It examines the fact that it can be difficult and complex for a community to ensure that the fundamental purpose or mission of an event that originates from within that community is protected and maintained even under constant pressure from external stakeholders such as the tourism industry.

TOPIC – CONTRADICTIONS AND COMPLEXITIES: THE SYDNEY GAY AND LESBIAN MARDI GRAS, LGBT TOURISM EVENTS AND SOCIAL REFORM

The Sydney Gay and Lesbian Mardi Gras (SGLMG), one of the world's largest LGBTQ events, is a three-week arts and cultural festival culminating in a three-hour night-time parade. The 2.4-km long parade begins in Oxford Street – the imagined 'queer heartland' of Sydney and, indeed, of Australia. In 2024, approximately 150,000 people watched the parade from the streets (Sergeant, 2024); 1.84 million viewed it on television (Molk, 2024); and over 12,000 people participated (Sydney Gay and Lesbian Mardi Gras, 2024). The festival and parade have become interwoven in Australian LGBT sexual identity and citizenship.

The parade began as a celebratory public expression of resistance to systemic prejudice against and injustices towards LGBTQ people. The first Mardi Gras, in June 1978, six years before the decriminalisation of homosexual acts in the state of New South Wales (NSW), ended in a violent riot with police, when 53 people were arrested (Markwell, 2002). This first parade was to commemorate the tenth anniversary of the Stonewall riots in New York, and had an overtly political flavour but was still saturated with celebration.

Over the course of the past 46 years, the parade has become synonymous with Australian LGBTQ culture and identity (Arrow & Boucher, 2022; Markwell & Waitt, 2013). But it has often traversed highly contested terrain, negotiating conflicts over its 'appropriateness' during the early era of HIV/AIDS; perceptions of increased commercialisation and commodification; shifting notions of gender and sexuality; and ongoing tensions between celebration, entertainment and social reform. Controversy, based on differing positions on these (and other) issues within the LGBTQ community, is never far from the surface.

These differences erupted in 2024 regarding the presence of police marching in the parade. They were initially uninvited from participating and then re-invited following negotiations between the GLMG Board and the NSW Police Force, literally a week or two before the parade. The withdrawal of consent to march was triggered by the murder of a local gay couple by a serving NSW policeman, who had been personally involved with one of the men. It also followed the release of the 3000-page Special Commission of Inquiry into LGBTQI hate crimes in NSW, which found that police had failed to investigate many potential gay hate crimes across a 40-year period.

The festival has also become a significant tourism event, the parade in particular, attracting visitors from interstate and overseas. Consequently, the Mardi Gras is now framed, at least in part, within a global LGBTQ tourism industry that desires a bigger and more spectacular parade each year. It is unlikely that any of the brave individuals caught up in the brutal riot on the night of 24 June 1978 would have imagined that the parade would become one of the world's most spectacular and enduring LGBTQ Pride events. It is doubtful also that they would have considered that the parade would become a nationally and – in the context of the global LGBTQ community – an internationally significant tourist event, attracting thousands of visitors from across Australia and the world. Indeed, it has become one of the most attended annual events in the country (Australia.com, 2024).

During the early years of Mardi Gras, from the late 1970s through to the early 1980s, the LGBTQ community in NSW was struggling for law reform and social acceptance. Systemic discrimination was commonplace, and gay men, lesbians and transgender people were frequently victims of hate crimes. Yet, in the space of 15 years, that marginalised and oppressed community began to be recognised as a lucrative market segment to be strategically targeted by companies selling everything from top-shelf alcohol to boutique holidays and hair remover. Marketers realised the opportunities that emerged from the creation of the 'gay consumer', with pockets supposedly full of so-called pink dollars and pounds.

LGBTQ tourism was one of the most targeted markets. The United Nations World Tourism Organization's Second Global Report on LGBT tourism (2017) describes the market as 'robust and resilient', comprising relatively cashed-up consumers with deep pockets and a strong desire to travel. While this is partially true in that there are many financially well off lesbian women and gay men who travel and indulge their consumerist aspirations, the LGBTQ community is diverse and encompasses the full spectrum of socioeconomic advantage and disadvantage.

Nevertheless, over the course of about ten years or so following the 1978 riot, the SGLM festival and parade cultivated the emergence of a growing LGBTQ tourism industry, paralleling the appearance of the gay consumer as a recognisable market sector. Mardi Gras has played a crucial role in the emergence of Australia, and particularly Sydney, as an internationally recognised LGBT tourist destination (Markwell, 2002). This global recognition led to the successful hosting of the International Gay Games in 2002 and, more recently, of World Pride in 2023.

One of the most overt early intersections between Mardi Gras and tourism occurred in 1999, when the Sydney Gay and Lesbian Mardi Gras Ltd, the entity with responsibility for organising the festival at the time, began its own LGBT travel agency – Mardi Gras Travel (Markwell, 2002). This development, although short-lived, nevertheless strengthened the sometimes contradictory connection between Mardi Gras as a festival embedded within a particular community and the commercial preoccupations of the tourism industry. Estimates of the economic impact of Mardi Gras to Sydney are around A$30 million (Sydney Morning Herald, 2009). Acknowledging its significant social, cultural and economic impact, the City of Sydney recognised Mardi Gras as a hallmark event in the early 1990s.

Hallmark events and festivals are powerful drivers for LGBT tourism. LGBT destinations are linked globally by an extensive calendar that includes more than 1,000 Pride events, film festivals and circuit-parties, as well as sporting events such as the International Gay Games and Eurogames, and quite idiosyncratic events such as the Gay Day phenomenon (Vorobjovas-Pinta & Fong-Emmerson, 2022; Waitt & Markwell, 2008).

A considerable body of research supports the fact that festivals and events can also be significant tools in regional economic and community social development. With sensitive and appropriate management – taking into consideration the needs and expectations of the host community as well as visitors – festivals can attract substantial numbers of LGBT tourists to regional and rural destinations, bringing considerable economic and social benefits to local communities (Lewis & Vorobjovas-Pinta, 2021).

The success of Mardi Gras as a distinctly Australian LGBT festival has spawned similar, albeit smaller, festivals in most of Australia's capital cities, and, importantly, a range of regional areas as well. LGBT festivals of various sizes and constituencies occur in regional areas across Australia – including Daylesford, Victoria; Alice Springs, Northern Territory; Newcastle, NSW; and Cairns, in Queensland. One of the newest of these is the Broken Heel Festival, which pays homage to the 1994 film *The Adventures of Priscilla, Queen of the Desert*, hosted in the outback town of Broken Hill, over 1100 kilometres from Sydney, and which celebrates drag cultures.

Simultaneously defiant and celebratory, the parade and the festival that has grown up around it have been pivotal in shaping and re-shaping relationships between the LGBTQ community and the broader Australian community. Undoubtedly, the interplay of capitalism and consumerism expressed through tourism, with sexual identities and communities, creates complexities, contradictions and controversies that sit uncomfortably at times with many individuals.

Nevertheless, the demonstration of the ability of Mardi Gras, and of LGBTQ tourism, to contribute significantly to the nation's economy has arguably been a useful strategy to advance social and political 'acceptance' of the LGBTQ community. The parade, for example, created a platform on which to advance the notion of same-sex marriage in Australia, which was legislated in 2017 (Ford & Markwell, 2017). Mardi Gras contributes far beyond any economic or corporate benefit; and the social, cultural and political impacts of this uniquely Australian event have been profoundly important in the shaping of LGBTQ identities, communities and cultures in the country.

Managerial implications

Those managing the SGLMG should curate the parade in such a way that it continues to maintain its connection with LGBTQ organisations and communities, and that it strives to balance corporate interests with community interests.

Policy implications

This chapter shows that parades such as the SGLMG, embedded within a particular community, can be effective platforms for advancing notions of equality and inclusion as well as cultural change, and can enhance social cohesion.

Research implications

A complex event like the SGLMG Parade can best be understood by fostering multidisciplinary research designs that encompass sociological, anthropological, geographic, economic and historical approaches.

QUIZ QUESTIONS

1. What are the origins of the Sydney Gay and Lesbian Mardi Gras Parade?
2. Identify three controversial issues that the parade has had to contend with.
3. Why are events and festivals so critical to LGBT tourism?
4. What are the benefits to regional towns of hosting an LGBT festival?
5. In what ways has the Sydney Gay and Lesbian Mardi Gras become interconnected with tourism?

DEBATE QUESTIONS

1. Has the Sydney Gay and Lesbian Mardi Gras Parade 'sold out' to corporate interests?
2. Given the history of police–LGBT community relations in New South Wales, should the police be allowed to march in the parade? What are the pros and cons?
3. The commercial interests/imperatives of tourism will always trump the interests of the LGBT community.
4. The Sydney Gay and Lesbian Mardi Gras has lost its purpose. It's all sequins and glitter with no real political goal.

Table 20.1 Alignment to United Nations Sustainable Development Goals

Goal	How
Good Health and Well-Being	The Mardi Gras Parade highlights safe sex messages and has been an instrument of public health in respect of HIV/AIDS. It aligns indirectly with well-being in terms of its role in helping to create a more accepting society regarding sexuality and gender.

(Continued)

Table 20.1 (Continued)

Goal	How
Gender Equality	Mardi Gras is inclusive of all gender identities, shines a light on gender diversity and thus can be affirming to people of divergent gender.
Decent Work and Economic Growth	The parade has a significant economic impact on the Sydney economy, helping strengthen Sydney's (and by extension Australia's) status as a globally significant LGBT destination.
Reduced Inequalities	Mardi Gras has been a platform to highlight issues around sexual and gender inequality; discrimination and prejudice towards LGBT people and communities.
Peace, Justice and Strong Institutions	The parade has contributed and continues to contribute to the creation of a more just and peaceful society, inclusive of sexual and gender diversity.

REFERENCES

Arrow, M. & Boucher, L. (2022). Sexual citizenship and the Sydney Gay and Lesbian Mardi Gras. *Journal of History*, 57(3), 336–361.

Australia.com (2024) Australia's biggest parties and celebrations. https://www.australia.com/en/things-to-do/arts-and-culture/australias-biggest-parties.html.

Ford, A. & Markwell, K. (2017). Special events and social reform: The case of the Sydney Gay and Lesbian Mardi Gras Parade and the Australian marriage equality movement. *Event Management*, 21(6), 683–695.

Lewis, C. & Vorobjovas-Pinta, O. (2021). Out of the closet and into the streets: Reflections on the considerations in hosting rural Pride events. In O. Vorobjovas-Pinta (Ed.), *Gay Tourism, New Perspectives* (pp. 211–223). Channel View Publications, Bristol.

Markwell, K. (2002). Mardi Gras tourism and the construction of Sydney as an international gay and lesbian city. *GLQ* 8(1–2), 81–99.

Markwell, K. & Waitt, G. (2013). Events and sexualities. In R. Finkel, D. McGillivray, G. McPherson & P. Robinson (Eds.), *Research Themes for Events* (pp. 57–67). CABI, Wallingford.

Molk, S. (2024, March 3). Saturday VOZ Ratings: Mardi Gras marches into first for the ABC. *TV Blackbox*. https://tvblackbox.com.au/page/2024/03/03/saturday-voz-ratings-mardi-gras-marches-into-first-for-the-abc/.

Sergeant, C. (2024, April 2). What the hell happened with Mardi Gras 2024? *Star Observer*. https://www.starobserver.com.au/news/what-the-hell-happened-with-mardi-gras-in-2024/229677.

Sydney Gay and Lesbian Mardi Gras (2024). Parade gallery. https://www.mardigras.org.au/parade-gallery/.

Sydney Morning Herald (2009, August 17). Sydney's Gay and Lesbian Mardi Gras worth $30m. http://www.smh.com.au/small-business-trends/sydneys-gay-nd-lesbian-mardi-gras-worth-30m-20090817-en8x.html.

Vorobjovas-Pinta, O & Fong-Emmerson, M. (2022). The contemporary role of urban LGBTQI+ festivals and events. *Event Management*, 28(6), 1801–1816.

Waitt, G. & Markwell, K. (2008). *Gay Tourism, Culture and Context*. The Hayworth Press, New York.

World Tourism Organization (2017). *Affiliate Members Global Reports, Volume 15: Second Global Report on LGBT Tourism*. UNWTO, Madrid.

21 EVENTS AND SOCIAL MEDIA

The #Euro2020 online firestorm

Nicole Ferdinand,
Nigel L. Williams and
John Bustard

AIM

This chapter aims to explore social media's role in mega-events, highlighting both the benefits and the dark side of this relationship.

DOI: 10.4324/9781003488729-26

LEARNING OBJECTIVES

1. To highlight how social media is used in events, especially mega-sporting events, by both organizers and other stakeholders, such as teams, athletes, and social media users.
2. To explain the nature of online firestorms and how they are driven by social media users.
3. To list a range of stakeholders that can potentially prevent or lessen the spread of hate online.

Theoretical focus and significance

The focus of this chapter is to explore the concept of online firestorms, including their causes, content, and the motivations of social media users who contribute to them. The chapter contributes to the relatively limited understanding of the dynamics of online social media firestorms within the specific context of events.

Practical focus and significance

The practical focus of this chapter is to explore both the positive aspects of social media's influence on events, such as its role in sponsorship activation and athlete representation, and its negative consequences, such as online harassment and the spread of hate speech, during mega-sporting events. The practical significance of the chapter lies in its examination of the interplay between social media and events, while also highlighting opportunities for positive change and increased awareness of societal issues such as the increasing prevalence of online hate and abuse.

TOPIC – EVENTS AND SOCIAL MEDIA: THE #EURO2020 ONLINE FIRESTORM

The influence of social media on events is profound, to the extent that contemporary event organizers and participants often perceive them as inseparable entities. The prevalence of 'Instagrammable' events, event-specific hashtags, and dedicated event social media accounts, coupled with the continuous social media activity by event audiences throughout all stages of their attendance, serves as unequivocal evidence of the symbiotic relationship between events and social media (Inversini & Williams, 2016; Ferdinand & Williams, 2020).

Bustard and Kitchin (2021) have also noted social media's increasing role in sponsorship activation. As businesses continue to place greater emphasis on social media over conventional media channels, more sponsorship resources will likely be allocated to social media platforms. This trend is of particular relevance to mega-sporting events such as the Olympics, the World Cup and the Euros, where sponsorship is paramount. Social media is also a crucial platform for athlete representation, with far-reaching implications for society. For example, it has emerged as a critical avenue for challenging traditional gender roles in sports (Litchfield & Kavanagh, 2019; Toffoletti & Thorpe, 2018; Tseng, 2020), particularly compared to traditional media. Additionally, social media coverage of events like the Paralympics has helped challenge stereotypes surrounding disability (Beacom et al., 2016). Finally, social media can be a powerful tool for individual athletes to raise awareness about important social issues such as racism, the gender pay gap, and LGBTQ+ rights during high-profile events (Everbach et al., 2021).

The relationship between social media and events also has a dark side. In particular, sports events and social media have been linked to a rise in online harassment, particularly during major championship events. In extreme cases, abusive comments can trigger an online firestorm, which can be defined as a surge of negative electronic or online word-of-mouth (WOM) and complaints against a person, company, or group on social media networks (Pfeffer et al., 2014). The aftermath of England's loss in the Euro 2020 final exemplifies this unfortunate trend. Researchers monitoring the X (formerly Twitter) hashtag #Euro2020final before, during, and after the match observed a sharp shift from positive and encouraging messages to racist comments targeting Bukayo Saka, Marcus Rashford, and Jadon Sancho - all Black players on the England team.

The hashtag #Euro2020final served as a stark reminder of the deep-seated divisions that persist within British society. For Black Britons, these tweets were a disheartening indication of their ongoing marginalization from mainstream British culture. An analysis of tweets showed that, before the match, there was an optimistic tone regarding the English team's international roots, immigration, diversity, and England's progressiveness. Additionally, during the match, discussions centred on the game itself, with Luke Shaw's historic early goal being one of the most widely discussed topics. However, post-match, the theme of racial abuse emerged in the aftermath of penalty misses by some players (Ferdinand et al., 2021).

It has been noted that social media users' anger, dislike, and desire to take revenge are important antecedents of online firestorms (Delgado-Ballster et al., 2021). These types of emotion could likely have applied to those social media users, who, upon experiencing their team's loss in the Euro 2020 final, lashed out against England's Black players by making racist comments. Another significant aspect of firestorms is that they are initiated by something negative rather than positive, also described in the social media marketing literature as NWOM or NEWOM, which has been noted to both spread faster and to more people than positive electronic word of mouth (PWOM/PEWOM) (Hornik et al., 2015). For example, it has been observed by marketing researchers that customers are more likely to engage in NEWOM than PEWOM (Packard & Berger, 2017; Kim & Hwang, 2022). One reason put forward for this is social media users' propensity for *Schadenfreude*, which "refers to the sense of joy sometimes experienced at the misfortune of another entity" (Hornik et al., 2019, p.83). Mixed in with the racist tweets using #Euro2020 were signs of *Schadenfreude* as some social media users seemed to take pleasure in pointing out that England's Black players had missed their penalty shots while their white teammates managed to score theirs.

Although only a small number of individuals posted hateful or racist content on Twitter/X, their comments quickly spread among users, and to such an extent that government officials were called upon to respond to the situation (Ferdinand et al., 2021), with arrests being made of the individuals found to have posted racist tweets. Ironically, the majority of tweets that contributed to the online firestorm were those condemning the racist or hateful content directed at the Black England players. Social media trolls often seek out this type of response, knowing that many users have a strong desire to denounce racist behaviour online to gain recognition. This phenomenon is commonly referred to as "slacktivism" or "low-cost, low-risk participation in a protest effort" (Smith et al., 2019, p.183). Social media users may also be motivated by personal involvement or moral stance (Gruber et al., 2020) – such as being fans of or connected to the Black English players, their own experiences of racism, or having strong anti-racist views. Whatever their motivations for engaging with the tweets, any engagement would have served to feed the online firestorm, which effectively overshadowed the many positives of the Euro 2020 championship – not least the significance of England's success in getting to the finals.

Amidst a largely negative situation that arose after Euro 2020, there is a silver lining in the form of increased awareness and discussions around the responsibility of various stakeholders in preventing the spread of online hate and abuse. These stakeholders range from social media platform owners to event organizers, broadcasters, law enforcement, educators, and individual users.

Additionally, the situation has shed light on the significant societal impacts of mega-sporting events, particularly when amplified by social media.

Managerial implications

Event organizers and other stakeholders involved in mega-events should be mindful of the dark sides of social media, such as online harassment and negative electronic word-of-mouth. They should therefore proactively monitor social media channels to effectively manage any potential crises and mitigate any negative impact.

Policy implications

To tackle online harassment during mega-events, policymakers can work with social media platforms to develop effective moderation policies, share data and insights, and advocate for platform improvements to enhance user safety.

Research implications

Researchers should conduct further studies into the triggers and dynamics of online firestorms in the context of sport and other events. This could involve qualitative analysis of social media conversations and interviews with individuals who have experienced or observed online harassment.

QUIZ QUESTIONS

1. According to the text, why is social media increasingly significant in the context of events such as mega-sporting tournaments?
2. What is "slacktivism" as mentioned in the text?
3. What term refers to the sense of joy experienced at the misfortune of another entity, as mentioned in the text?
4. According to marketing researchers, what type of electronic word-of-mouth (EWOM) is more likely to spread faster and to more people?
5. What is highlighted in the text as the silver lining amidst the negative situation described after the Euro 2020 championship?

DEBATE QUESTIONS

1. How can event organizers and sports governing bodies leverage social media to promote diversity, inclusion, and social justice initiatives during mega-sporting events?
2. What are the potential long-term consequences of online firestorms initiated by negative emotions, such as the ones observed during the Euro 2020 final, for both the individuals targeted and the broader societal discourse?
3. How can social media users be educated and encouraged to refrain from engaging in negative electronic word-of-mouth and instead promote positive electronic word-of-mouth during emotionally charged events like sports tournaments?
4. In what ways can stakeholders collaborate to effectively address the root causes of online hate and abuse, particularly in the context of mega-sporting events? What specific strategies or initiatives can be implemented to promote a safer and more inclusive online environment for participants and fans?

Table 21.1 Alignment to United Nations Sustainable Development Goals

Goal	How
Peace, Justice and Strong Institutions	This chapter relates to 16.1 of this goal – reduce all forms of violence everywhere, which includes psychological violence such as online hate speech and racist abuse.

REFERENCES

Beacom, A., French, L., & Kendall, S. (2016). Reframing impairment? Continuity and change in media representations of disability through the Paralympic Games. *International Journal of Sport Communication*, 9(1), 42–62.

Bustard, J. R., & Kitchin, P. J. (2021). Marketing events: an ecosystem perspective. In N. Ferdinand & P. J. Kitchin (eds.) *Events Management: An International Approach*, 2nd edition (pp. 117–141). London: SAGE Publications.

Delgado-Ballester, E., López-López, I., & Bernal-Palazón, A. (2021). Why do people initiate an online firestorm? The role of sadness, anger, and dislike. *International Journal of Electronic Commerce*, 25(3), 313–337.

Everbach, T., Nisbett, G. S., & Weiller-Abels, K. (2021). Rebel, rebel! How Megan Rapinoe's celebrity activism forges new paths for athletes. In M. Yanity & D. Sarver Coombs (eds.) *2019 FIFA Women's World Cup: Media, Fandom, and Soccer's Biggest Stage* (pp. 267–289). Cham: Palgrave Macmillan.

Ferdinand, N. & Williams, N.L. (2020). Event staging. In J. Connell & S.J. Page (eds.) *The Routledge Handbook of Events*, 2nd edition (pp. 350–365). Abingdon: Routledge.

Ferdinand, N., Bustard, J., & Williams, N. (2021, July 13). Euro 2020: Could Twitter stop racist abuse before it happens? *The Conversation*. https://theconversation.com/euro-2020-could-twitter-stop-racist-abuse-before-it-happens-164409.

Gruber, M., Mayer, C., & Einwiller, S. A. (2020). What drives people to participate in online firestorms? *Online Information Review*, 44(3), 563–581.

Hornik, J., Shaanan Satchi, R., & Rachamim, M. (2019). The joy of pain: A gloating account of negative electronic word-of-mouth communication following an organizational setback. *Internet Research*, 29(1), 82–103.

Hornik, J., Shaanan Satchi, R., Cesareo, L., & Pastore, A. (2015). Information dissemination via electronic word-of-mouth: Good news travels fast, bad news travels faster! *Computers in Human Behavior*, 45, 273–280.

Inversini, A., & Williams, N.L. (2016). Social media and events. In N. Ferdinand & P. J. Kitchin (eds.) *Events Management: An International Approach*, 2nd edition (pp. 271–287). London: SAGE Publications.

Kim, J. Y., & Hwang, J. (2022). Who is an evangelist? Food tourists' positive and negative eWOM behaviour. *International Journal of Contemporary Hospitality Management*, 34(2), 555–577.

Litchfield, C., & Kavanagh, E. (2019). Twitter, Team GB and the Australian Olympic Team: Representations of gender in social media spaces. *Sport in Society*, 22(7), 1148–1164.

Packard, G., & Berger, J. (2017). How language shapes word of mouth's impact. *Journal of Marketing Research*, 54(4), 572–588.

Pfeffer, J., Zorbach, T., & Carley, K. M. (2014). Understanding online firestorms: Negative word-of-mouth dynamics in social media networks. *Journal of Marketing Communications*, 20(1–2), 117–128.

Smith, B. G., Krishna, A., & Al-Sinan, R. (2019). Beyond slacktivism: Examining the entanglement between social media engagement, empowerment, and participation in activism. *International Journal of Strategic Communication*, 13(3), 182–196.

Toffoletti, K., & Thorpe, H. (2018). The athletic labour of femininity: The branding and consumption of global celebrity sportswomen on Instagram. *Journal of Consumer Culture*, 18(2), 298–316.

Tseng, Y. H. (2020). Representing sporting female discourse in social media: Taiwan women's basketball Facebook page 'Double Pump' as an example. *Sport in Society*, 23(12), 1908–1925.

22 #GENDEREQUAL OLYMPICS? Critical analysis of gender equality and the Olympic Games as a major multi-sport event

Michele K. Donnelly

AIM

The aim of this chapter is to critically examine claims made by the International Olympic Committee (IOC) about progress towards gender equality at the world's largest and most popular multi-sport event, the Olympic Games. Specific attention is paid to the claim that the Paris 2024 Summer Olympic Games would be the first "gender equal" Games because the IOC stipulated that there was an equal number of quota places for men and women athletes.

DOI: 10.4324/9781003488729-27

LEARNING OBJECTIVES

LEARNING OBJECTIVES

1. Understand and be able to distinguish between relevant concepts, including gender equality, gender parity, and gender balance.
2. Critically examine the intended and unintended consequences of the International Olympic Committee's approach to "fostering gender equality" and the subsequent actions of international sport federations.

Theoretical focus and significance

The theoretical focus of this chapter is gender equality as a widely accepted and promoted, but rarely defined and achieved, goal of sport organizations and events. Without a clearly stated, shared definition of gender equality, it is difficult to evaluate strategies to both achieve and monitor progress towards gender equality. Equality must be understood as more than a numerical goal of equal representation of men and women at sport events or in organizations.

Gender equality is one of the United Nations (UN) Sustainable Development Goals (SDGs), and is recognized in numerous UN, international, and national agreements as a human right. In the context of sport, gender equality is about more than the number of men and women participating in an event or of decision-makers included in an organization. Working towards 50/50 representation of men and women is about achieving gender parity or balance, which is one important aspect of gender equality. The theoretical significance of this chapter is the need to understand – and define – gender equality in its fullest sense in order to be able to address and achieve gender equality in sport organizations and events.

Practical focus and significance

It is wholly unacceptable that girls and women continue to be underrepresented to varying degrees in participation (as athletes, coaches, and officials) and decision-making at every level of sport worldwide. This includes all roles in the Olympic Movement and at the Olympic Games. Adopting a more comprehensive and accurate definition of gender equality in sport means paying attention to – and working to change – numerical representation *and* the conditions of men's and women's participation as athletes and decision-makers.

The number of women athletes has increased dramatically since women first competed at the Paris 1900 Summer Olympic Games. For the first time in the history of the modern Olympic Games, the IOC mandated that an equal number of men and women athletes would compete at the Paris 2024 Summer Games. However, the increases have been inconsistent, and there continue to be differences in men's and women's conditions of participation in many sports and events. Working towards gender equality in sport organizations and events requires us to celebrate incremental achievements alongside continued, thoughtful, intentional work to increase the number of opportunities for girls and women, and improve their status, value, and conditions relative to boys and men.

TOPIC – #GENDEREQUALOLYMPICS? CRITICAL ANALYSIS OF GENDER EQUALITY AND THE OLYMPIC GAMES AS A MAJOR MULTI-SPORT EVENT

In March 2024, the International Olympic Committee published a news story titled "#GenderEqualOlympics: Celebrating full gender parity on the field of play at Paris 2024", which claimed to "celebrat[e] a monumental achievement. ... The IOC has distributed quota places equally to female and male athletes – 50:50." Exactly 124 years after women first competed in the modern Olympic Games, Paris 2024 featured the highest proportion of women athletes ever. Although there were equal numbers of men and women, there were not equal numbers of men's and women's events. The programme at Paris 2024 – all the sports and events included at the Games – comprised 157 men's events, 152 women's events, and 20 mixed-gender events. "Full gender parity" was not being achieved on the field of play, and neither was gender equality.

Olympic sport programme

It is important to study the sport programme because it is the most visible aspect of the Olympic Games. According to the IOC (n.d.), "the Olympic programme is the fundamental core of the Olympic Games as decisions regarding the programme have an impact on virtually all other areas of the Olympic Games and Olympic Movement". The inclusion of specific sports and events, as well as how women and men athletes play those sports (and what they wear to do so), sends important messages about how the IOC and other international sport federations (IFs) define and attempt to achieve gender equality. In addition, the sport programme is highly contested, so IFs, athletes, Games organizing committees, broadcasters and the IOC itself all have an interest in its composition – and sometimes those interests conflict (Pavitt, 2020).

The IOC and gender equality

My research examines how the IOC has promoted gender equality at the Games, and its quest for gender equality. Most of the IOC's claims about gender equality achievements at the Games are focused on the sport programme. This includes the claim that there would be an equal number of men and women athletes, and that 28 of 32 sports would be "fully gender equal" at the 2024 Games in Paris. However, it is not always clear how the IOC defines gender equality.

In 2014, the IOC released a strategic plan for the future of the Olympic Games: *Agenda 2020*, where Number 11 of the 40 recommendations is "Foster gender equality". The IOC identified including an equal number of men and women athletes, and more mixed-gender events, at the Games as strategies to "foster gender equality".

Instead of "gender equality", claims about achieving "gender balance" were an integral part of all the IOC's statements about Paris 2024. It is crucial to critically examine what those claims meant and how they related to achieving gender equality. Ensuring gender parity (the more formal term for "gender balance") – the same number of men and women athletes – is important for gender equality at the Games; but it is limited because it does not address the conditions of men's and women's participation.

Gender differences in sporting events

The IOC's aim to achieve gender balance revealed an incomplete, number-focused commitment to gender equality (IOC, 2022). However, when men and women compete in the same sports, IFs continue to enforce differences between men's and women's events. These differences include: the length of races (e.g., Union Cycliste Internationale, 2023); weight categories (e.g., International Weightlifting Federation, 2020); the height, weight, size and spacing of equipment (e.g., World Athletics, 2024); the size of venues (Fédérational Internationale de Natation, 2019); and differences in judging (e.g., Fédération Internationale de Gymnastiques, 2024), rules (e.g., United World Wrestling, 2020), and uniforms (e.g., Fédération Internationale de Volleyball, 2021).

Using examples from the Fédération Internationale de Gymnastiques (2024), in artistic gymnastics, the differences between the men's and women's competitions include age requirements (18 and over for men and 16 for women); (e.g., parallel bars for men and uneven parallel bars for women); the number of apparatus (six for men and four for women); and uniform requirements (long or short pants for men, leotards or unitards for women). On the floor and vault – categories in which both men and women compete – the women's floor routines are set to music and include dance elements, while the men's do not; and when performing the same skills, men's eligible scores are lower than women's.

What the audience sees is women's gymnastics performed in ways that emphasize stereotypical femininity and minimize strength and power (Cervin, 2015). In contrast, men's gymnastics events are organized to emphasize the athletes' strength and power (Gurlly, 2020). These gender-based differences are examples of gender inequality – even if an equal number of men and women gymnasts compete at the Games.

Complete gender equality

In cases where sports are differentiated by gender, women's sports are designed to be a lesser version than the men's. For example, women's races are shorter, there are fewer weight categories, equipment and venues are lighter and smaller, and women wear more revealing uniforms.

Differences in men's and women's conditions of participation are the result of decisions made by those who control Olympic sports – decision-makers who continue to be predominantly men (Pape, 2019). The differences are not naturally occurring; nor are they universal. In fact, there are several sports and events on the Olympic programme that are not gender-differentiated. For example, men and women competing in archery and badminton use the same venue, equipment, and rules (World Archery, 2024; Badminton World Federation, 2024). This is evidence of internal contradictions in the Olympic programme: some events are constructed to be different for men and women, while others are not. This reinforces the need to identify and explain the remaining examples of gender-based differences.

These internal contradictions also require further attention from the IOC and the adoption of a more complete definition of gender equality – one that includes opportunity and status. The IOC needs to look beyond the numbers and work with IFs to address athletes' conditions of participation in the same sports. To do so, the IOC could adopt the definition of gender equality used by its long-term partner, UN Women (n.d.):

> Gender equality implies that the interests, needs and priorities of both women and men are taken into consideration, recognizing the diversity of different groups of women and men. Gender equality is not a women's issue but should concern and fully engage men as well as women.

Crucially, embracing and enforcing gender equality should not mean using men's sports as the standard (e.g., increasing the length of women's races to be the same as the men's distance). Rather, this is an opportunity for international federations to determine the best possible conditions for all athletes in their sports. Nor does it mean removing men's events and places for male athletes to add women's events and increase the number of women athletes at the Games. It is impossible to achieve gender equality at the expense of athletes.

QUIZ QUESTIONS

1. What milestone regarding gender parity did the Paris 2024 Olympics celebrate according to the International Olympic Committee (IOC)?
2. Although the Paris Olympics had equal numbers of male and female athletes, how did the number of events differ between genders?
3. According to the IOC, why is the sport programme considered the most visible aspect of the Olympic Games?
4. What are some of the gender-based differences in conditions of participation in sports that the IOC aims to address?
5. According to the chapter, what is a critical step the IOC needs to take to achieve a more complete definition of gender equality in the Olympic Games?

DEBATE QUESTIONS

1. Did achieving equal numbers of male and female athletes at the Paris 2024 Olympics truly represent gender equality, given the differing number of events and conditions of participation?
2. Should the IOC adopt a more comprehensive definition of gender equality, including the conditions of participation and event structures, to ensure true gender equality in the Olympic Games?

Table 22.1 Alignment to United Nations Sustainable Development Goals

Goal	How
Gender Equality	The chapter focused on how the IOC has attempted to work towards gender equality at the Olympic Games.

REFERENCES

Badminton World Federation (July 2024). *BWF Statutes, Section 4.1: The Laws of Badminton.* https://corporate.bwfbadminton.com/statutes/.

Cervin, G. (2015). Gymnasts are Not Merely Circus Phenomena: Influences on the Development of Women's Artistic Gymnastics during the 1970s. *International Journal of the History of Sport*, 32(16), 1929–1946. https://doi.org/10.1080/09523367.2015.1124859

Fédération Internationale de Gymnastiques (2024). *Technical Regulations 2024.* https://www.gymnastics.sport/publicdir/rules/files/en_1.1%20-%20Technical%20Regulations%20 2024.pdf.

Fédération Internationale de Natation (2019). *FINA Water Polo Rules 2019–2021*. https://resources.fina.org/fina/document/2021/01/12/a13c160d-b94a-4b63-93aa-a06fa370433f/2019_2021_wp_rules_congress_amended_06012020_0.pdf.

Fédération Internationale de Volleyball (2021). *Official Volleyball Rules 2021–2024*. https://www.fivb.com/volleyball/the-game/official-volleyball-rules/.

Gurlly, A.W. (2020). From Powerhouses to Pixies and Back: Boys, Men, and Troubled Masculinity in Artistic Gymnastics. In: Magrath, R., Cleland, J., Anderson, E. (eds) *The Palgrave Handbook of Masculinity and Sport*. Palgrave Macmillan, Cham. https://doi.org/10.1007/978-3-030-19799-5_8.

International Olympic Committee [IOC] (2014). *Olympic Agenda 2020: 20+20 Recommendations*. https://stillmed.olympic.org/Documents/Olympic_Agenda_2020/Olympic_Agenda_2020-20-20_Recommendations-ENG.pdf

International Olympic Committee [IOC] (2022). *IOC Gender Equality and Inclusion Objectives 2021–2024*. https://stillmed.olympics.com/media/Documents/Beyond-the-Games/Gender-Equality-in-Sport/IOC-Gender-Equality-and-Inclusion-Objectives-2021-2024.pdf.

International Olympic Committee [IOC] (n.d.). Olympic Programme Commission: Mission. https://olympics.com/ioc/olympic-programme-commission.

International Weightlifting Federation (2020). *Technical and Competition Rules and Regulations*. https://iwf.sport/wp-content/uploads/downloads/2020/01/IWF_TCRR_2020.pdf.

Pape, M. (2019). Gender Segregation and Trajectories of Organizational Change: The Underrepresentation of Women in Sports Leadership. *Gender & Society*, 34(1), 81–105. https://doi.org/10.1177/0891243219867914.

Pavitt, M. (December 7, 2020). IOC reject requests for additional Paris 2024 disciplines but weightlifting events and 50km race walk cut. *Inside the Games*. https://www.insidethegames.biz/articles/1101717/ioc-paris-2024-programme-rejections.

UN Women. (n.d.). Concepts and definitions. https://www.un.org/womenwatch/osagi/conceptsandefinitions.htm.

Union Cycliste Internationale (June 2023). *UCI Cycling Regulations – Part 2: Road Races*. https://assets.ctfassets.net/761l7gh5x5an/3zdJc5antr1dA3GYeDKdBu/bef82a9d7336e9b798c364066db92581/2-ROA-20230613-E.pdf.

United World Wrestling (2020). *International Wrestling Rules*. https://uww.org/sites/default/files/2019-12/wrestling_rules.pdf.

World Archery (January 2024). *Rulebook – Book 3: Target Archery*. https://rulebook.worldarchery.sport/PDF/Official/2024-01-15/EN-Book3.pdf.

World Athletics (January 2024). *Book of Rules – Book C: Competition*. https://worldathletics.org/about-iaaf/documents/book-of-rules.

23 STAGING THE AFRICAN RENAISSANCE AT AFRICA'S FIRST BLACK CULTURAL FESTIVAL

David Murphy

AIM

The aim of this chapter is to revisit the First World Festival of Negro Arts in Dakar, Senegal, in order to explore the role of such events in fostering a concrete sense of a shared Pan-African culture and identity.

DOI: 10.4324/9781003488729-28

LEARNING OBJECTIVES

1. To develop a greater understanding of the role of Pan-African cultural festivals in the political context of African decolonization.
2. To help understand why Pan-Africanism as an ideal has undergone a renaissance in recent decades.
3. To understand how Cold War politics intersected with African decolonization in the 1960s and 1970s.

Theoretical focus and significance

The theoretical focus of this chapter is an exploration of the ways in which the Dakar festival sought to stage or perform a Pan-African culture and identity: that is, Pan-Africanism was something produced by the event itself. The theoretical significance of this chapter lies in its focus on the importance of an ephemeral event which has previously been perceived as simply illustrating ideas previously developed in written publications. On the contrary, I argue that events such as the Dakar festival effectively performed or staged such ideas in complex and often contradictory ways.

Practical focus and significance

The practical focus of this chapter is the attempt to reconstruct the encounters and performances at a mega-event such as the Dakar festival through the consultation of multiple sources. The practical significance of the chapter is that events such as the Dakar festival are seen as worthy of study in their own right and not simply as illustrations of published materials.

TOPIC – STAGING THE AFRICAN RENAISSANCE AT AFRICA'S FIRST BLACK CULTURAL FESTIVAL

In April 1966, legendary African American jazz musician Duke Ellington travelled to Dakar with his orchestra to play at the first World Festival of Negro Arts. The festival was held against the backdrop of African decolonization and the push for civil rights in the US, and was hailed by its organizers as the inaugural cultural gathering of the Black world. More than 2,500 artists, musicians, performers and writers gathered in Senegal's capital for an event that spanned literature, theatre, music, dance and film, as well as the visual arts. Ellington's concerts were a highlight and, several years later, he still recalled them with great affection: "The cats in the bleachers really dig it … it gives us a once-in-a-lifetime feeling of having broken through to our brothers" (Ellington, 1973, p. 338). As was the case for many visitors from the African diaspora, Ellington's visit to Africa gave him a sense of coming home.

In 2016, on the 50th anniversary of the festival, an exhibition at the Quai Branly Museum in Paris acknowledged the significance of this first state-sponsored showcase of work by Black creative artists. *Dakar 66: Chronicle of a Pan-African Festival* (Murphy, 2017) captured the festival's idealism and practical successes but did not shy away from problematic issues, such as its entanglement in Cold War politics or the scathing criticism it received at subsequent, more radical, Pan-African festivals in Algiers (1969) and Lagos (1977).

As Duke Ellington's case demonstrated, the festival was imagined as an opportunity for Africa and its diaspora to be reunited through culture after the trauma of slavery and colonialism. The participation of artists and musicians from the US was particularly important to the then Senegalese president (and poet) Léopold Senghor. In 1930s' Paris, Senghor and other French-speaking students from Africa and the Caribbean had been inspired by the Harlem Renaissance and the jazz age to launch the Negritude movement, which promoted Black pride among France's colonial subjects. Ellington was thus among the most eagerly anticipated guests in Dakar, as were Langston Hughes, the elder statesman of African American literature, and an ageing Josephine Baker, the "Black Venus" from Missouri, who had stunned Paris in the 1920s with her sexually charged dance routines. Baker was, however, one of the few prominent female invitees, and it is only recently that scholars have begun to uncover the story of the many nameless female participants, particularly in various dance troupes, which provided the majority of female performers (Jaji, 2018).

Many contemporary critics noted that participants were largely drawn from an older generation, whom younger, more militant figures viewed as politically and aesthetically conservative. The US authorities, conscious that the racism exposed by the civil rights struggle had tarnished America's global reputation, did not want any radicals to travel to Dakar to "make trouble". Indeed, the participation of Ellington's orchestra was funded by the US State Department, which had been using its Jazz Ambassadors programme for over a decade as part of its Cold War diplomacy (Von Eschen, 2018). The country sent those they considered to be "safe" Black artists around the world to represent the US while, back home, they lacked basic civil rights.

The moderate Senghor was seen as a key ally by the US in its struggle for influence with the Soviet Union in West Africa. The Soviets did not play a formal role in the festival, but they did lend a cruise ship to the beleaguered hosts, who were desperate for additional hotel accommodation. The Soviets also sent Yevgeny Yevtushenko, a charismatic poet who enjoyed something akin to rock star status in the mid-1960s. As he had no formal role to play in the festival, Yevtushenko promptly teamed up with fellow poet Langston Hughes; and, according to the latter's biographer, they spent afternoons driving around town in a limousine, getting drunk on Georgian champagne (Rampersad, 1988, p. 401). The festival as a whole may have been bound up in Cold War politics, but the realities of individual encounters often tell a more nuanced story.

A vast exhibition of "classical" African artworks, entitled *Negro Art*, was, for Senghor, "the real heart of the festival" (Vincent, 2016). It was held at the newly built Musée Dynamique, a monumental Classical structure perched on a promontory overlooking the sea. The exhibition assembled almost 600 pieces of "traditional" African art, borrowed from over 50 museums and private collectors around the world. These were exhibited alongside a selection of works by Picasso, Léger and Modigliani, borrowed from the Museum of Modern Art in Paris, in a striking contrast between traditional sources and the modern masterpieces inspired by them. It was a remarkable diplomatic achievement to bring these artworks together, and it seems hard to imagine Western museums lending such priceless items to African partners today.

Senghor's idealism about the role that culture should play in postcolonial Africa was largely misplaced – by the late 1970s, the Musée Dynamique would house Senegal's Supreme Court (Murphy & Vincent, 2019) – but the festival still marked one of the high points of Black modernism in the twentieth century. In his opening speech, Senghor claimed that the event was "an undertaking much more revolutionary than the exploration of the cosmos" (Murphy, 2016, p. 1). While the Soviets and the Americans raced to conquer space, the "black world" was gathering together to do something more profound – to find its soul.

From an early twenty-first century perspective, Pan-African political and cultural initiatives of the 1960s and 1970s often appear strikingly utopian. However, the Pan-African ideal has continued to inspire various cultural and political actors on both sides of the Atlantic. It is thus important to revisit the First World Festival of Negro Arts not solely to explore what it tells us about the past but also in terms of the lessons we might learn for our present and our future.

What is so significant about the Dakar festival (and each of the subsequent Pan-African festivals) is that it provided a context in which Pan-Africanism could be performed in ways meaningful to a wide range of people. The festivals in Dakar, Algiers and Lagos effectively staged an African renaissance, announcing that the Black and African world was entering a new period of creativity following centuries of exploitation. Ultimately, though, perhaps what is most important about the festival is, in the words of Hoyt Fuller, the astute African American cultural critic:

> the mere fact that it opened, that it was held at all – for here were all but a few of the independent nations of Africa and the Caribbean, most of them desperately poor and with monumental problems, implicitly admitting that they nevertheless are bound together by certain historical and cultural imperatives, and that they wish to affirm and to strengthen those bonds. (Fuller, 1966, p. 101)

Over the past few decades, it has sometimes appeared as though the significance of the First World Festival of Negro Arts been entirely lost from view. However, there has recently been a revival in scholarly as well as public awareness of this landmark event (Murphy 2016), which is helping restore Dakar 66 to its rightful place at the heart of our understanding of a transnational Black culture and identity in the second half of the twentieth century.

Policy implications

The policy implications of this chapter are that African governments and the African Union should consider whether a revival of the great Pan-African festivals of the 1960s and 1970s might give greater impetus to cultural, economic and political collaboration on the continent, as well as fostering concrete ties with the African diaspora.

Research implications

The research implications of this chapter are that scholars in the field of African cultural studies now have a model on which to build wider discussions of festivals as complex events that are simultaneously political, cultural and commercial in their aims.

QUIZ QUESTIONS

1. Why did Pan-African festivals such as Dakar 66 emerge in the 1960s and 1970s?
2. How did such events become caught up in Cold War politics?
3. What was the significance of the event for members of the African diaspora?

DEBATE QUESTIONS

1. Are cultural festivals an effective means of promoting cultural and political unity?
2. Is the ideal of Pan-Africanism still meaningful in the early twenty-first century?
3. What might be the potential dangers of national governments organizing festivals seeking to promote certain forms of cultural identity?

Table 23.1 Alignment to United Nations Sustainable Development Goals

Goal	How
Peace, Justice and Strong Institutions	Pan-African festivals have sought to promote strong, peaceful relations between African nations and members of the African diaspora. They can productively be viewed as a form of reparative justice after the traumas of slavery and colonialism.

REFERENCES

Ellington, D. (1973). *Music is my Mistress*. Garden City, NY: Doubleday.

Fuller, H. (1966, July). World Festival of Negro Arts. *Ebony*, 90–106.

Jaji, T. (2018). *Bingo* Magazine in the Age of Pan-African Festivals: A Feminist Archive of Global Black Consciousness. *Nka: Journal of Contemporary African Art*, 42–43, 196–211.

Murphy, D. (2016). Introduction. The Performance of Pan-Africanism: Staging the African Renaissance at the First World Festival of Negro Arts. In D. Murphy (ed.), *The First World Festival of Negro Arts, Dakar 1966: Contexts and Legacies*. Liverpool: Liverpool University Press (pp.1–43).

Murphy, D. (2017). Dakar 66: Chronicles of a Pan-African Festival [Review]. *African Arts*, 50.1, 80–82.

Murphy, D., and C. Vincent (2019). Inside Dakar's Musée Dynamique: Reflections on Culture and the State in Postcolonial Senegal. *World Art*, 9.1, 81–97.

Rampersad, A. (1988). *The Life and Times of Langston Hughes*, vol. 2, *1941–67: I Dream a World*. New York and Oxford: Oxford University Press.

Vincent, C. (2016). "The Real Heart of the Festival": The Exhibition of *L'Art nègre* at the Musée Dynamique. In D. Murphy (ed.), *The First World Festival of Negro Arts, Dakar 1966: Contexts and Legacies*. Liverpool: Liverpool University Press (pp.45–63).

Von Eschen, P. M. (2018). Soul Call: The First World Festival of Negro Arts at a Pivot of Black Modernities. *Nka: Journal of Contemporary African Art*, 42–43, 124–35.

24 TRANSFORMATIVE EVENTS

A migrant narrative of identity and belonging at the Edinburgh Festival Fringe

Lina Fadel

AIM

By examining a personal case study of performing research on stage, this chapter seeks to highlight how narrative performance can challenge prevailing stereotypes and singular narratives about migration. It considers the impact of such storytelling events on both individual lived experiences and broader academic practices, contributing to the discourse on the intersection of events, scholarly activism and social transformation.

DOI: 10.4324/9781003488729-29

LEARNING OBJECTIVES

1. Understand the intersections between events, storytelling, identity, and belonging within contexts of migration;
2. Assess the impact of narrative events and how they enable individuals to express their cultural identities and claim belonging within new social and academic contexts;
3. Understand how narrative events can contribute to fostering a sense of inclusion and community.

Theoretical focus and significance

The theoretical focus of this chapter is on the intersection of narrative performance and event theory, examining how storied events serve as transformative agents for social change, identity formation, and belonging. By analysing the performative nature of storytelling within the context of migration and displacement, the chapter explores how these events challenge dominant narratives and foster cultural resistance.

Practical focus and significance

The practical focus of this chapter is on the application of narrative performance as a method for engaging public audiences and creating spaces for dialogue and resistance. The practical significance of this chapter lies in highlighting how performing personal and collective stories at events can foster a deeper understanding of marginalized experiences and contribute to social change by challenging stereotypes.

LEARNING OBJECTIVES

TOPIC – TRANSFORMATIVE EVENTS: A MIGRANT NARRATIVE OF IDENTITY AND BELONGING AT THE EDINBURGH FESTIVAL FRINGE

When approached about turning my previous article (Fadel, 2022) into a chapter for a book on how events transform societies, I felt a sense of unease. I am not an 'events scholar', my work does not directly tie to this field, and the relevancy of my article to 'events' was not something I had considered before. In the article, I wrote about my experience as a Syrian scholar performing my research on stage at the Edinburgh Festival Fringe, Scotland, in the summer of 2022, reflecting on that experience using a narrative lens and drawing on my research interests. However, my encounter with Mike Duignan, the editor of this volume, prompted a different line of thought. My curiosity led me to explore the literature on 'events' (Carnegie and McCabe, 2008; Duignan et al., 2022; Kirby et al., 2018; McClinchey, 2008) to understand how my research on narrative, autoethnographic, and anti-colonial methods within contexts of migration and displacement connects to the concept of 'events' both theoretically and methodologically.

A new understanding

To my relief, the literature revealed a meaningful connection between events-based research and other fields of study. Events-related disciplines now engage with anthropology, sociology, cultural studies, and other areas, indicating that events are no longer merely economic phenomena but spaces for studying human interactions within their social and political environments. Duignan (2023) describes them as 'complicated, dynamic entities', and observes that events research has undergone a paradigm shift, evolving to include debates on identity, memory, agency, representation, marginalization, community, borderlands, diversity, cultural understanding, space, place, cultural belonging, and performativity.

With this new appreciation, I revisited my article, re-examining my experience of being a migrant academic performing on stage, and its significance. My initial reflections on participating in the Fringe still hold: the significance of that experience for me was not about public engagement or the thrill of performing. It was an act of claiming my story and narrative, an act of activism and resistance. Reflecting further, I now realize that my Fringe performance was an event, and that my experience and its affective connotations constituted an event in themselves. Events create spaces for sharing experiences, values, and interests, and my performed experience created a spatial event that transcended public engagement. As a former refugee driven by my migrant experience, performing in the city I now call home was a major, even life-changing, event.

Performing on stage: an 'identity' event

The Cabaret of Dangerous Ideas, established in 2003 as a collaboration between Edinburgh-based universities and the Edinburgh Festival Fringe, provides academics with the space to engage with the public by performing their research on stage. For my performance, I developed a show called *Become a Sexy Refugee in 5 Easy Steps*.

In truth, I wasn't just performing my research. I transformed my experiences as a migrant academic into an event where I could perform my identity narrating present and past experiences. Being on stage was terrifying and exhilarating. It allowed me to distance myself from the detached and supposedly sophisticated objectivity required in academic debates. Performing on stage was an event that enabled the sharing of my fragmented self with the community. If 'gender is the repeated stylization of the body' as Butler (1990/1999, p. 25) would argue, then identity is the repeated narrativity and performativity of my lived experiences as a Syrian woman and academic. Like gender, identity 'is a sequence of repeated acts that harden into the appearance of something that's been there all along' (Salih, 2007, p. 57). Like gender, identity is a 'strategy' that has cultural survival as its end, since those who do not 'do' their identity correctly are punished by society (Butler, 1990/1999, pp. 139–140). But being on stage was not just about that; it was also about equal opportunities and social justice.

Performing home and belonging: a reorientation event

Exposing the double standards at the UK border and in the media's portrayal of refugees was a reorientation for me. This was my chance to publicly address the injustices faced by migrants, refugees, and asylum seekers and reflect on how we discuss them in everyday conversations. Speaking out was a reorientation through which I practised my belonging to the city I now call home. Like identity, belonging is a complicated notion and often used as if it were self-explanatory (Antonsich, 2010). But someone like me who has experienced unbelonging knows that belonging is not self-explanatory. Belonging is hard work, especially for people plagued by otherness (Fadel, 2019, 2020) and strangeness (Ahmed, 2012).

When I was up on stage, I was no longer a 'stranger ... passing by, at the edges of social experience' (Ahmed, 2012, p. 3). The event was not happening to me, and I was not just part of it. I was it; the event opened up a space for belongingness and inclusion. I belonged to the stage, the audience, the city, and the country. If home 'is where we have our "sense of place" and we feel we belong, if it is not necessarily where we are from but where we are "towards"' (Strani, 2024, p. 39), then I was making home on stage. I was, in the words of Ahmed (2012, p. 3), a stranger whose 'experience can teach us about how bodies come to feel at home through the work of inhabitance, how bodies can extend themselves into spaces creating contours of inhabitable space, as well as how spaces can be extensions of bodies'. I was also in dialogue with the city. Duffy (2005, p. 679) reminds us that events involve 'on-going dialogues and negotiations within communities as individuals and groups attempt to define meaningful concepts of identity and belonging'.

Storied events as transformative encounters

I found my cultural voice on that stage. My performance enabled the transformation of my narrative into an event of resistance, belonging, and identity. By telling my story – a different story that demonstrated diverse ways of being and becoming in this world – I challenged a toxic singular narrative that treated 'all Syrians – all refugees – as one amorphous mass of people, rather than individuals in their own right with lives, children, careers, homes, hopes, and dreams' (Fadel, 2022). Standing there and challenging the stereotypes and preconceptions that had been attached to me during my time in the UK turned my narrative into a transformative encounter. While this experience may not have significantly altered the perception of refugees and migration-related issues, it profoundly transformed my academic practice and enriched my lived experience of migration in the UK.

Research implications

The research implications of this chapter suggest that integrating narrative performance and autoethnographic methods into academic practice can enrich our understanding of home-making, identity, and belonging within contexts of migration. This approach provides valuable insights into how personal and collective stories can be leveraged as powerful tools for social change, informing future research on the impact of events in transforming societal perceptions of migration.

Table 24.1 Alignment to United Nations Sustainable Development Goals

Goal	How
Gender Equality	The chapter is written by a migrant woman and former refugee, who is based at a UK institution, and draws on the significance of such individuals being able to tell their unique stories, irrespective of nationality, ethnicity, gender, or social status
Reduced Inequalities	The chapter engaged with equal opportunities in research by highlighting the experience of a migrant academic engaging with a local community through performing on stage
Sustainable Cities and Communities	Connecting with the city and the community through narrative performance
Peace, Justice and Strong Institutions	See the point in response to Reduced Inequalities

REFERENCES

Ahmed, S. (2012). *On being included: Racism and diversity in institutional life*. Duke University Press. https://doi.org/10.2307/j.ctv1131d2g.

Antonsich, M. (2010). Searching for belonging: An analytical framework. *Geography Compass*, *4*(6), 644–659. doi: 10.1111/j.1749–8198.2009.00317.x.

Butler, J. (1990/Anniversary edition 1999). *Gender trouble: Feminism and the subversion of identity*. New York: Routledge.

Carnegie, E., & McCabe, S. (2008). Re-enactment events and tourism: Meaning, authenticity and identity. *Current Issues in Tourism*, *11*(4), 349–368.

Duffy, M. (2005). Performing identity within a multicultural framework. *Social and Cultural Geography*, *6*(5), 677–692, doi:10.1080/14649360500258153.

Duignan, M. B. (2023). Thirty years of events-related research (1992–2022): Published works in annals of tourism research and annals of tourism research empirical insights. *Annals of Tourism Research*, 100, 103556. doi.org/10.1016/j.annals.2023.103556.

Duignan, M. B., Everett, S., & McCabe, S. (2022). Events as catalysts for communal resistance to overtourism. *Annals of Tourism Research*, *96*, 103438.

Fadel, L. (2019). Syrian, Scottish, British: How I came to belong before I became a UK citizen. *The Conversation*. Available online: https://theconversation.com/syrian-scottish-british-how-i-came-to-belong-before-i-became-a-uk-citizen-108226 (accessed on 30 May 2024).

Fadel, L. (2020). When hope is a dinghy in the Channel: How racism in Britain is a crisis of belonging. *The Conversation*. Available online: https://theconversation.com/when-hope-is-a-dinghy-in-the-channel-how-racism-in-britain-is-a-crisis-of-belonging-144513 (accessed on 30 May 2024).

Fadel, L. (2022). A Syrian academic at the Fringe: Why I put on a show to reclaim the stories of refugees like me. *The Conversation*. Available online: https://theconversation.com/a-syrian-academic-at-the-fringe-why-i-put-on-a-show-to-reclaim-the-stories-of-refugees-like-me-190119 (accessed on 30 May 2024).

Kirby, S., Duignan, M., & McGillivray, D. (2018). Mega-sport events, micro and small business leveraging: Introducing the 'MSE-MSB Leverage Model'. *Event Management*, *22*(6), 917–931. https://doi.org/10.3727/152599518X15346132863184.

McClinchey, K.A. (2008). Urban ethnic festivals, neighborhoods, and the multiple realities of marketing place, *Journal of Travel & Tourism Marketing*, *25*(3–4), 251–264, doi:10.1080/10548400802508309.

Salih, S. (2007). On Judith Butler and performativity. In K. Lovaas & M. M. Jenkins (Eds.), *Sexualities and communication in everyday life: A reader* (pp. 55–68). SAGE Publications.

Strani, K. (2024). On places, roots and rhizomes: Place and belonging through the work of Ullrich Kockel. In M. Nic Craith, K. Strani, & A. Mackie (Eds.), *Heimatkunde: Explorations of Place and Belonging* (pp. 27–41). LIT Verlag. https://www.lit-verlag.de/isbn/978-3-643-91443-9.

25 CHALE, LET'S GO
The case of the Chale Wote Street Art Festival

Nduka Mntambo

AIM

The aim of this chapter is to explore the impact of the Chale Wote Street Art Festival in shaping discourse about public art practice in Accra, Ghana.

DOI: 10.4324/9781003488729-30

LEARNING OBJECTIVES

1. To assess the significance of art practices in challenging conventional narratives within the context of the Global South.
2. To examine the case of Chale Wote as a catalyst for event-led social change in artistic practice.

Theoretical focus and significance

The chapter focuses on how public art festivals produce knowledge through art as a form of "worlding". The theoretical significance of this chapter is to illuminate the potency of artistic encounters in public spaces as platforms for cultural and social reimagining, particularly in the Global South.

Practical focus and significance

The aim of this chapter is to explore how the Chale Wote festival uses artist projects and participatory engagements to bring about transformative effects on public spaces. The practical significance of this chapter lies in demonstrating how artistic interventions can reconceptualize marginalized urban spaces.

TOPIC – CHALE, LET'S GO: THE CASE OF THE CHALE WOTE STREET ART FESTIVAL

This chapter explores the transformative power of the Chale Wote Street Art Festival in Accra, Ghana, as an argument for how cultural events can transform marginalized urban spaces. The chapter's objectives include the evaluation of public artistic praxis as a mode for effecting transformation. The potential significance of this exploration lies in its contribution to understanding culture-led urban regeneration within the context of the Global South. Additionally, the chapter focuses on the practical aspects (artist projects) of Chale Wote, examining it as a case study for championing alternative public space narratives. Through this lens, the chapter attempts to contribute to academic discourse on event-led social change in artistic practice.

Following Maharaj's (2009) idea of art practice as knowledge production, I consider the iteration of the Chale Wote Street Art Festival held in 2016 in Jamestown, Accra, as the epistemic engine that stages a radical encounter of urban world-making. To understand complex urban environments such as Jamestown, creative and artistic practices can help articulate fringe processes. In reading the

Figure 25.1 Jamestown (2016). Author own image.

possibilities of "worlding" that Chale Wote offers, I draw on the idea Maharaj calls an "agglutinative mode" of enquiry, which brings into play associative manoeuvres, juxtapositions, blends and splices, and non-inflexional modes of elision and stickiness. The Chale Wote festival thrives on the register of the agglutinative, both in political and aesthetic terms.

The Chale Wote Street Art Festival is an annual event held in Accra that showcases a range of artistic expressions in urban spaces. The festival is located in the Ga neighbourhood of Jamestown and is guided by the iconic lighthouse. The organizing collective is a hub for African alternative music, video, and art, and informs the festival's programming, which is based on local and historical knowledge systems. The festival not only reimagines black diasporic experiences but also reconfigures public and civic spaces.

The Ga phrase "Chale Wote", which translates to "Man, let's go!", encapsulates the spirit of movement and liberation that the festival embodies. The festival offers a range of performances, screenings, and discussions that inspire a re-examination of our role in the world. The festival theme "Spirit Robot", challenged and reshaped accepted narratives of urbanity. This thematic underpinning symbolizes a rejuvenation of perspective, encouraging participants to actively engage in the construction of their realities. The duality of spirit and robot serves as a conceptual framework for interpreting the interactions with black artists and their works. The concept of "Spirit Robot" encapsulates a transformative vision, offering festival-goers a departure from traditional artistic constraints. This framework represents a break from the limitations imposed on African art practices by more conventional spaces and academic institutions.

Throughout the festival, the everyday life of Ga-Jamestown is theatrically elevated, weaving the community's collective narrative into the fabric of the event. A diverse group of artists – including performance artists, filmmakers, dancers, visual artists, and writers – come together in the area's vibrant streets. Below is a vignette of some of their encounters.

Encountering American performance artist Autumn Knight at the Untamed Empire, one of the lab spaces in the event, was a profound experience. She is an artist who describes herself as a black magician and afro-trickster. One of Autumn's affecting video pieces is called *Lagrimas Negras* (Black Tears), in which she offers her black tears at the seawall in Galveston, Texas. She wanted to see if expressing grief as a black woman would elicit any empathy from the public. For an hour Autumn wept, but no one stopped to ask what was wrong – except for some children, whose parents quickly pulled them away.

Ghanaian Realpen pencil is a young Instant Live Drawing artist with a photographic memory. He lives and works in Accra. I witnessed his extraordinary ritual of creation while he worked on the streets of Ga-Jamestown. This was not an artist in his studio drawing a supine model, but a public act of creation. For hours he was surrounded by a cheering and at times impatient audience. The artist

Figure 25.2 Autumn Knight (2016). Author own image.

danced, scribbled, and cajoled the portrait of a beautiful young black woman into being, using techniques that illuminate the processes of creation. Beyond the kinetic beauty of his performance, Realpen pencil reminds us of the embodied nature of birthing works of the imagination.

Walking the streets of Ga-Jamestown, one cannot help but marvel at the sartorial aesthetic sensibility so boldly exhibited by both women and men. The project of beauty, memory, and imagination takes flight in the poignant fashion film *To Catch a Dream* by the prolific Nest Collective from Nairobi, Kenya – a cutting-edge, multi-disciplinary art collective that collapses and blurs the uninteresting lines between fashion, film, music, and visual arts. This collective describes itself as an army of thinkers, makers, and believers invested in subverting, reimagining, and dissecting layers of African identities, (in)visibilities, (in)abilities, mobilities, and acts of enunciation.

The economic and social ramifications of Chale Wote are significant, particularly for the historically marginalized community of Ga-Jamestown. The festival stimulates local economies and fosters innovative spaces for artistic and intellectual growth. Chale Wote not only initiates economic activity but also serves as an experimental ground for radical thought and creative practice.

In a conversation with the director of cultural network Accra[dot]Alt and producer of Chale Wote, Mantse Aryeequaye, we explored the contestation of

Figure 25.3 Realpen pencil (2016). Author own image.

knowledge centres, recasting and decentring art practices, strategies of self-funding, and the transformative economic infrastructures that Chale Wote offers the neglected community of Ga-Jamestown. Speaking about the evolution of Chale Wote over the past decade, Aryeequaye asserts that it is essential for young black people at this time to create new knowledge – knowledge that is not centralized within the academic sphere because, a lot of the time, we have not been able to put into practice many academic theories for transformative setups. Speaking about the economic pressures of running Chale Wote within a hyper-capitalistic society, Aryeequaye reminds us that the whole of Ghana was once the Wall Street of the transatlantic slave trade. As such, he argues that the culture of exploitation is embedded in the psyche of the people, especially those with access to resources.

Chale Wote sparks a lot of economic activities, but also is an essential site for experimentation for participants. Aryeequaye speaks about how international artists would come to the festival with complete ideas about the work they want to make. Still, after a two-hour tour of Ga-Jamestown – with its complex political history, rhizomatic layout, and textures of the everyday – these artists cannot help but reframe their work and question their premises.

Chale Wote's theme – Spirit Robot – has come to mean different things to different people; but the underlying theme is liberation. Aryeequaye sees the Spirit Robot as our liberation theory, expressed through performance or digitally conceived moments. A dance with multiple realities and possibilities is fashioned out of the emancipatory technologies of the self, which are rooted in the understanding of our troubled past and confident knowledge of imagining and creating interesting futures.

Research implications

Researchers should consider art-making processes as a legitimate and elegant site of knowledge production.

QUIZ QUESTIONS

1. How does the Chale Wote Street Art Festival contribute to the transformation of marginalized urban spaces in Accra, Ghana?
2. Discuss the significance of the festival theme "Spirit Robot" and how it challenges traditional narratives of urbanity.
3. Explain Maharaj's (2009) concept of the agglutinative mode of enquiry and how it is applied in the context of the Chale Wote Street Art Festival.

DEBATE QUESTIONS

1. To what extent can cultural events like the Chale Wote Street Art Festival be considered effective tools for urban regeneration in marginalized communities?
2. How does the theme "Spirit Robot" at Chale Wote challenge or reinforce existing perceptions of African art practices within academic and traditional art spaces?
3. Can the agglutinative mode of enquiry, as proposed by Maharaj, be effectively utilized to understand and address complex urban environments beyond the context of artistic festivals like Chale Wote?

REFERENCE

Maharaj, S. (2009). Know-how and No-How: stopgap notes on "method" in visual art as knowledge production. *Art and Research*, 2(2), pp. 1–11.

SECTION

5 TRANSFORMING OUR ENVIRONMENT

26 GLASTONBURY AND CLIMATE CHANGE

How the world's most iconic music festival puts the spotlight on climate challenges and solutions

Richard Betts

AIM

To use Britain's world-famous Glastonbury Festival as an illustration of how the world as a whole needs to both reduce its impact on the climate and increase its resilience to climate change and extreme weather, whilst continuing to function effectively and allowing its citizens to thrive and enjoy life.

DOI: 10.4324/9781003488729-32

LEARNING OBJECTIVES

LEARNING OBJECTIVES

1. Humans are causing climate change by emitting greenhouse gases, and its effects are already being seen.
2. The worst effects of climate change, such as catastrophic sea level rise, can be avoided if we reduce emissions; and there are many ways to do this.
3. However, we need to adapt to the changes we have already caused, such as increased extreme weather.

Theoretical focus and significance

The chapter focuses on how the rich complexity of society (as illustrated by the Glastonbury Festival) brings both challenges and opportunities in dealing with environmental issues. Human-caused climate change is an extremely urgent issue – some describe it as an emergency – but addressing it is far from simple. Awareness and understanding of the interconnected challenges and the numerous possibilities to contribute to addressing climate change are therefore vital.

Practical focus and significance

This chapter focuses on practical solutions to cutting greenhouse gas emissions, such using renewable energy instead of fossil fuels, reducing private car use and/or moving to electric vehicles, and changing diets to reduce meat and dairy consumption. Also required is planning ahead to be more resilient to extreme weather; and taking action on climate change – both reducing emissions and adapting to new climate conditions – is urgent. Arming people with knowledge of what can be done, both at the individual and the system level, will help enable them to take action themselves and push for large-scale changes.

TOPIC – GLASTONBURY AND CLIMATE CHANGE: HOW THE WORLD'S MOST ICONIC MUSIC FESTIVAL PUTS THE SPOTLIGHT ON CLIMATE CHALLENGES AND SOLUTIONS

Glastonbury, Britain's largest and most famous music festival, is also a symbol of the many faces of the global climate change debate. It's full of people enjoying life and relying on technology, reliable supplies of energy and food, and consumer goods; yet it's also deeply rooted in environmental and social justice concerns.

And, of course, it's also hugely exposed to extreme weather. If the party is to keep going, can all these factors be reconciled? And what will it look like in the future? Will it need to adapt to survive?

The global climate is of course already changing. So far, humans have increased global temperatures by about 1.3°C since we first began large-scale burning of fossil fuels in the 1700s; and most of that increase – about 1.0°C – has occurred since the time of the first Glastonbury festival in 1970. The effects of this are clearly emerging (IPCC, 2021), with extreme weather events increasingly posing risks to all manner of outdoor events, including festivals. For example, in 2023, numerous music events around the world were cancelled or badly impacted by various weather extremes (Bain, 2023).

Glastonbury is famous for some very wet years when the festival became a mud bath, and extreme daily rainfall is increasing across much of the UK and elsewhere (Hawkins et al., 2020; IPCC, 2021). In January 2023, an Elton John concert in Auckland, New Zealand was cancelled due to heavy rain. In June, golf ball-sized hail injured dozens of people at a Louis Tomlinson concert in Colorado, USA; and in August, the Wacken Open Air music festival in Germany turned away 35,000 fans as the mud-soaked ground could not cope.

But a more insidious threat, which even risks lives, is heightened in heatwaves. Although hot, sunny weather is often welcomed by festival-goers, there can be too much of a good thing: becoming too hot brings the risk of heat stroke, which can lead to severe illness or even death. Take the year 2023: in April, 13 people died from heatstroke at an outdoor awards event in India; in August, the ThumpTown music festival in British Columbia, Canada, was postponed due to the threat posed by a nearby wildfire; and in November, a fan died at a Taylor Swift concert in Rio de Janeiro in the midst of Brazil's severe heatwave, prompting the postponement of the show.

Rising temperatures are melting glaciers and ice sheets, and global average sea levels have already risen by about 20cm over the last century, with some further rise already inevitable. This is a particular threat to the low-lying area near Glastonbury known as the Somerset Levels, which suffered a devastating flood some centuries ago due to a severe storm surge coinciding with a very high tide. Despite improved flood protection, this will become increasingly challenging as sea levels continue to rise. The Glastonbury Festival site itself is not at risk from the sea, but major road and rail links to the site traverse the Levels.

What is Glastonbury doing about it?

The various facets of Glastonbury's unique character both illustrate the challenge facing society in reducing our impact on the environment and set an example of how progress can be made and hearts and minds inspired. Huge public address systems, lighting rigs, catering facilities and mobile phones are all hungry for power, and we take easily available energy for granted – but it is also a major driver of climate change. For decades, we have been burning fossil fuels to power our worldwide increase in welfare and living standards, and deforesting land to make way for food production. Globally, how can we keep the benefits and share them more widely while reducing the collateral damage to the climate before it becomes too severe? Frankly, how can we keep the party going without trashing the place? Glastonbury has been helping show the way.

The festival has strong environmental traditions, with its Green Fields area having been entirely run on wind, solar and pedal power since 1984. By 2023, the power needs of the entire festival were met by renewable energy – including on-site solar or wind power, fossil-free fuels from anaerobic digesters or waste cooking oil, or grid electricity from a non-fossil fuel provider. Festival-goers are actively encouraged to use public transport through the sale of combined festival and coach tickets ahead of the main ticket sales and the provision of a free shuttle bus from the nearest railway station, and 40,000 attendees use these options. High-quality vegetarian and vegan food – with its lower carbon footprint and more efficient use of land than meat and dairy – is widely available and extremely popular.

As well as these practical steps to encourage sustainability, there are many strong educational and advocacy actions promoting environmental awareness. Global campaigning organization Greenpeace has long sponsored the festival, with its own stage and mass events with environmental messaging. In 2019, broadcaster and natural historian Sir David Attenborough enthralled a vast crowd at the Pyramid Stage, as did Swedish environmental activist Greta Thunberg in 2022; and the Speakers Forum stage has hosted talks and discussions by leading environmentalists for many years. The new Science Futures area has its own stage, The Laboratory, and stalls with hands-on activities for people to learn about topics such as ecology, climate science and potential climate solutions. In the late-night party area of Shangri-La, crowds dance beneath evocative art with hard-hitting messages of sustainability and social justice.

But even with all this, there are clearly further challenges to be met. In particular, well over 100,000 attendees still arrive by private car. While these numbers could be reduced further, some attendees will always either need or want to drive. As drivers switch to electric vehicles, how will the festival be able to meet the demand for vehicle charging points? And with many of the acts coming from abroad, should more priority be given to artists who do not need to fly? This would be a major limitation for a festival of such global repute. Or should these aspects be viewed as unavoidable emissions and compensated by measures to actively remove carbon from the atmosphere? These practical challenges for keeping the festival viable whilst minimizing its environmental impact are shared by the world as a whole – how can we continue to live fulfilling, joyful lives without damaging our only home?

Alongside this, we already need to live with the damage we have caused to the global climate, and again Glastonbury is at the front line here. The duty of care to festival-goers and workers includes being ready for extreme weather. Glastonbury will need to plan ahead for a range of extreme weather that could occur, including heavy rain and heatwaves. The festival already provides free water, a vital service in hot weather; but other practical safeguarding measures could include providing more shade, and potentially even avoiding scheduling acts drawing major crowds during the hottest parts of the day. Actively encouraging festival-goers to look after themselves and others will be even more important than ever.

These are the challenges we need to address to live with the changes we have already caused to the climate whilst limiting even worse changes in the future, illustrated by 200,000 people enjoying themselves for a few days in Somerset.

Managerial implications

Managers of large music festivals and similar outdoor events need to pursue ways to reduce the carbon emissions associated with their event to reduce their contribution to climate change. They also need to plan events that are resilient to extreme weather to safeguard those attending.

Policy implications

Policymakers at national levels need to transform energy, transport and food systems so that all aspects of life – including music festivals – can continue to be enjoyed without contributing to climate change. They also need to put in place measures to enable adaptation to climate change, particularly extreme weather – for example by upgrading energy and transport infrastructure to better withstand high temperatures, heavy rainfall and high winds, and managing the land to reduce flooding risks.

Research implications

Research is needed on the most efficient and effective ways for festivals to reduce their carbon emissions, either directly or indirectly. Studies are also needed of the implications of climate change for multi-hazard and cascading risks affecting festivals to understand potentially complex situations that may need to be managed to safeguard large numbers of people.

QUIZ QUESTIONS

1. How much global warming had occurred by 2023 since the time of the Industrial Revolution (18th/19th centuries)?
2. By how much have global sea levels risen over the last century?
3. In 2023, how much of the Glastonbury Festival's power needs were met by renewable energy?

DEBATE QUESTIONS

1. Should Glastonbury stop inviting performers who need to fly to get there?
2. What priority should Glastonbury give to discouraging festival-goers from using private cars compared to providing electric vehicle charging points?
3. Should the organizers of Glastonbury consider holding the festival at a different time of year?

Table 26.1 Alignment to United Nations Sustainable Development Goals

Goal	How
Affordable and Clean Energy	By pointing out that Glastonbury now meets all its power needs with renewable energy
Industry, Innovation and Infrastructure	By prompting thinking on how to provide temporary electric vehicle charging for up to 100 people
Responsible Consumption and Production	By prompting thinking on the consequences of consumption and production
Climate Action	By prompting thinking on how festivals can reduce emissions and increase resilience to climate change

REFERENCES

Bain, K. (2023) Here are all the concerts affected by climate change in 2023. *Billboard*. https://www.billboard.com/lists/concerts-affected-climate-change-2023-full-list/july-4/.

Hawkins, E., Frame, D., Harrington, L., Joshi, M., King, A., Rojas, M., & Sutton, R. (2020). Observed emergence of the climate change signal: From the familiar to the unknown. *Geophysical Research Letters*, 47, e2019GL086259. https://doi.org/10.1029/2019GL086259.

Intergovernmental Panel on Climate Change [IPCC] (2021). Summary for Policymakers. In: *Climate Change 2021: The Physical Science Basis. Contribution of Working Group I to the Sixth Assessment Report of the Intergovernmental Panel on Climate Change*. Cambridge University Press, Cambridge, pp. 3–32. doi:10.1017/9781009157896.001.

27 CONCERNS ABOUT THE SOCIAL IMPLICATIONS OF SPORTING EVENTS IN NATURAL AREAS

David Newsome and
Michael Hughes

AIM

This chapter reflects on continuing trend of the 'sportification' of nature that may be impacting the natural environment and influencing the way that humans view the natural environment.

DOI: 10.4324/9781003488729-33

LEARNING OBJECTIVES

LEARNING OBJECTIVES

1. Understand what the 'sportification' of nature means.
2. Appreciate concerns raised about negative biophysical impacts.
3. Comprehend that there are conflicting values about what people do in natural environments.

Theoretical focus and significance

The chapter explores the question of how it is possible to combine and/or reconcile the notions of conquering nature for individual gratification with appreciation of nature and the putative benefits for humans when they visit natural and protected areas. Research demonstrates that holding sporting events in nature conveys negative environmental and social impacts.

Practical focus and significance

The 'sportification' of nature is a threat to the wider social importance of natural and protected areas. The global natural environment is in a state of decline, and some of the pressures, such as climate change, are very difficult to manage. At the same time, we have choices about what we do and where, and the implications of such choices need to be considered carefully.

TOPIC – CONCERNS ABOUT THE SOCIAL IMPLICATIONS OF SPORTING EVENTS IN NATURAL AREAS

Following from the publication of earlier work (Newsome & Hughes, 2017, 2018), we reflect on the continuing trend regarding 'outdoor enthusiasts' who wish to engage in activities that may be impacting the natural environment and, importantly, influencing how humans view their recreational activities in natural settings. The problematic attitudes promoted through the extreme sportification of natural areas are exemplified by promotion of the Antarctic Ice Marathon (2024), which states that:

> Adventure marathoners and ultra-athletes are always looking for the next big challenge. It could be a remote desert marathon, a high-altitude mountain marathon or a jungle marathon. However, mainland Antarctica represents the last frontier, the final great wilderness to be conquered. And now adventure athletes like you can do it.

The idea of wilderness frontiers in need of conquering reflects a 'humans taming nature' colonialist perspective that underpins past and present ecological destruction (Adams & Mulligan, 2003, pp. 1–15; Oelschlaeger, 1995).

Viewing protected natural areas as places to be 'conquered' in the pursuit of extreme sporting competition arguably contravenes the core values of nature appreciation, conservation and biodiversity protection. We again ask the question: How is it possible to combine the notions of conquering nature for individual gratification with appreciation of nature and its benefits in natural and protected areas? There may be arguments about equity for all participants in recreational activity (Curry, 2001; Bradshaw & Doak, 2022), and that an extreme sporting event has as much place in a national park as a bird-watching group; but we reject this notion.

It still appears that humans are now more focused on seeking thrills to validate ourselves as worthy and successful. A plethora of websites, YouTube postings and promotions, sports shops and adventure equipment retailers encourage participation by profiling young men and women using off-road vehicles, engaging in adrenaline-fuelled activities and running marathons in wild nature spaces. The principal objective is to compete in a demanding outdoor competition and prove that you can master something, often touted as the natural environment (for example in the quote above from Antarctic Ice Marathon). It is a global phenomenon promoted and supported by the media and commercial interests, with activities supported by politicians, local communities and companies that sell outdoor clothing and equipment (for example, Newsome et al. 2011; Newsome & Hughes, 2018). For example, note words like 'muscle', 'big show', 'mega test' and 'hammer time' on the cover of motoring magazines in Figure 27.1.

We contend that, while there may be social and personal benefits derived from such events, such benefits could also come from events that do not take place in remote, ecologically sensitive natural places, including protected areas. Moreover, as previously reported by Ewert et al. (2006), Arnegard and Sandell (2012), Newsome (2014) and, more recently, Newsome and Hughes (2018), Bartoletti et al. (2019) and Malchrowicz-Mośko et al. (2019), significant environmental concerns and management issues associated with extreme events in natural areas remain to be addressed.

There is persuasive evidence that contact with nature is beneficial at the individual and the community scale. A large body of evidence points to the individual health benefits of being in 'green spaces', amongst 'unspoilt nature' and experiencing the diversity of wildlife in natural settings (for example, see Kaplan, 2001; Berman et al., 2008; La Puma, 2019; White et al. 2019; Randler et al. 2022). There is also ample evidence regarding the wider social benefits of contact with, recreation in or simply proximity to natural areas (Kweon et al., 1998; Maas et al., 2008; Hughes, 2014). However, we contend that the benefits of

Figure 27.1 Motoring magazines on sale at a busy international airport. Author own image.

'being in nature' will be difficult to realise for many in an atmosphere of a large-scale extreme sports event, especially if it involves vehicles. All of this can be compounded by showcasing the apparent exhilaration of conquering nature during an event (as in the ice marathon).

We therefore pose the question of whether the increasing use and interpretation of nature as a backdrop for sporting events leads to the possibility of relegating the experience of nature and degrades restorative mental health benefits as people continue to lose sight of the purpose of natural and protected areas (Newsome & Hughes, 2017, 2018). Is it possible that such a trend could lead to a loss of support for our natural and protected areas, resulting in political support for change in user emphasis and paving the way for profit-driven proposals – such as events that could damage the wildlife and biodiversity values of natural environments?

However, we also acknowledge that the situation is complex. For example, Buckley (2023) discusses the mental health benefits of being in nature from different standpoints; and Brymer and Schweitzer (2013) and Clough et al. (2016) consider the mental health benefits of extreme sport. Indeed, Brymer et al. (2009)

and Brymer and Gray (2010) posited that extreme sport in natural settings can promote feelings of being at one with the natural world, or may foster a sense of connection through what was identified as life-enhancing energy. As a side note, the study by Brymer et al. (2009) focused on extreme sport participants who were older than average, and who were prepared to deconstruct and reflect on their extreme sport experience in natural areas. This suggests a sample unrepresentative of general extreme sports participants.

Beyond the individual benefits, marathons and other sporting events like mountain bike endurance races and motorised events are often described as being for a 'social cause' – for example, alleviating poverty (Oxfam Trailwalker, 2024), helping tackle child exploitation (Valkyrie Racing, 2021) or raising awareness of global warming (FIA Formula E, 2016). Clearly the topic of people's interests and what they do outdoors is highly diverse and complex. Some would argue that this is the way of the future; but the trend raises the question that organised events, especially if large scale, are not likely to be good for natural areas. There is the risk of ecological damage, trail erosion, trampling of vegetation, disturbance of wildlife and displacement of those visitors who seek less of a domineering approach and more contemplative and/or appreciative natural experiences (Newsome, 2014).

We have previously raised concerns about how the rise in adventure sporting activities in protected areas may result in negative impacts on both the biophysical environment and social nature appreciative values, alongside the proliferation of a wider message to the community that natural areas are open to anything that might be considered as fun or good exercise (Newsome & Hughes, 2017, 2018). Marathons, adventure racing or the sportification of nature are firmly established as regular global phenomena. Furthermore, the commercialisation of these activities has given rise to events that are highly organised, often with many spectators in attendance, attracting media attention and supported by advertising, retail interests, local community stakeholders and political interests.

We therefore feel it remains important to ask questions about our use of, and our attitude towards, the natural environment. Why do we need to extend activities that belong in gymnasiums, sports and entertainment arenas, playing fields, degraded land and other modified landscapes into the last frontiers of nature like Antarctica? This is especially pertinent given that many natural areas are the last refuge for wildlife of all kinds and the only place where we might find the true song of nature and find peace, quiet and tranquillity (Figure 27.2). Sports enthusiasts already have ample opportunity to do all the things they want to do in other places. We assert that getting in touch with nature does not have to be part of an event!

Figure 27.2 Antarctica is about peace, tranquillity and wildlife, and for travellers who wish to experience awe and wonder. It is not for the sportification of nature. Author own image.

Managerial implications

Event organisers need to develop guidelines that seek to prevent inappropriate activities in highly valued nature spaces and protected areas. Where events are permitted in natural areas, they should be subject to rigorous management planning.

Policy implications

Legislation should be amended to limit events and sporting activities in protected and important natural areas.

Research implications

Studies should collect further data on how sporting and allied events impact the values of other users of protected areas.

QUIZ QUESTIONS

1. What are the key social benefits of protecting natural areas and wild spaces?
2. What is the central purpose of conservation reserves?
3. To what extent do you think sporting events impede the enjoyment of passive visitors to natural areas?

DEBATE QUESTIONS

1. Should we ban sporting events from all protected areas?
2. Is conservation of nature more important than recreational access to protected areas?
3. Why is it not acceptable to allow car rallies and marathons in remote and pristine areas?
4. Are some sporting events less harmful to the conservation of nature than others?

Table 27.1 Alignment to United Nations Sustainable Development Goals

Goal	How
Good Health and Well-Being	Promotion of responsible connections to nature
Sustainable Cities and Communities	Promotion of responsible connections to nature
Climate Action	Arguing against damage to protected areas is a key aspect of biodiversity conservation
Life on Land	Arguing against damage to protected areas is a key aspect of biodiversity conservation

REFERENCES

Adams, W., & Mulligan, M. (2003). *Decolonizing nature: Strategies for conservation in a post-colonial era*. London: Earthscan.

Antarctic Ice Marathon (2024). Welcome to the world's southernmost marathon. www.icemarathon.com (accessed 10 February 2024).

Arnegard, J., & Sandell, K. (2012). Outdoor recreation in times of change. In: *6th international conference on monitoring and management of visitors in recreational and protected areas: Outdoor recreation in change – current knowledge and future challenges. Stockholm, Sweden, August 21–24, 2012.*

Bartoletti, C., Magro-Lindenkamp, T. C., & Sarriés, G. A. (2019). Adventure races in Brazil: Do stakeholders take conservation into consideration? *Environments*, *6* (7), 77.

Berman, M. G., Jonides, J., & Kaplan, S. (2008). The cognitive benefits of interacting with nature. *Psychological Science*, *19* (12), 1207–1212.

Bradshaw, K., & Doak, C. (2022). Making recreation on public lands more accessible. *Notre Dame Law Review*, *97* (1), 35–56.

Brymer, E., & Gray, T. (2010). Developing an intimate 'relationship' with nature through extreme sports participation. *Leisure/Loisir*, *34* (4), 361–374.

Brymer, E., & Schweitzer, R. (2013). Extreme sports are good for your health: A phenomenological understanding of fear and anxiety in extreme sport. *Journal of Health Psychology*, *18* (4), 477–487.

Brymer, E., Downey, G., & Gray, T. (2009). Extreme sports as a precursor to environmental sustainability. *Journal of Sport & Tourism*, *14* (2–3), 193–204.

Buckley, R. (2023). Tourism and mental health: Foundations, frameworks, and futures. *Journal of Travel Research*, *62* (1), 3–20.

Clough, P., Houge Mackenzie, S., Mallabon, L., & Brymer, E. (2016). Adventurous physical activity environments: A mainstream intervention for mental health. *Sports Medicine*, *46*, 963–968.

Curry, N. (2001). Rights of access to land for outdoor recreation in New Zealand: Dilemmas concerning justice and equity. *Journal of Rural Studies*, *17* (4), 409–419.

Ewert, A., Attarian, A., Hollenhorst, S., Russell, K., & Voight, A. (2006). Evolving adventure pursuits on public lands: Emerging challenges for management and public policy. *Journal of Park & Recreation Administration*, *24* (2).

FIA Formula E (2016, September 14) All electric racing car runs on Arctic ice cap. https://www.fiaformulae.com/en/news/6342/all-electric-racing-car-runs-on-arctic-ice-cap.

Hughes, M. (2014). Researching the links between parklands and health. In Voigt, C. & Pforr, C. (Eds), *Wellness tourism: A destination perspective* (pp. 147–160). London: Routledge.

Kaplan, R. (2001). The nature of the view from home: Psychological benefits. *Environment and Behavior*, *33* (4), 507–542.

Kweon, B.-S., Sullivan, W. C., & Wiley, A. R. (1998). Green common spaces and the social integration of inner-city older adults. *Environment and Behavior*, *30* (6), 832–858.

La Puma, J. (2019). Nature therapy: An essential prescription for health. *Alternative and Complementary Therapies*, *25* (2), 68–71.

Maas, J., van Dillen, S. M. E., Verheij, R. A., & Groenewegen, P. P. (2008). Social contacts as a possible mechanism behind the relation between green space and health. *Health and Place*, *15* (2), 586–595.

Malchrowicz-Mośko, E., Botiková, Z., & Poczta, J. (2019). 'Because we don't want to run in smog': Problems with the sustainable management of sport event tourism in protected areas (a case study of National Parks in Poland and Slovakia). *Sustainability*, *11* (2), 325.

Newsome, D. (2014). Appropriate policy development and research needs in response to adventure racing in protected areas. *Biological Conservation*, *171*, 259–269.

Newsome, D., & Hughes, M. (2017). Jurassic World as a contemporary wildlife tourism theme park allegory. *Current Issues in Tourism*, *20*, 1311–1319.

Newsome, D., & Hughes, M. (2018). The contemporary conservation reserve visitor phenomenon! *Biodiversity and Conservation*, *27*, 521–529.

Newsome, D., Lacroix, C., & Pickering, C. (2011) Adventure racing events in Australia: Context, assessment and implications for protected area management. *Australian Geographer*, *42* (4), 403–418.

Oelschlaeger, M. (1995). Soul of the wilderness: The wild, the tame, and the folly of sustainable development. *International Journal of Wilderness*, *1* (2), 5–7.

Oxfam Trailwalker (2024). Oxfam Trailwalker Melbourne 2024: Together for adventure for the last time ever. https://trailwalker.oxfam.org.au/ (accessed 11 February 2024).

Randler, C., Murawiec, S., & Tryjanowski, P. (2022). Committed bird-watchers gain greater psychological restorative benefits compared to those less committed regardless of expertise. *Ecopsychology*, *14* (2), 101–110.

Valkyrie Racing (2021). Press and media. https://www.valkyrieracing.com/press-media (accessed 11 February 2024).

White, M. P., Alcock, I., Grellier, J., Wheeler, B. W., Hartig, T., Warber, S. L., … & Fleming, L. E. (2019). Spending at least 120 minutes a week in nature is associated with good health and wellbeing. *Scientific Reports*, *9* (1), 1–11.

28 THE GOOD THE BAD AND THE NOISY

The paradox(s) created by motorised events in green spaces

Jim Macbeth, David Newsome and Cheryl Jones

AIM

The fundamental aim of this chapter is to alert you to the complexities involved in hosting events, specifically the siting of motorised events in protected areas. By interrogating political power inequalities in leisure and tourism, you will be more aware of the dynamics driving the social, political and economic forces involved in holding events.

DOI: 10.4324/9781003488729-34

LEARNING OBJECTIVES

1. You should become more cognisant of the conflicting values involved in holding and siting events, but also recognise that most decisions, public and private, involve conflicting values.
2. Events are not neutral; nor simply positive for the so-called host community or for governing bodies.
3. You can learn to use the concept of 'paradox' in planning and decision-making, and recognise issues surrounding diversity, including gender, wealth and ethnicity; who misses out.

Theoretical focus and significance

Central to this chapter are two conceptual positions, one from sociology and one from environmental science. The sociological theory of social capital allows us to understand the value conflicts that can and do arise in situations such as major events. At the same time, the underlying knowledge base from environmental science reminds us that there are impacts on the environment, usually negative. We are emphasising that having a more complex understanding of social dynamics and conflicting values highlights the practical value of analysis using complex concepts and theories. Events represent conflicting value positions; and, for motorised events in green spaces, the value conflicts are stark.

Practical focus and significance

The practical value of this discourse is in giving you an understanding of the complexity of value conflicts where motorised events are being proposed. Further, our four-stage model can be adapted to help you understand an existing or proposed event. You should become a more aware and complex thinker. You should recognise that all events sit within the contemporary context of severe climate uncertainty and political upheaval, including issues of autocracy and democracy, diversity and inequality.

TOPIC – THE GOOD THE BAD AND THE NOISY: THE PARADOX(S) CREATED BY MOTORISED EVENTS IN GREEN SPACES

Now to the case study and understanding a situation with fundamental value conflicts. We are using two paradoxes to focus attention on the value conflict inherent in the siting of motorised events in green spaces. The first paradox is between the values and intentions underlying the creation of green spaces in cities *as opposed to* the underlying values that 'ride' along with competition, aggression and noise when we slot in motorised events. Parks, including marine and urban parks, along with simply 'wild' areas, provide an escape from our urban everyday life to the tranquillity of nature.

But there is another fundamental paradox when we consider the social capital that develops within the various and contradictory 'camps' involved in motorised events: simplistically, between those for and those against motorised events in protected areas.

This chapter addresses these paradoxes. The context is the siting of the 1996 Australian Formula 1 Grand Prix within an urban green space – namely Albert Park in Melbourne, Victoria, Australia. It is worth noting here that the decision by the Victorian State government, led by then State Premier Jeff Kennett, to establish this event in a park can also be understood in the context of the rise of neo-liberal power in Australia, as elsewhere (Lowes, 2004).

Population pressure, including from tourism and events, is obviously often in direct conflict with the purposes for which protected areas and urban green spaces are intended. Motorised events are not the only pressure as uncontrolled individual use, infrastructure development and other events can all contribute to the degradation of both conserved and created green areas and their purposes. Our focus here is on motorised events.

> Urban and national parks have specific purposes, including the protection of special environments, flora and fauna. They provide spaces for Australians and visitors to understand our unique landscape and to learn how to 'tread lightly' on the land. Tranquillity and peaceful enjoyment are crucial to these objectives. Motors, especially mass motor events and their helicopters, are incompatible with these objectives, including in urban areas. (Macbeth et al., 2014)

In our previous publications we provided environmental context and outlined a possible model for understanding the structural and social meaning of motorised events, using the Australian Grand Prix (see Macbeth et al., 2014; Jones et al., 2016 a, 2016b). This annual event is held in an urban park close to the centre of

Melbourne, including proximity to hundreds of apartments. Such an event held in a protected park will, by definition, conflict with intended natural values, including environmental protection, solitude and serenity – not to mention the joy of being able to see wildlife (Lowes, 2004).

All motorised events have some sort of corporate structure, whether a car club day out or a Grand Prix, and all events have environmental impacts in one way or another. We have conceptualised motorised events into four layers – micro, meso, macro and mega – to help explain impacts and structures, as outlined in the following extracts from Macbeth et al. (2014):

> Micro level events are local, run by volunteers and often sponsored by a vehicle club. These events are primarily about having a good time in the bush, sometimes with light competition. The only spectators, if any, will be family and friends, and other club members – Sunday afternoon fun such as family picnic days, working bees, tag-along-tours, intra and inter club events.

Meso level events are generally larger, such as Variety Club events – still amateur and voluntarily managed, but attracting participants from outside the local area, possibly interstate. Again, these are not-for-profit operations but supported by sponsorship from local and/ or national … businesses.

Macro level events take us into the professional and for-profit realm of motorised events. They may be 'feeders' into larger events attracting international competitors and spectators from interstate. State and local governments often seek and sponsor such events. This level will attract media attention and includes events such as Australasian Safari, part of an adventure genre of which the Dakar rally is the global pinnacle.

Mega events are international competitions, run by international organisations, professional and for-profit such as the Australian Grand Prix and Australian Rally Championship. Competitors are also professionals. These events are highly prized by governments to promote tourism and investment involving global financial and global media coverage with international spectators.

These models allow us to understand the events themselves; but, when we shift our gaze to the social, there is a fundamental paradox: social capital is strengthened for both 'sides' of the debate surrounding such hosting. The concept of social capital is about networks and clubs, advocacy groups and employee networks, all of which can generate positive social capital for their 'members'. There are two main types of social capital – bonding and bridging (or linking). Bonding social capital is primarily about relationships within a group (informal or formal). The current analysis of singer Taylor Swift's fandom, the Swifties, is a good example of an informal, sometimes face-to-face, network (Macbeth, 2024). Bonding social capital is often shown as good for mental health, partly because of the activity and commitment and partly because of the connectedness it creates with other people. The research around fandom uses the term parasocial *relationships* (Hoffner and Bond, 2022), which can become counterproductive when fandom becomes parasocial *attachments* (Stever, 2017).

The paradox with bonding social capital is there will be competing interests reflected in the simplistic notion of those for and those against motorised events in protected areas. *Advocacy* groups form strong bonds because they share a view for or against motorised events in protected areas. Social capital also develops for fans who follow such events, for example Grands Prix. The Australian Grand Prix Corporation (AGPC, 2024) claimed 452,055 attendees in 2024, so this shared experience creates strong social capital.

Likewise, the anti-Grand Prix advocacy group in Melbourne shares a commitment to protect Albert Park from the racing cars. The 'Save Albert Park' group (www.savealbertpark.org) was formed before the city's first race, protesting from 1994 (Save Albert Park, 2020 [1995]), and was still active at the time of writing in 2024 (Florance, 2015). In fact, it has filed freedom of information (FOI) requests about disputed attendee numbers (OVIC, 2023). The group's longevity is evidence of very strong bonding social capital.

Bridging social capital is also evident in the links made by both sides of the debate over the Melbourne Grand Prix with, of course, clear international connections in the Grand Prix 'community'. The competition is obviously international, and indications are that Australians travel to other countries to attend Grands Prix; thus international relationships are established at personal, government and corporate levels.

It appears that the main supporter 'group' of the Grand Prix comprises the AGPC and the State of Victoria government, along with sponsors. The linking of social capital between these parties appears to be strong given the costs absorbed by the State (actual amounts were unavailable due to the ongoing FOI dispute at the time of writing). However, in March 2023 *The Age* newspaper claimed the government had spent $78.1 million supporting the AGPC (Waters, 2023).

The overall message we wish to convey in this chapter is that our environment is the platform for all life, and vital for our physical and mental health. However, we now live in a world of degraded and declining natural areas, alongside massive urban expansion and an increasing human population. The environment has many pressures placed on it. Some of these are difficult to manage, for example, climate change. At the same time, we have choices about what we do and where. With motorised events taking place in nature and urban green space it appears that the social capital developed and fostered by governments, big business and advertising has considerable sway when compared to the environmental movement. It can thus become noise, pollution and 'aggression' versus quiet contemplation and the appreciation of nature. The social capital surrounding the diversity of environmental issues is fragmented and complex, and for now it would seem that the 'paradox' remains. But for how long?

Managerial implications

All managers, including public officials and politicians, have personal value conflicts when dealing with stakeholders (including staff) while also having to understand the conflicting value positions of public, political and corporate interests. We have written this chapter to help highlight these value conflicts. Of course, you then have to work with those conflicts to arrive at decisions. Often, they will be made politically, which may undermine managerial decisions. How you deal with public policy issues will be part of your task, and in too many cases will undermine what you see as the best outcome. Students and other researchers in this area need to unpack the value conflicts, which means also understanding their own value perspectives. Research papers and reports should therefore make such value conflicts clear to readers and decision-makers.

Policy implications

From a policy perspective, events should not be seen in a value and power vacuum. Events are not simply leisure activities; for millions of people they are occupational sites, while for other millions they are tourism experiences. Policy should therefore recognise this, along with critical social issues of diversity and environmental issues of species diversity, all in the context of social change. Arguably, the United Nations Sustainable Development Goals (UNSDGs) are now outdated due to obvious climate change chaos and the subsequent SD ethical issues (Macbeth, 2005). But they are still a useful starting point. The policy question(s) for proponents of macro- and mega-level events require that the UNSDGs and issues in the 1987 Brundtland Report (*Our Common Future*) be addressed (United Nations, 2015, n.d.; Brundtland, 1987).

Research implications

Macro and mega events, for example, are justified or disputed on many levels by various actors, ranging from business lobbyists to social dissidents, and from politicians to environmental scientists. Theoretically informed research will seek to 'unpack' the complexities of such events. You might ask why in 2023 the Victorian State government cancelled its plan to host the Commonwealth Games, a major international sporting event. Economics is not the only aspect worth understanding. Each of the quiz/debate issues below imply research needs in themselves.

QUIZ QUESTIONS

1. What is a paradox? Give examples from your life experience (not from this chapter).
2. Explore the meaning of each level of event – micro, meso, macro, mega. Give examples in your country.
3. What gender or ethnicity issues should be explored in relation to any event – whether existing or proposed, micro, meso, macro or mega?
4. Explore event planning and hosting in the context of forms of government, including, for example, democratic, authoritarian or theocratic.

DEBATE QUESTIONS

1. Explore social capital issues in your local community, university or local government area.
2. Can motorised events ever be compatible with communities and environmental protection?
3. Select an aspect of the 1987 Brundtland Report and debate the impacts of a macro- or mega-level event. Alternatively, do the same for the UNSDGs.
4. Debate the UNSDGs as now outdated (or not) due to obvious climate change chaos and the SD ethical issues that arise (Macbeth, 2005).
5. Debate the policy question(s) that face proponents of macro- and mega-level events using the UNSDGs and issues in the Brundtland Report.

Table 28.1 Alignment to United Nations Sustainable Development Goals

Goal	How and Desirable
Good Health and Well-Being	Connectedness to communities
Affordable and Clean Energy	Use of renewables
Reduced Inequalities	Diversity
Sustainable Cities and Communities	Resolution of the paradox
Responsible Consumption and Production	No plastics
Climate Action	Compatibility with environmental protection
Life on Land	Compatibility with environmental protection
Peace, Justice and Strong Institutions	Resolution of the paradox

REFERENCES

Australian Grand Prix Corporation. (2024). https://www.grandprix.com.au/#:~:text=Circuit%20in%202025.-,After%20all%20the%20adrenaline%2Dfuelled%2C%20heart%2Dpumping%20action%20at,welcome%20you%20back%20once%20again.

Brundtland, G. H. (1987). *Report of the World Commission on Environment and Development: 'Our common future'*. New York: United Nations. https://sustainabledevelopment.un.org/content/documents/5987our-common-future.pdf.

Florance, L. (2015, March 11). In pictures: Melbourne's Formula One Grand Prix protests in the early years. *ABC News*. https://www.abc.net.au/news/2015-03-12/in-pictures-grand-prix-protests-in-the-early-years/6282724.

Jones, C., Newsome, D. and Macbeth, J. (2016a). Governance and environmental implications of motorized events: Insights from Australia and avenues for further Inquiry. *Current Issues in Tourism*, *19*, 680–696.

Jones, C., Newsome, D. and Macbeth, J. (2016a). Understanding the conflicting values associated with motorised recreation in protected areas, *Ambio*, *45*, 323–330.

Lowes, M. (2004). Neoliberal power politics and the controversial siting of the Australian Grand Prix motorsport event in an urban park. *Loisir et Société / Society and Leisure*, *27*(1), 69–88.

Macbeth, J. (2005). Towards an ethics platform for tourism, *Annals of Tourism Research*, *32*(4), 962–984.

Macbeth, J. (2024). Personal observation and analysis of Taylor Swift's Eras tour of Australia.

OVIC. (2023). 'Save Albert Park Inc' and Australian Grand Prix Corporation (Freedom of Information) [2023] VICmr 84 (14 August 2023). Office of the Victorian Information Commissioner.https://ovic.vic.gov.au/decision/save-albert-park-inc-and-australian-grand-prix-corporation-freedom-of-information-2023-vicmr-84-14-august-2023/.

Save Albert Park. (2020 [1995], October–November). *SAPIENS: Newsletter of Save Albert Park Inc.*, 294. https://nla.gov.au/nla.obj-3169818762/view.

Stever, G. S. (2017). Evolutionary theory and reactions to mass media: Understanding parasocial attachment. *Psychology of Popular Media Culture*, *6*(2), 95–102. https://doi.org/10.1037/ppm0000116 (accessed May 22, 2024).

United Nations (2015). *Transforming our world: The 2030 Agenda for Sustainable Development.* New York: UN. https://sdgs.un.org/sites/default/files/publications/21252030%20Agenda%20for%20Sustainable%20Development%20web.pdf.

United Nations (n.d.). *The 17 Goals*. https://sdgs.un.org/goals (accessed May 22, 2024).

World Commission on Environment and Development (1987). *Report of the World Commission on Environment and Development: 'Our common future'* [Brundtland Report]. New York: United Nations.

Macbeth, J., Jones, C. and Newsome, D. (2014, March 14). Does the Australian Grand Prix belong in a public park? *The Conversation*. https://theconversation.com/does-the-australian-grand-prix-belong-in-a-public-park-23594.

Hoffner, C. A. and Bond, B. J. (2022, June). Parasocial relationships, social media, & wellbeing. *Current Opinion in Psychology, 45*, 101306. https://doi.org/10.1016/j.copsyc.2022.101306.

Waters, Cara. (2023, March 31). How the Australian Grand Prix brings in the millions. *The Age*. https://www.theage.com.au/national/victoria/how-the-australian-grand-prix-brings-in-the-millions-20230330-p5cwk6.html.

29 LONDON 2012 What the Olympic Games' legacy of sustainability means for events today

Verity Postlethwaite, Eleni Theodoraki and Mike Duignan

AIM

The aim of the chapter is to review the framing of sustainability during the London 2012 Olympic and Paralympic Games event lifecycle, with a particular focus on the role of the Commission for a Sustainable London 2012 (CSL).

LEARNING OBJECTIVES

1. Contextualize the sustainability claims made across the hosting of the London 2012 Olympic and Paralympic Games.
2. Frame a number of key actors in the management of sustainability during the London 2012 Olympic and Paralympic Games.
3. Review the evolving narratives on sustainability, assurance and being a 'critical friend' in the Commission for a Sustainable London 2012's lifecycle.

Theoretical focus and significance

The theoretical focus of this chapter is the notion and interpretation of sustainability, with a focus on how different organizations interpreted the process of framing and assuring sustainability measures for an international sport event. It is important to talk about the concepts of sustainability performance and assurance right now given the climate emergency and the lessons learned from the organization of the London 2012 Olympic and Paralympic Games.

Practical focus and significance

A number of practical sustainability measures and programmes have been evidenced and illustrated since the hosting of the London 2012 Olympic and Paralympic Games – a key point being the notion that the London Games were the boldest modern Olympiad to claim sustainability across the life course of the event. A number of events have continued in the footsteps of those Games to assure various audiences that sustainability is at the heart of event planning and delivery. However, the actors who hold events to account have differed, and measures of sustainability remain inconsistent.

TOPIC – LONDON 2012: WHAT THE OLYMPIC GAMES' LEGACY OF SUSTAINABILITY MEANS FOR EVENTS TODAY

From the outset, the bid and preparation for the London 2012 Games aimed to make it a groundbreaking sustainable event. According to the United Nations, sustainability is "development that meets the needs of the present without compromising the ability of future generations to meet their own needs" (Theoradaki,

2016, p.197). This concept is as much about legacy as it is about environmental impact. Postlethwaite et al. (2022) noted that the BBC comedy *Twenty Twelve*, which satirized the organization of London 2012, highlighted this point. In one episode, the (fictional) head of sustainability describes the Games as a "catalyst for change" and "improving the quality of life in London's East End"–outcomes echoed in the actual UK government and mayor of London's joint report on the Games' legacy.

Beyond satire and official reports, recognition has come from multiple voices and actions lauding the London 2012 organizing efforts to reach their sustainability goals. For example, in 2012, Achim Steiner, executive director of the UN's environmental management group, praised London 2012 for demonstrating that "sustainability is not theory but infinitely doable" in practice (Degun, 2012). Ten years later, local school groups continue to use the Olympic Park site as an outdoor classroom to learn about how East London's polluted waterways and brownfield land were transformed into a new public park (Queen Elizabeth Olympic Park, n.d.). From a management perspective, understanding how this was achieved–specifically the governance in place–is crucial to gauging how London 2012 has influenced subsequent events in the UK, from football tournaments to festivals. More importantly, London's hosting of the Olympic Games effectively changed the way we, as consumers of such events, talk about sustainability.

In business terms, hosting an edition of the Olympic and Paralympic Games is akin to managing a fast-food franchise. The host city signs a contract with the International Olympic Committee (IOC) agreeing to specific operational guidelines concerning time, budget, and quality. Hosting the Games is an extremely risky business (Flyvbjerg et al., 2003) – if a global recession hits (as it did during the lead-up to London 2012) or a global pandemic disrupts plans (as with Tokyo 2020), the host city bears the financial burden, often using public funds originally earmarked for legacy plans. The challenge is that "the host city" is not a single entity but a cacophony of actors, with no specific individual or organization in charge. Jeremy Beeton, director general of the temporary government agency coordinating London 2012, described the complex delivery structure: "you have this marvellous situation where you've got powerful figures all over the place running departments, boroughs and the city, [but] they're not governance structures because you can't govern" (Postlethwaite et al., 2022). This is often referred to as the "problem of many hands".

In the late 1990s and early 2000s, the UK did not have a strong record of delivering complex projects on a national scale (Postlethwaite, 2020). London, in particular, suffered reputational and economic damage during the "Picketts Lock affair" of 2001, which reportedly cost London its bid to host the 2005 World Athletics Championships. However, London's successful stewardship of the 2012 Olympics demonstrated the UK's transformation. A key factor in achieving its sustainability goals was the ability of disparate stakeholder groups across the public and private sectors to work together under a common vision. London first submitted its application to host the Olympics in 2003 and was formally announced as the winner in 2005. During the initial planning and preparation period, several authorities with varying connections to sustainability were created. For example, the London Organizing Committee for the Olympic Games (LOCOG) had an autonomous role in delivering London 2012 on behalf of the UK government, the City of London, and the International Olympic Committee. Although sustainability goals were part of the common vision, they were not always the highest priority for LOCOG and others.

Early in the development of London 2012, political and management actors formed the Commission for a Sustainable London 2012 (Theodoraki, 2018). This commission oversaw the Games' sustainability programme, including monitoring sustainability claims and practices by LOCOG and the Olympic Delivery Authority. Sebastian Coe, chairman of LOCOG, highlighted that the Games aimed to demonstrate sustainability on an "unprecedented scale". He noted that London 2012's relentless pursuit of sustainability influenced every decision in developing the Olympic Park and staging the Games (Institute for Government, 2013). These Games were the first to meet the sustainable event management British Standard (BS) 8901 on events sustainability management systems, which paved the way for a new international standard on sustainability, showcasing the impact of these Games on international sustainability policy.

The initiatives and planning of London 2012 were scrutinized by the Commission for a Sustainable London 2012, which adopted the WWF-endorsed One Planet Living sustainability framework, used Dow insulation within the Olympic Stadium, committed to zero-waste targets, and "greened" the Games' supply chain. However, when results were inconsistent or negative, this was documented. For instance, before the Games began, *The Guardian* newspaper's environment correspondent, Fiona Harvey (2012), wrote that the "greenest Olympics ever" could have been greener. Similarly, Shaun McCarthy, chair of the Commission for a Sustainable London 2012, bluntly stated in early 2013 that, although London delivered the most sustainable Games ever, no Olympic or Paralympic Games could be truly sustainable given the excessive resource use. The Commission ultimately positioned itself as a "critical friend", championing the use of London 2012's learnings in future event management infrastructure (see McCarthy, 2013).

Research from various sources shows that collective efforts since 2012 have contributed to better practices and conversations around event hosting (see McCarthy, 2013). For example, in September 2021, English Premier League team Tottenham Hotspur partnered with Sky for the #GameZero initiative, putting on the world's first net-zero football match; and the city of Birmingham claimed that its 2022 Commonwealth Games was the most sustainable multisport event to date. Both events were results of the sustainable legacy pioneered by the London 2012 organizers. However, since London 2012, no equivalent commission for a sustainable event has been established or legally codified, raising concerns about who assures and takes responsibility for sustainability practices during an event's lifecycle.

Managerial implications

Managers should critically reflect on who, beyond the claims of the event, can act as a "critical friend" to ensure that sustainability claims, measures, and practices are delivered to the standard set out by the event organizing committee.

Policy implications

Policy makers should consider the sustainability framing and monitoring across the life course of the event (i.e. the pre-bid, bid, preparation, delivery, and legacy phases) and what bodies are appropriately resourced and positioned to hold the event organizers to account in relation to sustainability claims.

Research implications

The conclusions are relevant to scholars considering aspects of event management, sustainability and sport, and governance of sporting events as they contribute learning from over a decade since delivery of the Games in London 2012. This chapter's findings and discussion emphasize the discursive complexity of defining sustainability and assurance across the Games' lifecycle by the Commission for a Sustainable London 2012. The chapter raises questions about how the contribution and value of the Commission can be understood; and, perhaps most importantly, how this knowledge and learning can be used in the current context of the "new norm" event model being promoted by the International Olympic Committee and others. In terms of sustainability, there was one form of assurance conceived and another form of assurance delivered. This contributes to an important revisiting of the professional or accepted standards around sustainability claims and events.

QUIZ QUESTIONS

1. Who authored and produced the sustainability strategy for London 2012?
2. What problem did the management of sustainability claims for London 2012 face?
3. What role did the Commission for a Sustainable London 2012 have?
4. What sustainability management standard did London 2012 influence?

DEBATE QUESTIONS

1. How can we prevent the gigantism and associated unsustainable aspects of the summer Olympic and Paralympic Games?
2. As "owner" of the Olympic Games, should responsibility for sustainability rest with the International Olympic Committee?
3. Is it clear what sustainability means in the context of an international sporting event?

Table 29.1 Alignment to United Nations Sustainable Development Goals

Goal	How
Sustainable Cities and Communities	Cities as hosts affect and are directly affected by (mostly) government-led infrastructure projects that precede the staging of the Olympic Games. In recent years we have seen a plethora of negative impacts stemming from unsustainable behaviours, poor long-term legacy planning and the event's sheer gigantism.
Peace, Justice and Strong Institutions	Considering the scale and scope of Olympic-related projects, strong institutions are needed to ensure the projects aim to serve post-Games, long-term *legacy requirements* rather than short-term *Games requirements*. The CSL was envisaged as an independent organization with a fixed-term assurance role and a remit to ensure live, ongoing event preparations. This is not the typical *ex post* assurance role that is performed by auditors. This deviation from standard practice can be explained by: (a) the one-off opportunity to influence, as they happen, the sustainability performance of events that are not periodic; and (b) the particular ethos of the Olympic Games undertaking, patriotism and national branding.

REFERENCES

Degun, T. (2012, September 22). Glowing praise for London 2012 sustainability measures. *Inside the Games*. https://www.insidethegames.biz/articles/1010936/glowing-praise-for-london-2012-sustainability-measures.

Flyvbjerg, B., Bruzelius, N., & Rothengatter, W. (2003). *Megaprojects and risk: An anatomy of ambition*. Cambridge: Cambridge University Press.

Harvey, F. (2012, July 19). London 2012 falls short of "greenest ever" targets, report shows. *The Guardian*. https://www.theguardian.com/sport/2012/jul/19/olympic-games-green-targets.

Institute for Government (2013). Making the Games. https://www.instituteforgovernment.org.uk/our-work/policy-making/making-policy-better/making-games.

McCarthy, S. (ed.). (2013, February). London 2012: Sustainable legacy? Environmental Scientist, Special edition. https://www.the-ies.org/sites/default/files/journals/env_sci_feb_13.pdf.

Postlethwaite, V. (2020). *Inspiring a generation(?): Interconnecting discourses between governing actors, policy, and legacy around London 2012*. PhD Thesis, University of Worcester. https://eprints.worc.ac.uk/10117.

Postlethwaite, V., Theodoraki, E., & Duignan, M. (2022, August 11) London 2012: what the Olympic Games' legacy of sustainability means for events today. The Conversation, https://theconversation.com/london-2012-what-the-olympic-games-legacy-of-sustainability-means-for-events-today-187308.

Queen Elizabeth Olympic Park (n.d.). Things to do for schools. https://www.queenelizabetholympicpark.co.uk/the-park/things-to-do/for-schools.

Theodoraki E (2016). The problem with sporting mega-event impact assessment. In Transparency International (Ed.), *Global corruption report: Sport* (Chapter 3.3). Routledge. doi:10.4324/9781315695709.

Theodoraki, E. (2018). Third-party assurance of sustainability reporting: The case of the London 2012 Olympic and Paralympic games. In B. P. McCullough & T. B. Kellison (Eds.), *Routledge handbook of sport and the environment* (pp. 241–252). Routledge. https://doi.org/10.4324/9781315619514-18.

30 MARCH MADNESS AND THE ENVIRONMENTAL IMPACTS OF SPORT EVENTS

Brian McCullough

AIM

Discuss the factors that contribute to the comprehensive environmental impact of large sporting events.

DOI: 10.4324/9781003488729-36

LEARNING OBJECTIVES

LEARNING OBJECTIVES

1. Identify the challenges with calculating the environmental impact of events.
2. Describe the challenges that practitioners encounter to reduce the impacts of events.
3. Discuss the factors that may put environmental impacts of sport events into context.

Theoretical focus and significance

The concepts focus predominately on impacts of fan travel and impacts of attending a sporting event. The chapter highlights the theoretical and methodological challenges to calculating the environmental impact of sporting events.

Practical focus and significance

The practical focus is on the difficulties for practitioners to predict and then eliminate their environmental impacts of sporting events. It suggests that practitioners should improve their efforts while also considering what constitutes an acceptable limit of environmental impacts.

TOPIC – MARCH MADNESS AND THE ENVIRONMENTAL IMPACTS OF SPORT EVENTS

The March Madness tournament, hosted by the US National Collegiate Athletic Association (NCAA) for 68 men's and women's basketball teams, takes place at various sites across the country. This annual sporting event is a part of the nation's sports culture, with 50 million Americans filling out team brackets (tree diagrams for knock-out tournaments) to predict the winners of each game. Consequently, viewership is so widespread, encompassing sport and non-sport fans alike, that estimates of a decrease in US gross domestic product (GDP), or American work output, can total $1.4 billion per hour during the men's tournament (Challenger, Gray & Christmas, 2014).

Across this three-week tournament, games are played at various host sites that rotate annually across the country. Basketball fans travel to these sites to support their respective collegiate team, along with local fans wanting to experience March Madness. The men's tournament generates $1.3 billion in annual revenues for the NCAA from ticket sales, merchandising, broadcast rights, and sponsorship (AP News, 2024). Therefore, producing and consuming such a widespread event, culminating in the semi-final and final games in a football stadium for greater attendance, has a tremendous economic impact. However, the event also has an immense environmental impact when you consider the production and consumption for games hosted on neutral sites – where teams (and their fans) may need to travel up to 3,000 miles from college campuses to host locations.

Despite the economic gains, it is worth examining the environmental impact of sporting events like the NCAA March Madness tournament. Previously, researchers have explored the environmental impact of mega-events like the Olympics and other hallmark events hosted at multiple sites but in the same city (Cooper & McCullough, 2021). They typically look at participant and spectator travel to the event since that is the largest contributing factor to an event's carbon footprint. However, much of this research ignores other economic activities associated with a sporting event but that are commonly included in the scope of an economic impact assessment. McCullough et al. (2020) found that, while economic impact assessments use broader scopes to maximize such impacts (see Crompton, 1995), sport organizations typically limit the scope of their environmental impact to the stadium only. The researchers argued that both the consumption and production of a sporting event should be included in an environmental impact assessment, as in an economic impact assessment.

Given the limited research into lengthy, multi-site events like March Madness and the limited scope of previous environmental impact studies on sporting events, Cooper and McCullough (2021) used the 2019 men's tournament as a context to apply the earlier framework and rationale of McCullough et al. (2020) to assess the environmental impact of a sporting event. Cooper and McCullough found that fan and team travel was the biggest source of carbon emissions (79.95%) of the total; and hotel stays (6.83%), food (6.37%), stadium operations (5.9%), and general waste (0.95%) were also assessed. While the study made certain assumptions based on peer-reviewed methods to calculate each category's carbon emissions or equivalents, these assumptions may have overestimated some categories, and other carbon emission categories (e.g., onsite transportation estimates) were not included. The authors argue that such tradeoffs present a fair, albeit not complete, assessment of the event's environmental impact. In total, "463 million pounds of CO2 equivalent emissions. That's about 1,100 pounds (499 kilograms) for every player, coach and fan who attends. That amount is the same as driving over 1,200 miles (1,930 kilometers) in a typical sedan" (McCullough, 2023).

Practical implications

This chapter presents various ways to reduce the environmental impact of the March Madness tournament. First is more regional placement of teams, which may be a pressing need as there are suggestions that the tournament may expand beyond its current 68-team format to 100+ teams. While it would be extremely difficult, if not impossible, to discourage fans from attending games, thus reducing carbon emissions from travel, a regional format, especially in earlier rounds involving more teams, could greatly reduce the environmental impact of those rounds.

Second, the NCAA could require that bidding host cities and venues meet specific environmental credentials. It already stipulates a minimum number of hotel beds within a particular radius of the host venue. Additional requirements could include environmentally friendly credentials for accommodations in that radius and prioritizing more environmentally sustainability managed venues, resulting in decreased energy and utility usage and the possibility of reduced landfill waste generated for the event.

Third, the NCAA could prioritize cities with more accessible public transportation infrastructure for travel between airports, hotels, and host venues. While Cooper and McCullough did not examine this aspect, the reduction of onsite carbon emissions has been a priority for other sporting events (Martins et al., 2022; Trail & McCullough, 2021).

Research implications

While reducing environmental impacts across all business sectors is essential, we must recognize that we all have such impacts through simple human activities. This is not to excuse sporting events from their responsibility to be as sustainable as possible. Still, it raises the point that mass gatherings like the NCAA March Madness tournament and other sporting events will have environmental impacts. Research such as by Cooper and McCullough (2021) indicates potential areas to reduce the environmental impact of such events and improve the methods and measures to refine and improve future environmental impact assessments.

It is also worth discussing what are considered 'acceptable' levels of carbon emissions. While some may take a cost-benefit analysis approach, weighing environmental impacts against economic gains, others may suggest significantly reducing or eliminating attendance (Cooper & Alderman, 2021; Gammelsæter & Loland, 2023). While barring spectators is not practical – since the sport is a social event – economic principles still apply whereby individuals will choose other activities over attending such events, which does not eliminate their environmental impact. Instead, it shifts their impact to another activity.

Finally, the 2024 Women's March Madness tournament attract record viewership and attendance figures, so there is no doubt it is gaining popularity and will continue to expand. Such expansion suggests that the highest-ranked team will not host the initial rounds of the tournament, but instead the women's games will follow the neutral site format of the men's tournament. While it will be important to reduce the environmental impact of both the men's and the women's tournaments, it is vital to consider acceptable levels of environmental impact as the women's tournament expands and is more heavily attended.

DEBATE QUESTIONS

1. What are acceptable levels of environmental impact for sporting events?
2. What are the biggest priorities for sport events to reduce their impact?
3. What policies should be mandated to reduce the impact of sporting events?

QUIZ QUESTIONS

1. What are the biggest contributing factors to the environmental impact of a sporting event?
2. What can be done to reduce the environmental impact of sporting events?
3. Are there additional environmental impacts that must be considered? If so, what?

Table 30.1 Alignment to United Nations Sustainable Development Goals

Goal	How
Industry, Innovation and Infrastructure	Sustainable transportation and location of facilities
Sustainable Cities and Communities	Sustainable transportation and location of facilities
Responsible Consumption and Production	Environmental impacts of economic activity
Climate Action	Reducing the environmental impacts of sporting events

REFERENCES

AP News. (2024, February 2). *NCAA generates nearly $1.3 billion in revenue for 2022–23: Division I payouts reach $669 million.* https://apnews.com/article/ncaa-revenue-mens-basketball-tournament-d721a558bed2cdcd7b5539173b454945.

Challenger, Gray & Christmas. (2014, March 11). *March Madness could cost employers $1.2B: Challenger 2014 March Madness report.* https://www.challengergray.com/blog/march-madness-could-cost-employers-12b/.

Cooper, J. A., & Alderman, D. H. (2021). Cancelling March Madness exposes opportunities for a more sustainable sports tourism economy. In Lew, A. A., Cheer, J. M., Brouder, P., & Mostafanezhad, M. (Eds.), *Global tourism and COVID-19: Implications for theory and practice* (pp. 71–81). Routledge.

Cooper, J. A., & McCullough, B. P. (2021). Bracketing sustainability: Carbon footprinting March Madness to rethink sustainable tourism approaches and measurements. *Journal of Cleaner Production*, *318*, 128475. https://doi.org/10.1016/j.jclepro.2021.128475.

Crompton, J. L. (1995). Economic impact analysis of sports facilities and events: Eleven sources of misapplication. *Journal of Sport Management*, *9*(1), 14–35.

Gammelsæter, H., & Loland, S. (2023). Code red for elite sport: A critique of sustainability in elite sport and a tentative reform programme. *European Sport Management Quarterly*, *23*(1), 104–124. https://doi.org/10.1080/16184742.2022.2096661.

Martins, R., Pereira, E., Rosado, A., Marôco, J., McCullough, B., & Mascarenhas, M. (2022). Understanding spectator sustainable transportation intentions in international sport tourism events. *Journal of Sustainable Tourism*, *30*(8), 1972–1991. https://doi.org/10.1080/09669582.2021.1991936.

McCullough, B. P. (2023, March 15). *What's the carbon footprint of March Madness?* The Conversation. https://theconversation.com/whats-the-carbon-footprint-of-march-madness-201540.

McCullough, B. P., Orr, M., & Watanabe, N. M. (2020). Measuring externalities: The imperative next step to sustainability assessment in sport. *Journal of Sport Management*, *34*(5), 393–402. https://doi.org/10.1123/jsm.2019-0254.

Trail, G. T., & McCullough, B. P. (2021). A longitudinal study of sustainability attitudes, intentions, and behaviors. *Sustainability Science*, *16*(5), 1503–1518. https://doi.org/10.1007/s11625-021-00954-7.

CONCLUSIONS AND RECOMMENDATIONS

Mike Duignan

Events and Society delved into the multifaceted impacts of events on individuals and communities, exploring themes of social connection, cultural identity, economic inequality, and environmental sustainability. The book reveals the transformative power of festivals, sports events, and cultural celebrations, emphasizing their potential to foster deep connections, combat loneliness, and promote social change.

Festivals play a crucial role in fostering meaningful connections between individuals and their environments. The concept of 'festival landscapes' highlights how these events can alter participants' sense of place and community, promoting stewardship of the landscape. For instance, festivals in Lutruwita/Tasmania demonstrate how such events can cultivate a profound appreciation of natural spaces, urging event organizers to prioritize fostering these interactions to enhance positive impacts. The historical analysis of 17th-century Naples illustrates the importance of civic festivals in combating loneliness and fostering social connections. These insights advocate for integrating historical practices into contemporary event planning to nurture community solidarity and well-being, particularly in post-pandemic contexts.

The London 2012 Olympics and Paralympics highlight the challenges of translating elite sports success into widespread grassroots participation. While the Olympics boosted the UK's elite sports infrastructure, the broader claim of inspiring a generation remains contentious. The Paralympics advanced elite parasports and disability awareness but did not substantially overcome societal barriers for disabled people. These findings underscore the need for sustained, inclusive initiatives to foster genuine engagement

DOI: 10.4324/9781003488729-37

and societal change through sports. The London 2012 Games' volunteering programme aimed to create a lasting volunteer culture, but sustaining this momentum proved challenging. Effective volunteer management involves creating supportive structures that address motivations and expectations, ensuring long-term engagement and integration into broader community strategies. This emphasizes the importance of nurturing a sustainable volunteer legacy through strategic collaboration with local sectors.

Mega-events like the Olympics and the FIFA World Cup often bring infrastructural and economic benefits, but can also exacerbate inequalities and displace marginalized communities. The analysis of Tokyo 2020 and various World Cup events reveals the adverse impacts of such displacements, stressing the need for inclusive and equitable planning. Policymakers must ensure that the benefits of mega-events are equitably distributed, avoiding further marginalization of vulnerable populations. Environmental sustainability is a recurring theme, with festivals like Glastonbury highlighting the role of events in advocating for climate action. Emphasizing sustainable practices throughout the event lifecycle is crucial. Event organizers are encouraged to adopt rigorous sustainability measures to minimize their ecological footprint and promote environmental consciousness among attendees.

Cultural events, such as the Sydney Gay and Lesbian Mardi Gras and small-town Pride celebrations, play a vital role in promoting LGBTQ+ visibility and acceptance. These events challenge urban-centric notions of LGBTQ+ culture, fostering a sense of belonging and community in rural areas. However, balancing commercial aspects with cultural authenticity remains critical. Ensuring inclusivity and maintaining connections with community organizations are essential for preserving the events' core values.

The integration of digital technologies, such as virtual reality and smartphones, presents both opportunities and challenges. While these technologies can enhance engagement, they also risk detracting from communal aspects of events. Developing policies that balance digital interaction with meaningful social engagement is vital for maximizing the positive impacts of technological innovations. Robust security measures and risk management practices are paramount in ensuring the safety of event attendees. Recent security failures at live events underscore the need for comprehensive strategies, including public–private partnerships and intelligence sharing. Event organizers must conduct thorough security risk analyses and implement appropriate treatment strategies to safeguard attendees and maintain public trust.

In conclusion, *Events and Society* emphasizes the transformative power of events and the complex interplay of social, cultural, economic, and environmental factors. By adopting inclusive, sustainable, and strategic approaches, event managers and policymakers can harness the potential of events to foster positive societal change and address the myriad challenges they present. This comprehensive analysis highlights the importance of thoughtful event planning, community engagement, and policy development in maximizing the benefits of events while mitigating their potential negative impacts. Through these efforts, events can become powerful tools for promoting social cohesion, cultural identity, and environmental sustainability.

MANAGERIAL AND POLICY RECOMMENDATIONS

Understanding stakeholder needs is fundamental to successful event planning and legacy creation. Collaborating with local residents and communities ensures that events are not only desired but also supported by those who are most affected by them. Engaging marginalized groups in the planning process helps develop inclusive cities and public spaces that cater to diverse populations. To achieve this, events should be co-designed with local residents, ensuring their voices are heard and their needs met. Additionally, securing legacy funding in advance is crucial to prevent budget cuts from undermining planned legacies, thereby safeguarding the long-term benefits promised to the community.

Sustainability and environmental management must be at the forefront of every stage of an event's lifecycle, from pre-bid through to the legacy phase. Rigorous management planning is essential to prevent activities that could harm protected natural areas and to ensure that the event's environmental impact is minimized. Establishing consistent sustainability frameworks and monitoring practices throughout the event's duration allows for accountability and ensures that organizers adhere to their sustainability claims. This approach not only preserves the environment but also enhances the event's reputation and public trust.

Security and risk management are vital for the safe execution of live events. Developing comprehensive security plans that include public–private partnerships and intelligence sharing can significantly mitigate potential threats. By conducting thorough security risk analyses and implementing appropriate risk treatment strategies, event organizers can enhance public safety and maintain trust in their operations. Furthermore, governments should create policies that improve the vetting and review processes for public events, ensuring that security measures are robust and effective.

Volunteer management plays a crucial role in the successful execution of events. Creating supportive structures that address volunteers' motivations and expectations can enhance their engagement and satisfaction. Diversifying recruitment efforts and matching volunteer roles to individual skills and profiles will not only improve volunteer experiences but will also ensure that a broader segment of the population is involved. Collaborating with local volunteer sectors helps create sustainable volunteer legacies, providing individuals with valuable skills that can lead to continued volunteering and potential paid employment opportunities.

Balancing social and cultural elements with economic impacts is essential for ethical legacy management. Long-term outcomes should be considered from the outset, with funding for legacies secured in advance to ensure that planned benefits are realized. Mega-events must avoid exacerbating existing inequalities or displacing local communities. Transparency about potential legacy outcomes and realistic expectations are crucial, along with effective evaluation systems to assess the impacts of policies. This balanced approach helps ensure that the benefits of hosting events are equitably distributed and that negative impacts are minimized.

Technological integration in events requires thoughtful policies that engage audiences without detracting from their overall experience. Understanding how mobile technology can enhance or harm event satisfaction is crucial for developing a balanced digital engagement strategy. Properly integrating technology can enrich the event experience, providing additional layers of interaction and information without overwhelming or alienating attendees.

Cultural sensitivity and inclusivity are imperative for the success of events. Addressing problematic traditions, such as blackface, in organizations and their products/services is necessary to promote inclusivity and respect for all cultures. Maintaining the cultural authenticity of hallmark events while managing their commercial aspects ensures that they remain true to their roots. Parades and festivals should balance corporate interests with community values by maintaining strong connections with community organizations and reflecting the local culture.

Effective crowd management involves implementing agreed principles for managing large groups, including effective communication methods and surveillance. Understanding different crowd behaviours and preparing for potential risks are essential to ensuring the safety of attendees. This proactive approach helps prevent incidents and ensures that events run smoothly.

Policy development should focus on enhancing transparency and committing to human rights in the context of hosting mega-events. Adjusting legislation to support sustainable practices and protect natural areas during events will promote long-term environmental stewardship. These policies help ensure that events do not compromise the environment or the rights of the communities involved.

Research implications include conducting interdisciplinary studies to understand the impacts of cultural economies on vulnerable groups. Studying the long-term impacts of event legacies helps develop best practices for achieving sustainable outcomes. These research efforts provide valuable insights that can inform future event planning and policy development.

Finally, event and urban development should leverage investments in mega-events to promote urban social development. Ensuring that infrastructure created for events has clear post-event use and sustainability plans will contribute to lasting positive impacts on host communities. By integrating these recommendations, event managers and policymakers can enhance the positive impacts of events, address potential risks, and ensure sustainable and inclusive outcomes for all stakeholders.

INDEX

9781032786209